KU-443-942

THE FILMS OF
CLINT EASTWOOD

by Boris Zmijewsky & Lee Pfeiffer

A Citadel Press Book
Published by Carol Publishing Group

DEDICATION

*To Janet and Nicole for all the wonderful real life memories,
and to Clint Eastwood for all the great "Reel" life memories.*
—L.P.

For Peter and Ashley
—B.Z.

First Carol Publishing Group Edition 1993

Copyright © 1982, 1988, 1993 by Boris Zmijewsky and Lee Pfeiffer
All rights reserved. No part of this book may be reproduced in any form,
except by a newspaper or magazine reviewer who wishes to quote brief
passages in connection with a review.

A Citadel Press Book
Published by Carol Publishing Group
Citadel Press is a registered trademark of Carol Communications, Inc.
Editorial Offices: 600 Madison Avenue, New York, N.Y. 10022
Sales & Distribution Offices: 120 Enterprise Avenue, Secaucus, N.J. 07094
In Canada: Canadian Manda Group, P.O. Box 920, Station U, Toronto,
Ontario M8Z 5P9
Queries regarding rights and permissions should be addressed to
Carol Publishing Group, 600 Madison Avenue, New York, N.Y. 10022.

Carol Publishing Group books are available at special discounts for bulk
purchases, for sales promotions, fund-raising, or educational purposes.
Special editions can be created to specifications. For details, contact:
Special Sales Department, Carol Publishing Group,
120 Enterprise Avenue, Secaucus, N.J. 07094.

Manufactured in the United States of America

10 9 8 7 6 5 4 3 2 1

ISBN 0–8065–1094–3

CONTENTS

ACKNOWLEDGMENTS

Since the original edition of *The Films of Clint Eastwood* was published, numerous individuals and companies have generously helped make it a success. The authors are indebted to the following for their contribution to the 1982 edition of the book: the late Mark Ricci of New York's legendary Memory Shop, Bill Kenly, Lou Valentino, Paramount Pictures, MGM, United Artists, Warner Brothers, Universal Pictures, 20th Century Fox, Malpaso Productions, ABC-TV, Marc Zubatkin, Gary Knudson, Tom Conroy, Jim Ouchterloney, Lisa Graff, Vinnie Bellotti, Karrie Bellotti, Mike McDermitt, Wide World, UPI, and Shelly Stein.

Updated material for the 1988 and 1993 editions was written by Lee Pfeiffer, and the author extends his thanks not only to the aforementioned, but to the following for having been so helpful in chronicling the achievements of Clint Eastwood: Jerry Ohlinger's Movie Memorabilia Store, 242 West 14th Street, New York, N.Y.; Photofest of New York; Bill Gold; Dave Turner of the Clint Eastwood Appreciation Society; Steve Clark, the U.K.'s number one Clint fan; Walter Brinkman; *Variety*; Tony Grimando of T.J.'s World of Stuff, Inc.; Kevin Clement of Chiller Theatre; Karen and Robert DeFelice; Fred Schenk; Rich Varrone; Phil Lisa; and from Carol Publishing, Allan J. Wilson, Bruce Bender, Steve Schragis, Alvin Marill, Gary Fitzgerald, and Mike Lewis.

Special thanks to Ron Plesniarski, whose catalog of movie memorabilia features an extensive number of rare Eastwood items. This can be obtained by sending $2.00 to: *Spy Guise*, Box 205, 261 Central Ave., Jersey City, N.J. 07307. Reader comments are appreciated. Please address all correspondence to: Box 152, Dunellen, N.J. 08812.

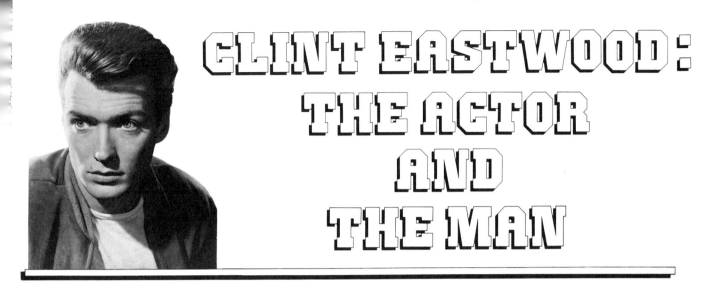

CLINT EASTWOOD: THE ACTOR AND THE MAN

A tall detective strolls into his favorite diner for a quick lunch on a hot summer's day in San Francisco. As he begins to devour a hot dog, he is alerted by a burglar alarm that sounds in the bank across the street.

The detective's face betrays a resigned look of irritation at this infringement on his free time; nevertheless, he walks outside to investigate. As he nears the bank, he withdraws from his shoulder holster an ominous .44 Magnum. A second later one of the bank robbers dashes outside toward a waiting getaway car.

The detective shouts for the man to halt. His command is answered by a shotgun blast from the criminal. In the flash of a second, the detective's gun is blazing, and the bank robber lies severely wounded on the pavement.

A second bandit dashes outside and leaps into the getaway car, and the vehicle speeds toward the tall detective, who is the only obstruction to the men's freedom.

As the car approaches, the police officer coolly raises his handgun and, with a series of devastatingly accurate shots, sends the car careering into a nearby fire hydrant, causing the death of the occupants.

Still holding the hot dog in his free hand, the detective walks briskly over to the wounded bank robber. He sees that the man is looking at a gun that is lying next to him.

The detective stands before the bandit and points his Magnum at him, saying, "I know what you're thinking, punk. You're thinking, *Did he fire five shots or six?* Well, to tell the truth, in all this confusion I forgot myself. But being as this is a .44 Magnum, and the most powerful handgun in the world—it can blow your head clean off—you've got to ask yourself one question: *Do I feel lucky?* Well, do you, punk?"

Not surprisingly, the robber does not feel so lucky this day, and the tall detective is not forced to risk his life one more time.

The above sequence, from the 1971 thriller *Dirty Harry,* typifies the hard-hitting action and nail-biting suspense that have become the trademark of one of the most popular screen actors in the history of motion pictures: Clint Eastwood.

Since the late 1960s, audiences around the world have been fascinated by Eastwood's style. His no-nonsense approach to resolving the most demanding of situations has left women swooning and men filled with envy. With the possible exception of John Wayne, no other actor has accumulated the box-office successes of Clint Eastwood. Small wonder that near the end of his career, Wayne pronounced Eastwood "my only logical successor."

Eastwood's track record of successful motion-picture ventures is all the more amazing when one considers just how broad a base his popularity has. His films are virtually all designed to appeal to American audiences through the stable, traditional genres of the U.S. cinema (the western, the detective story, the country-western comedy); still, almost all his films have been enormous successes around the world. One can understand the universal acceptance of Eastwood's action-adventure films, since there has traditionally been a market for these kinds of movies. However, it is to his credit that the popularity of a film such as *Every Which Way but Loose,* a humorous satire on the current country-western craze, can meet with the same appreciation and enjoyment from Japanese audiences as from American moviegoers.

Just what is it about Eastwood that makes his popularity so universal? Certainly, critical acclaim has never been a factor in his success, although one can see a certain acceptance of his talents by many film critics who once considered Eastwood's brand of films to be a short-lived fad. Eastwood has survived and thrived often in spite of—not because of—his treatment from international film critics. He once said that he was not bitter about the generally negative response critics have given his work. "I've had my share of good notices along the way," he stated, "but I've found that most film critics don't know too much about movies anyway."

In a sociological framework, much of Eastwood's success can be attributed to the era in which his brand of character was introduced. The mid-sixties were violent, exciting times in which young people seemed to rebel against all traditional symbols of the Establishment. People's desires to change things were reflected in their choice of heroes and the people they emulated. Nowhere were these changes more apparent than in the public's demand for new types of motion-picture entertainment. In this changing environment in the entertainment field, Clint Eastwood found himself embraced as a pop-culture hero, even though a few short years before, the films that would make him a star would have been largely ignored by the general moviegoing public.

Probably no one fit more perfectly into the antihero mold than Clint Eastwood. True, his contemporaries and immediate predecessors had their share of memorable "cad" roles, most notably Paul Newman in his brilliant characterization of *Hud* and, a decade earlier, Marlon Brando in his classic interpretation of the Stanley Kowalski role in *A Streetcar Named Desire*. Yet as unappealing as these characters were, the audience had a certain intrinsic understanding of them. Their actions may not have been forgivable, but the backgrounds of the characters always showed them to be either victims of their environments (therefore enticing the audience to pity them) or lovable rogues whose charms made it impossible to hate them for their actions.

Eastwood was to change all this with his first appearance in a starring role on the international movie scene. His characterization of The Man with No Name in *A Fistful of Dollars* portrayed a human being who was seemingly devoid of the simplest emotions or sympathetic actions. Why, then, did international audiences embrace such a cold-blooded figure as a hero? Possibly because Eastwood directed all his actions with the type of fast thinking and correct decision making that all of us would like to possess. In real life, we were restrained by the laws of the system, which often protected criminals at the expense of the victims, but at least we could see on screen a no-nonsense figure who could take the law into his own hands and get away with it.

This was often done with cold, calculated planning on the part of the Eastwood character. His enemies often suffered horrendous fates at his hands. Yet these victims evoked no sympathy from the audience, because they were embellished in such a villainous way as to make Eastwood's violence not only tolerated, but enthusiastically welcomed.

His screen image personified the very qualities that the audiences of the sixties wanted to see in their heroes. He was—and still is—the fantasy answer to our real-life problems. He leaves alone those who do not get in his way. However, when someone seeks to harm him or forcefully manipulate him, he takes action and fulfills the desires of the moviegoers, who all too often feel that society has rendered them impotent in defending themselves.

Richard Harmet of the *Los Angeles Free Press* showed an understanding of the Eastwood acceptance by international audiences when he wrote:

> There was something about this part that Eastwood played so naturally that almost immediately made him one of our top boxoffice attractions. On the screen there seemed about him the absolute certainty that he stood above the rest of mankind, and that there was no one he couldn't take with his gun or his fists. Unconcerned about a higher moral order, he shot those who stood in his way.
>
> Above all, he was in complete control of his environment, certain of his actions and sure there was no obstacle he could not overcome and no human he could not dominate.
>
> And there is his appeal. Modern man—trampled on by government, beset by pollution, and manipulated by advertising—can only dream of control over his environment, and it is Eastwood who supplies that dream come to life.

In order to trace Clint Eastwood's rise to the top of the box office, one must understand the ingredients that brought about the changes in Hollywood philosophy that necessitated the studio's search for a new type of hero. Hollywood in the early sixties might have been described, paraphrasing Dickens as "the best of times and the worst of times." Film technology was making great advances, and more money than ever was being spent creating epic films that showed off these technical achievements to the fullest. The blockbuster "road show" movies, which so long had been the staple of Hollywood's bread and butter through such films as *Gone with the Wind*, *Ben-Hur*, and *The Ten Commandments*, reached new heights financially (if not artistically) in the early sixties as the studios tried to duplicate the success of those earlier films. Millions of dollars were poured into giant spectacles like *The Alamo*, *55 Days at Peking*, *Mutiny on the Bounty*, and *Cleopatra*. However, by the time these films reached the screen, Hollywood found, much to its horror, that this was no longer the product that the audience wanted to buy. The result: Major studios hovered on the verge of bankruptcy while these films struggled to break even at the box office.

Even the B movie, so long the mainstay of second-run-movie houses, was becoming unprofitable, owing to the impact of television. Audiences felt they could see films of the same quality on television, and many of these movies began to play to nearly empty theaters.

Clearly, Hollywood had to satiate its audience's desires for something different. While filmmakers agonized endlessly about what they could offer the public, one of the answers was quietly being formulated in Europe, where in 1964 two men—a little-known Italian director and a moderately successful American television actor—were quietly filming a low-budget western called *A Fistful of Dollars*. No one suspected it at the time, but this modest little film would revitalize the entire trend of action-adventure movies from the mid-sixties on, and the two men filming it would soon be catapulted into international prominence. Their names were Sergio Leone and Clint Eastwood.

A rare photo of Clint Eastwood as an infant.

For many years Eastwood had struggled to carve a name in the acting community. It is ironic that the Europeans had more confidence in his acting than did the natives of his own country, who originally told him he had no future in movies. Eastwood's success, when it did come, was remarkable, and in 1971 *Life* magazine proclaimed on its cover, "The world's favorite movie star is—no kidding—Clint Eastwood!"

Eastwood's beginnings were conspicuously humble and in no way foreshadowed the international achievements that would later make him so wealthy. He was born Clinton Eastwood, Jr., on May 30, 1931, in San Francisco. It is appropriate that one of Eastwood's most memorable screen characters is the drifter who never knows where the next day will find him. The same can be said for Eastwood's early years. With the Depression wreaking havoc on the American economy, Eastwood's parents, Clinton and Ruth, found that steady employment for the man of the house was nonexistent. Therefore, the family had to move wherever Clint's father could secure a temporary job. This period was not easy for

Eastwood's parents, and it was particularly difficult for Clint and his younger sister, Jean. Eastwood would later recall in an interview, "I must have gone to ten different schools in the first ten years of my schooling. We moved so much that I made very few friends. Moving has become sort of a lifestyle for me. Basically, I've been a drifter."

Eventually, Clint's father found steady employment with the Container Corporation of America in Oakland, California. Eastwood attended the Oakland Technical High School, and unlike other future rebel superstars like Steve McQueen and Marlon Brando, he proved to be a conscientious and successful student. He tried hard to please his parents, both of whom he respected a great deal. He placed great emphasis on being the best at whatever he did. This he attributed to a philosophy his father professed. Eastwood once recalled, "My father always kept telling me you don't get anything for nothing, and although I rebelled, I never rebelled against that. . . . I always got along great with my parents."

It was often difficult to maintain close family ties in the Eastwood family. His mother had long sympathized with the plight of her children, and she tried very hard to give them some sort of family stability. For many years, she would send Clint and Jean to spend time on their grandmother's chicken ranch in Sunol, California. Eastwood spent his formative years living intermittently on this ranch, and these visits provided many of the fun times Eastwood enjoyed in those otherwise bleak years. He appreciated his parents' efforts then, and he still does. He stated not long ago, "I think my parents and my grandmother—she was quite a person, very self-sufficient, lived by herself on a mountain— probably had more to do with my turning out the way I am than any educational process I may have gone through. . . . I was lucky to have them."

Eastwood, at seventeen.

While in high school, Eastwood became a star of sorts on the basketball court, largely because of his height. He usually towered over the other students in his class, and although this often made him feel uncomfortable, his height probably aided him later, in his acting career. While in high school, however, acting appeared be the last thing on Clint's mind. An introverted and shy youth, he had little desire to make himself the center of attention. However, his imposing build and rugged good looks attracted not only girls, but teachers who were always looking for student talents to be displayed in class plays.

It was at this time that Eastwood was first exposed, however reluctantly, to the acting profession. He recalls, "I had a teacher decide we were going to put on a one-act play, and she made up her mind I was going to be the lead. It was really disastrous. I wanted to go out for athletics; doing plays was not considered the thing to do at that stage in life—especially not presenting them before the entire senior high school, which is what she made us do. We muffed a lot of lines. I swore that was the end of my acting career."

With his acting "career" a shambles, Clint turned his sights on more practical—and profitable—pastimes. After school and during the summers, he held a variety of odd jobs, which helped him pay his own way and ease his father's financial burden somewhat. The jobs that held his interest were mostly related to working outdoors. He baled hay in Yreka, California, cut timber near Paradise, California, and fought forest fires for the forestry service in the northern part of the state.

Eastwood's temporary employment afforded him a luxury he had long dreamed of—his first car. Actually, the car was barely drivable. In addition to this problem, Clint purchased it when he was still underage for a driver's license. Nevertheless, the auto provided him with many hours of enjoyment as he practiced driving on back roads and in fields. His total cost for the car amounted to a little more than fifteen dollars.

Upon graduating from Oakland High School in 1948, Eastwood decided to strike out on his own. He had a diploma, a few dollars, a suitcase, and little else. His family extended their offer to continue supporting him, but Eastwood did not want to move with them to Texas, where his father had secured another job. Clint wandered aimlessly around California, finding temporary employment wherever he could.

He eventually heard of some opportunities available for hardworking young men who wished to try their hands at being lumberjacks in Springfield, Oregon. Arriving at the lumber camp, Clint was immediately hired, and he set right to work at the backbreaking labor the job required. The pay was good, but there was little else to recommend the job. It was almost impossible to spend any money, because the nearest major town, Eugene, proved to be an arduous drive through the Oregon mountain passes.

Eastwood stayed at the lumber camp for a little more than a year, then left. He says, "The dampness finally got to me, and I moved on. Around Eugene, in the Willamette Valley, it's beautiful, but in the winter it socks in. You go six, seven months without seeing blue."

Perhaps because of a need to know that the family was within reach in case of hard times, Eastwood eventually drifted to Texas, although he did not reside with his family. He found employment with the Bethlehem Steel Company, working a furnace. "My job was general maintenance around the big blast furnaces, and the heat got so intense you felt as if your skin would peel right off your body. I didn't like the work, even though the pay was good. I was working the graveyard shift, from midnight until nine in the morning. I had my days free, but I was too tired to enjoy them."

Following his brief tenure at the steel company, Clint found a position as a lifeguard in Renton, Texas, as a county employee. Eastwood was also required to give swimming instruction—a task he was ably suited for, having excelled as a swimmer in high school. The work tended to be pleasing and uneventful. The main benefit, he would say later, was enjoying the sight of all the girls clad in their bathing suits. They would often stop by and flirt with him. "Believe me," he jokes, "those jobs were hard to get."

Never one to stay with an unchallenging job too long, Clint left the lifeguard position and found work with the Boeing plant, near Seattle. Here, he was assigned to the parts department, where he spent most of

As a student at the Red Cross National Aquatic School in 1953.

his time filling out forms—hardly the type of work that would seem enticing to the future Dirty Harry.

In 1949, Eastwood determined that he should return to school to major in—of all things—music. (This may seem a surprising interest for Clint, but one must remember that even during his career in show business, his little-talked-about love for music was shown more than once. In *Paint Your Wagon*, he made his big-screen singing debut, and Clint actually cut a record for a small recording company during the years he was filming the *Rawhide* television series. He recalls an occasion in which he was sent on tour to promote the record—called "Unknown Girl"—while wearing a ridiculous "cool" outfit provided by the record company. "The pants they gave me to wear were not pants; they were leotards. To rebel, I sometimes showed up wearing my western costume, smelling of cow manure. The record-promotion company didn't like it, but the teenagers did." Twenty years later, Clint had a hit record of "Barroom Buddies," which he sang with Merle Haggard in *Bronco Billy*.)

Eastwood's plan to return to school was thwarted when he was drafted into the army. He reported to Fort Ord, California, for basic training. Soon after the army accepted him, the Korean conflict erupted. But Eastwood's swimming prowess would once again prove quite valuable. He explained to Arthur Knight in an interview for *Playboy* in 1974,

11

They needed a couple of guys to help out at the pool there. So I got up and went into my act as a Johnny Weismuller type. . . . I told them I was absolutely the greatest swimmer going, things like that, and I ended up getting the job. When we started out, there was this buddy of mine and I, and a master sergeant and four sergeants over us, and a lieutenant over them. Everybody got shipped to Korea except me; my name just didn't come up. So I figured I'd make the best of it and went and talked to the captain. I said, "Look, I'm only a private, but I think I can handle this swimming-pool thing," and he said, "Well, I don't even know how to swim, so go ahead and run it. You're wearing a sweat shirt; nobody will know you're just a private." So I stayed there and hired four other guys to work for me. We had a pretty good swimming-instruction program going, got quite a few excellent ratings—like four-star movie reviews. I even lived down at the pool; it was a terrific deal, for being in the service.

Eastwood was able to use his leisure hours to earn money by working in jobs outside the base. One such job was at the Spreckles Sugar Refining Company, where he worked on a loading dock. He felt the money was worth giving up his spare time for, because his salary from the army amounted to a whopping $67 a month. Eventually, however, the government demanded that Eastwood resign from his part-time jobs and save his strength for the army.

Eastwood's strength was much needed for one incident that nearly cost him his life. One of Clint's friends, a pilot on a navy bomber, suggested that Eastwood use a weekend pass and accompany him on a routine flight to San Francisco. Clint agreed, even though he had to ride in the rear compartment above the bombbay.

No sooner was the plane over open water, than for some inexplicable reason, the bombbay door fell open. The air pressure was so tremendous that Eastwood had to use all his strength to prevent being sucked out into the sea. Somehow, he managed to close the bombbay door.

Screaming for help over the intercom, he found that it had gone dead between the bombing compartment and the cockpit. In addition to these troubles, the plane began to lose both altitude and oxygen. The pilot had to make a dramatic crash landing in the open sea.

With waves pounding him, and darkness settling in, Eastwood and his friend began the seemingly endless swim toward shore. To add to his worries, he encountered a school of jellyfish, which caused him great pain. He remembers, "I thought I might die. But then I thought, *Other people have made it through these things before.* I kept my eyes on the lights on shore and kept swimming." Fortunately, both men made it to safety. Characteristic of his nature, all these hardships didn't bother Eastwood as much as did the five-mile walk to a highway in wet clothes.

During his army years, Eastwood first met his future wife, Maggie Johnson. One of Clint's friends had arranged for him to meet her through a blind double-date. Their relationship grew gradually. Clint escorted Maggie on many modestly budgeted dates, which grew more and more frequent. Eventually, he would spend all his free time with her. Eastwood claimed that he was attracted not only by Maggie's good

A young Clint Eastwood

looks, but also by her independence and ability to profess her own opinions. At the time of their first meeting, Maggie was a student at the University of California at Berkeley.

With his army career coming to an end and his relationship with Maggie heading toward possible marriage, Eastwood contemplated what he would do with his life. Several of his army buddies, including Martin Milner and the late David Janssen, had been actors trying to make it big in civilian life. They constantly harassed Clint to try his hand at acting, and although he seemed to take the idea more seriously than he ever had in the past, he decided instead to go a more practical route. When he was discharged from the army, he enrolled in Los Angeles City College to major in business administration. This decision he later attributed more to self-pressure to choose a good-paying career, than to any real interest in the business world.

During his school semesters, Eastwood again found part-time employment. He worked as an attendant in a gas station and later took on the responsibilities of being a janitor in an apartment building.

When these jobs came to an end, Clint found employment digging foundations for swimming pools. On this job, an incident occurred that well illustrates Eastwood's allegiance to old friends and just how far he is willing to carry his fierce loyalty. While on the job one day, Eastwood and an old buddy found themselves in a verbal altercation with the foreman. The incident flared to the point where Eastwood's friend was fired. Suddenly, Clint also put down his shovel and began to walk. The foreman asked increduously why he was leaving. Eastwood replied, "This man is my friend. If he doesn't work here, neither do I."

To this day, most of Eastwood's inner circle of friends go back to his days as a struggling actor, if not before. While he has kept company with some of the people in the movie industry, he refuses to "go Hollywood" and attend parties and functions simply to get more publicity. In the company of old friends, he finds himself more relaxed and doesn't have to be pretentious in order to be accepted.

Eastwood continued to hear from friends that he was definitely suited for the movies. More out of desperation than interest, he reluctantly went to Universal Studios to attempt to make an appointment for a screen test. At the time the major studios were still using contract players, which meant that an aspiring young actor or actress would be hired by the studio to play small parts in various films. Each contract guaranteed the player a specified salary for a certain number of weeks, after which the studio could renew or drop the actor's contract. In addition to having steady work and receiving monetary benefits, the contract players were also required to attend classes on filmmaking. This, coupled with experience on the set, was often more valuable to the aspiring thespians than their salaries.

Eastwood's gamble on securing a screen test was a success. The studio brought him into a well-lighted room, sat him down, and interviewed him in an informal, rambling conversation. It soon became apparent that the studio was not the least bit interested in what Eastwood was saying. Rather, this was just a test to see whether he photographed well enough to decorate the background as an extra. Apparently he did, and much to his surprise, he was signed for a contract that guaranteed him forty weeks' work at seventy-five dollars per week.

Astounded by his success, Eastwood decided to give acting his fullest effort. With his steady income supplemented by Maggie's part-time work as a bathing-suit model for a swimwear company, the couple felt the time was right to get married. On December 19, 1953, Maggie Johnson became Maggie Eastwood.

Eastwood's first assignment in motion pictures was a small role in a minor horror film titled *Revenge of the Creature*. His appearance was brief and completely forgettable, not only for audiences, but for himself as well. Other films followed in rapid succession. He appeared in such ''epics'' as *Tarantula*, *Francis in the Navy* (with old friend Martin Milner), *Lady Godiva*, and *Never Say Goodbye*. All the roles offered him in these films were far too brief for Clint to make an impression; yet the employment was steady, and his salary had increased to a hundred dollars per week.

At this time, however, Eastwood was nearly faced with a tragedy. Maggie contracted a severe case of hepatitis, and for several days her prospects for survival looked grim. Eastwood kept working in order to pay the doctor bills, but finances were becoming strained with Maggie out of work and in poor health. Fortunately, she eventually overcame her sickness and managed to return to work to supplement the couple's income. Eastwood was relieved enough, now that he could stop worrying about his wife's health, to concentrate on his upcoming new contract

Clint as he appeared in his early days in Hollywood.

Clint and Maggie seen relaxing by their pool.

14

*Eastwood in an early
studio pose.*

with Universal.

The studio brass were to give Eastwood a raise to $125 per week, but for some reason they had a change of heart. The studio informed him that if he wanted to continue with Universal, it would have to be at the present rate of $100 a week. Eastwood swallowed his pride and accepted the offer, only to allow him more time to gain acting experience. After six months, however, the studio decided they had no use for him at all and dropped his contract.

Shocked by this latest blow to his ego, Clint went to RKO, at that time the haven of the B movie. RKO saw great promise in his acting abilities and signed him for a Ginger Rogers comedy titled *The First Traveling Saleslady.*

Despite high hopes, the film was a failure with the public and quickly vanished from sight. However, the studio rapidly signed Eastwood for a bit role in another comedy, this one titled *Escapade in Japan,* in which he played a sailor with the memorable name of Dumbo.

Before this film could be released, RKO was sold, and the studio went out of business shortly thereafter. Ironically, *Escapade in Japan* was purchased for distribution by Universal Pictures. Not surprisingly, this undistinguished little feature also failed to light any fires with the moviegoing public. Eastwood knew that Universal would have no interest in him, since they had recently fired him.

Eastwood landed a job as a co-star in a 20th Century-Fox western called *Ambush at Cimarron Pass.* Although the film offered him his largest role to date, Eastwood would later describe the movie as "maybe the worst film ever made."

By 1958, Clint found himself digging swimming pools once again. His brief love affair with acting was beginning to fade rapidly, and he had begun to wonder if his dreams of success hadn't been foolish. He continued to accept parts wherever they were offered, and he did manage to secure a few unimpressive roles in short-lived TV series like *Navy Log* and *Men of Annapolis.* An appearance on *Highway Patrol* garnered him his first piece of fan mail.

Clint's next big-screen work was a promising war film, *Lafayette Escadrille,* which starred heartthrob Tab Hunter. The director was the distinguished William Wellman, and for a moment Clint's optimism was reawakened. Unfortunately, *Lafayette* went the way of Clint's other films—it died at the box office.

Although Eastwood had little practical reason to be high spirited at this time, fate was about to step in and reward him for his long struggle and constant disappointments. In fact, if it hadn't been for a simple luncheon date, Eastwood might never have become the star he is today. Good fortune finally tapped him one day when he was having lunch with Sonia Chernus, an employee of CBS Television's story department. Eastwood caught the eye of CBS executive Robert Sparks, who was looking for someone to cast in one of the two lead roles for an upcoming western series called *Rawhide.* Sparks approached Eastwood and asked whether he was an actor. Clint replied in the affirmative and gave

Sparks a brief rundown of his acting career, making sure he particularly overemphasized his contribution to *Ambush at Cimmarron Pass*. This nearly backfired on Clint when Sparks and *Rawhide* producer Charles Marquis Warren asked to see a print of the film. Convinced they would find it a disaster, Eastwood gave up and went home in despair, certain he was out of the running.

Much to Clint's surprise, Warren phoned him later to tell him they wanted him for the role of Rowdy Yates, the second lead in *Rawhide*. Eastwood was set to co-star with Eric Fleming, as a kind of father-son cattle-driving team. Clint was ecstatic. He signed a contract and filmed ten of the thirteen episodes the network had agreed to air. His salary went up to what he felt was an astronomical plateau. However, his luck was short-lived. CBS was having second thoughts about running the show, owing to suspicions that the glut of TV westerns and the decline in popularity of hour-long programming would make the series unprofitable.

Eastwood would later describe this period as the lowest point in his career. He recalled, "Here was my career, lying in the basement of CBS, because the word was out that hour-long shows were out. So I decided to go up and visit my parents. . . . On the way I got a telegram saying that the series had been sold after all, and to be ready to work on such and such a day. Mag and I did a little champagne trick and yelled a lot: I shouted a lot of profane things out the window."

Rawhide premiered on January 9, 1959. Its initial ratings were far from spectacular but were good enough for CBS to keep it on the air. By its second season, the series was a major hit and proved to be immensely profitable not only for CBS, but for Eastwood as well. The basic story line of the series involved the adventures of a group of cowboys on a seemingly endless cattle drive. In essence, the show was inspired by Howard Hawks's 1948 western classic *Red River*. Fleming and Eastwood portrayed the John Wayne and Montgomery Clift roles respectively. By all standards, it was a superior series. Eastwood was not given the most fascinating character in the world to work with, but he did try to innovate various idiosyncrasies to make Rowdy Yates a little more interesting.

In addition to benefiting from the show in terms of salary, Eastwood learned a tremendous amount about filmmaking techniques through watching such directors as Ted Post work on the series. Eastwood claims that working on *Rawhide* was one of the most valuable acting assignments he's ever taken, and he credits this experience with expanding his acting technique. "Having the security of being in a series week in, week out gives you great flexibility; you can experiment with yourself, try a different scene different ways. If you make a mistake one week, you can look at it and say, 'Well, I won't do that again,' and you're still on the air next week."

Rawhide brought Eastwood great exposure to American audiences, but he still strove to make a mark for himself in the world of feature films. At every turn he was rejected by the CBS brass, which maintained that his contract didn't allow him to star in anything but *Rawhide*. The normally calm Eastwood lost his temper pubiicly for the first time and told *Hollywood Reporter*, "I haven't been allowed to accept a single feature or TV guesting offer since I started the series. Maybe they figure me as the sheepish guy I portray in the series, but even a worm has to turn sometime. Believe me, I'm not bluffing—I'm prepared to go on suspension, which means I can't work here, but I've got offers from London and Rome that will bring me more money in a year than this series has given me in three." CBS relented, and Eastwood won his case.

In early 1964, Eastwood found himself on a shooting hiatus from *Rawhide*. His agent called to let him know that there was an offer to do a western in Spain titled *The Magnificent Stranger*. Eastwood was unimpressed, particularly when he learned that the film was to be financed by a German-Italian-Spanish production company with an Italian director, Sergio Leone. Eastwood was certain that no European studio could make a successful, realistic American western. Yet when he read the script, he was impressed. He recognized the story as a remake of Japanese director Akira Kurosawa's masterpiece *Yojimbo*. Eastwood had known that a few years before, a remake of Kurosawa's *Seven Samurai* had resulted in *The Magnificent Seven*, a notable western that helped launch such future superstars as Steve McQueen, Charles Bronson, Robert Vaughn, and James Coburn. Eastwood felt that in the right hands, lightning might strike twice.

Eastwood chats with Bob Reisdorff and Beverly Noga at a 1964 party.

17

30 Dpf.

ILLUSTRIERTE
film-Bühne
Nr. 7613

MALEDETTO GRINGO

(IL MAGNIFICO STRANIERO)

*An early publicity pose
for the* Rawhide *series.*

*Clint Eastwood and Kim
Hunter.*

*Clint Eastwood
promoting* Rawhide.

There were other, more practical reasons for Eastwood's eventually accepting this film. For one, he desired to see Europe, and this was an expense-paid trip for him and Maggie. In addition, he was to receive a fifteen-thousand-dollar fee. He decided that if the film were a success, it could only help his career, whereas if it proved to be the disaster it very well might be, no one outside Europe would ever see it anyway. This move also allowed Clint to demonstrate his independence from CBS, as well as giving him totally free rein to virtually create a character out of the paper-thin hero of the script.

The director and crew looked to Clint as the only authentic Yankee available, and Eastwood found that he alone on the set had any real feeling for the American West. He decided to have a field day with his character and play it as exactly the opposite of the mild-mannered character he portrayed on *Rawhide*. He purchased the seediest wardrobe he could find, in order to give his character—the Stranger with No Name—the gravest appearance possible.

Although Eastwood learned to respect director Sergio Leone during the brief shooting schedule, he was confident that the film would never be shown in the U.S. He also felt that the character he portrayed—a ruthless, mercenary drifter—was too off-beat to be accepted as a hero in his native land.

Eastwood returned directly from Europe to begin shooting *Rawhide* again. Clint had all but forgotten about *The Magnificent Stranger* until he picked up an issue of *Variety* one day long after he had returned from Spain. "I read an article which said the big deal in Italy was that everybody was enthusiastic about making westerns after the success of this fantastic new film *A Fistful of Dollars*. That meant nothing to me, because the title we had used during shooting was *The Magnificent Stranger*. Then, about two days after that, there was another item from Rome, and it said, '*A Fistful of Dollars*, starring Clint Eastwood, is going through the roof here.' And I said, 'Clint Eastwood. . . . !' Then I got a letter from the producer—who hadn't bothered to write me since I left—asking me about making another picture."

Obviously, European audiences were far more eager to accept this new type of hero than was the American public. Other than *Rawhide*, no other acting opportunities presented themselves to Clint in the United States. Appreciative, and still stunned by his hero status in Italy, Eastwood returned in 1965 to begin shooting *For a Few Dollars More*, once again with Sergio Leone directing. The plot was similar to that of its predecessor, and Eastwood broke no new acting ground, other than having a few good scenes with fellow American actor Lee Van Cleef. Yet audiences lined up by the thousands for a chance to see Eastwood on screen.

Clint was no longer embarrassed by his stature in European westerns. He proudly stated that only Marcello Mastroianni made more money in Italian films than he did. Word had reached America about the hits Eastwood was producing overseas; yet no major studio expressed an interest in releasing the films. Apparently Hollywood was not even willing to front the small amount of money it would take to secure distribution rights for two proven box-office winners.

In Europe, it was different. Already, enterprising film studios sought to exploit Clint's name by editing various *Rawhide* episodes together and releasing them under the guise of a major new Clint Eastwood film. The threat of legal action ended such schemes, but they did signify yet another example of what European producers would do to get Clint's name on a film.

On the domestic front, various changes had been made in *Rawhide*. Eric Fleming had had a major falling-out with CBS over a variety of differences. The result was his dismissal from the series and Eastwood's elevation to the starring role in the series. This proved temporarily satisfying, but Eastwood's taste of motion-picture success had made him impatient with the series. In 1966, this situation was resolved for him when CBS canceled *Rawhide*. The show had run for nine years—an amazing achievement for any television series. It might have run longer if CBS hadn't refused to film the series in color. *Rawhide* was the last remaining network show to be filmed exclusively in black-and-white.

Eastwood did not have time to cry over the cancellation. In fact, he saw it as an opportunity to pursue other projects for theatrical distribution. He did not have to wait long. In 1966, Sergio Leone informed him that he had written a screenplay for the third—and, as it turned out, the last—of the Man with No Name films, this one entitled *The Good, the Bad, and the Ugly*. Once again, Eastwood ventured to Europe for the start of another western. This time, however, there was a difference. For his efforts on this film, Eastwood was paid the staggering sum of $250,000. For the producers, Eastwood's price was worth it. This film far outgrossed its predecessors and became one of the highest-grossing films of the decade in Italy.

A studious Eastwood on the set of The Witches, *about 1965.*

Eastwood's work overseas was not limited to the Leone westerns. Following *The Good, the Bad, and the Ugly*, he appeared briefly in a film called *The Witches* for producer Dino de Laurentiis. Eastwood's character was unmemorable, as was the film. It was not a critical or a financial success.

While Clint was away those years working in Europe, America was in the midst of a social upheaval. Youth riots, anti-Vietnam-war demonstrations, civil rights protests, and the drug culture swept America. With people seemingly so dissatisfied with tradition, United Artists thought the time was appropriate to introduce a new form of hero to the public. That hero was Clint Eastwood. For quite some time U.A. had courted the idea of buying the Leone trilogy for domestic distribution. In 1967, the company decided to take the plunge and purchased the rights to present all three Leone-Eastwood films in America. The modest sum U.A. paid for this privilege proved to be one of the best-spent investments the company made in the sixties. The films were released in chronological order, to the anticipated disastrous reviews. But although critical reaction may have been predictable, audience reaction was unexpectedly enthusiastic. It is doubtful that even U.A. expected the enormous success of these films.

A Fistful of Dollars, released early in 1967, proved to be one of the company's biggest money makers in years. Losing no time in exploiting a hot trend, the company was very easily able to satisfy the cravings of the public by releasing *For a Few Dollars More* in early summer of the same year. *The Good, the Bad, and the Ugly* opened to huge audiences in early 1968. Each of the films outgrossed its forerunner by considerable sums. America had found a new hero, and his name was Clint Eastwood.

Armchair sociologists and frustrated film critics wrote endlessly of various hypotheses to explain the popularity of these crudely made films. Perhaps David Dowing and Gary Herman express the most insight to the question in their book *Clint Eastwood: All American Anti-Hero*, wherein they write:

> It's not hard to see why these films were made in the sixties, or why they proved so popular. It was a decade of revolt, sandwiched between the false optimism of the fifties and the unalleviated pessimism of the seventies. There were many reasons for this revolt, but one connecting thread was clearly a growing feeling that people were slowly losing control over their own lives. And there were many ways in which it was expressed; two of them were indisputably the cult of indifference, of stylish "cool," and the use of revolutionary violence. For such a social situation, it is hard to imagine a more fitting hero than the Man with No Name, who is in control of his life and environment, who smiles knowingly and bows to no one, who looks good and keeps free of ties, who kills with passionless artistry. . . . No Name is Guevara without the encumbrances, without a future, a permanent revolution that will never risk the corruption of statehood.

Having become an "overnight" success, Eastwood found himself in great demand, at last, in his native land. 1968 proved to be one of his most hectic years, and if anyone thought that the Eastwood craze was merely a passing phenomenon, they would soon learn just how wrong they were. In the course of this year, many events were to affect Clint, all of which were to have a significant impact on his career. U.A., still reaping enormous profits from the spaghetti westerns (as critics came to dub Leone's films), quickly hired Eastwood to appear in an Americanized western titled *Hang 'Em High*. Critics were no more impressed by this effort than they had been by Eastwood's previous work, but his increased value to the audience reflected itself in his salary. For this undemanding role, Clint received four hundred thousand dollars.

Eastwood's personal life was also booming with new developments. Using his newfound wealth, Clint and Maggie moved into the outskirts of Carmel, California. There, they financed the construction of a huge house, situated on more than two hundred acres of beautiful countryside. (Eastwood would later allow his love for this part of the country to figure prominently in *Play Misty for Me*, wherein the gorgeous landscapes are shown off to full advantage.) Eastwood helped with much of the custom-designed construction of his house.

Eastwood dreamed of making himself a success in the motion-picture industry, and one of his prime incentives was his ultimate desire to start his own production company, with which he could maintain strict control over all aspects of his films. Soon after filming *Hang 'Em High*, Clint turned his energies toward making this dream a reality. Other actors had attempted to organize their own production companies, often with less-than-impressive results. Burt Lancaster and John Wayne were among the more notable stars who had found that both starring in and producing their own films could lead to a great variety of problems. Yet Eastwood's decision would prove to be one of the wisest and most profitable of his career.

Clint had long been a critic of wastefulness in film production. As he became more successful, he observed time and again how major studios allowed millions of dollars to be spent unnecessarily. Clint felt that with his own company, he could streamline budgets drastically and, with a minimum number of people on his staff, produce successful first-rate films. After several years of planning, his efforts resulted in Malpaso Productions, over which he maintains virtually total control.

When asked once why he desired to trouble himself with starting a production company, he explained, "My theory was that I could foul up my career just as well as anyone else could foul it up for me, so why not try it? And I had this great urge to show the industry that it needs to be streamlined so it can make more films with smaller crews. The crews will be employed more, so there'll be just as much work. What's the point of spending so much money producing a movie if you can't break even on it? So at Malpaso, we don't have a staff of twenty-six and a fancy office. I've got a six-pack under my arm, and a few pieces of paper and a couple of pencils, and I'm in business. What the hell, I can work in a closet."

Eastwood named Malpaso after a creek that runs through some land he owns. In Spanish, it means "bad step." Yet Malpaso has proved to be anything but a bad step. Although it had been active since 1968, Malpaso did not play a major role in Eastwood's career until the early seventies. At that time the production company began to work in full gear. Keeping in line with his pledge to maintain a staff at the minimum required, Malpaso originally consisted solely of Eastwood, producer Bob Daley (who has produced many Eastwood films), and Sonia Chernus, Clint's old friend from his CBS days on *Rawhide*. The three people reviewed all possible film products, and Malpaso was rarely dormant. The entire company worked out of trailers on the lots of major studios, thereby allowing Malpaso to be the most mobile production company in Hollywood. Since 1968, Malpaso has been associated with every Eastwood film. Clint's wisdom in forming the company has reaped him millions of dollars and has kept many actors and technicians employed on his films during some of Hollywood's dimmest days.

1968 also saw another important development unfold in Eastwood's professional and private lives: his first association with director Don Siegel. The two men met while filming Clint's modernday western

Coogan's Bluff, which Siegel directed. The film proved to be among the high points in both men's careers, and its success was responsible for Clint and Don collaborating over the years on some very notable achievements. Both Eastwood and Siegel, who had directed some of the finest B movies ever made, including the original *Invasion of the Bodysnatchers* and *Riot in Cell Block 11*, formed a strong personal bond of friendship that has extended to their lives outside of the filmmaking industry.

With Don Siegel and Don Stroud on the set of Coogan's Bluff *(1968).*

About Siegel, Eastwood once told Stuart Kaminsky in his book *Clint Eastwood*:

> I like his attack on directing. . . . He never gets bogged down, even in disaster. I think he's fantastic. We have worked a lot together, and probably will in the future. I feel he's an enormously talented guy who has been deprived of the notoriety he probably should have had much earlier because Hollywood was going through a stage where the awards went to the big pictures and the guys who knew how to spend a lot of money. As a result, guys who got a lot of pictures with a lot of effort and a little money weren't glorified. So Don had to wait many years until he could get to do films with fairly good budgets. He's the kind of director there's not enough of.

This heartfelt respect was obviously mutual. Siegel is quoted by Kaminsky in another book, *Don Siegel: Director*, as stating:

> I found Clint very knowledgeable about making pictures, very good at knowing what to do with the camera. I also found that he is inclined to underestimate his range as an actor. I think he is a very underrated actor, partly because he is so successful. . . . He started to come up with ideas for camera set-ups. I started to call these Clintus shots and even if I decided not to use them they invariably gave me another idea [which we called] a Siegelini shot. . . . Clint is a very strong individual on and off the screen. He doesn't require, and I don't give him, much direction. . . . Clint knows what he's doing when he acts and when he picks material. That's why he's the number one box office attraction in the world.

On May 19, 1968, while Clint was in Europe filming the blockbuster World War II epic *Where Eagles Dare* with Richard Burton, he received news from home that Maggie had given birth to the couple's first child, a boy, whom they decided to name Kyle Clinton Eastwood. Eastwood was elated at the news but irritated that his contract with MGM required him to be away from his wife and newborn son in order to complete the lengthy shooting of *Eagles*. For many years thereafter, Clint tried to have

Clint and son Kyle outside Kyle's school.

his family on location with him, wherever that might be.

Almost directly after returning from Europe, Eastwood—family in tow—flew to Oregon for *Paint Your Wagon*, Paramount's overblown musical in which Eastwood made himself the darling of the critics for once by turning in the only low-key performance in the entire film. With this film, Eastwood went against type not only by singing on screen, but also by playing a quiet, peace-loving man. The result: good notices for Clint but one of the few box-office duds of this career.

Eastwood's film career provided him with little in the way of leisure time. He felt that as long as fans were willing to pay money to see him, he would turn out the type of films they wanted at the fastest possible rate. In rapid succession came another World War II adventure, this one titled *Kelly's Heroes*, which required Eastwood to move to location shooting in Yugoslavia. This film was followed by *Two Mules for Sister Sara*, which reunited Clint with Don Siegel in a minor western that few Eastwood fans cite as among their favorite films. It should be noted, however, that both of these movies were major financial successes. It appeared that every film Eastwood's name appeared in looked certain to bring in enormous profits. Perhaps because of this security, Clint and Siegel felt it was time to branch out and explore other avenues for their talents. The two agreed to take a gamble on filming a Gothic-psychological drama titled *The Beguiled*, which cast Eastwood as a wounded Union soldier who manipulates his protectors and benefactors: a house filled with conniving, frustrated women of varying ages.

The Beguiled was a superb, yet completely unusual film for Clint to star in. For Eastwood's fans, it was a disappointment because Clint was the villain of the piece and the action was at an almost nonexistent level. Although modestly budgeted, *The Beguiled* was a box-office failure and a great disappointment for Eastwood, who had hoped his fans would not be misled by a poor ad campaign that promised standard Eastwood fare, though the film was anything but that. He hoped *The Beguiled* would stand on its own. It didn't, and Eastwood had to endure the frustration of giving one of the finest performances of his career in the film which played to the smallest number of his fans.

Never one to be afraid of taking risks, Clint followed *The Beguiled* with another uncertain venture: He decided to try his hand at a directing career. Directing had long fascinated Eastwood, and as early as his *Rawhide* days, he had observed the techniques of directors he had admired. In fact, he had requested that CBS allow him to direct an episode of *Rawhide*. The network refused, on the basis that Clint was not a member of the Directors Guild and therefore would have been in violation of union rules.

Now Eastwood had Don Siegel nominate him for membership in the Directors Guild. Siegel signed Eastwood's membership card, and for the first time in his career Clint was allowed to exercise his creative juices in the field of directing.

For his debut behind the camera, Eastwood chose no easy subject matter. In this film, titled *Play Misty for Me*, the Eastwood character is

A light moment with Geraldine Page on the set of The Beguiled.

menaced by an overpossessive, eventually maniacal woman (Jessica Walter) who attempts to kill Clint after he scorns her advances. To his credit, the film was a major success both critically and financially.

Eastwood is a man of great energy, vitality, and talent. Critics are often all too content with dismissing him as a one-dimensional actor of no consequence. Fortunately, those attitudes are changing. And well they should. It is no easy chore for one man to act and direct simultaneously. Yet Eastwood has had great success in eliciting very effective performances not only from himself, but from his actors as well. Perhaps this is because he has experienced working on both sides of the camera and can sympathize with and understand both the actor's and the director's strong points and limitations. He attempts to build an *esprit de corps* on the set, and the results have shown his efforts to be successful.

Over the years, Eastwood has built up his stock company of actors and technicians, in much the same manner as John Ford once did. There is a reason why these talented professionals return time and time again to work with Eastwood. Perhaps William Holden stated the reason most eloquently when, after Clint had directed him in *Breezy*, he was quoted as saying, "I had forgotten what it was like to make a picture this agreeably. I'll work with Clint any time he asks. Besides, he can't pull any crap on me, because he is an actor too. He's also even tempered, a personality trait not much in evidence among directors. The crew is totally behind him, and that really helps things go smoothly. There's been no tempera-

27

ment, nothing. We all do our own work and like it."

Eastwood involves himself in all aspects of his films. If he is not an expert in a particular field, he is willing to learn. Ferris Webster, an editor on several Eastwood films, has stated, "Clint's a great student. He can run all the equipment, too, which is a great help, and when there's second-unit work to be shot, it's probably Clint behind the camera. He knows what he wants to do." And what Eastwood wants is cost-cutting efficiency right down the line. This includes doing away with all unnecessary frills not only in acting and directing, but also in editing. He is one of the few filmmakers who will have all the editing on a film done on location. This not only saves time and money, but also allows him to see the effectiveness of the entire editing process while still on the set.

Eastwood followed his directorial debut in *Play Misty for Me* with the most controversial film of his career, *Dirty Harry*, a fast-paced detective story directed by Don Siegel. The film quickly became a *cause célèbre*, with the media arguing heatedly about whether the film should be condoned or condemned for its viewpoint of police tactics. Many felt that Eastwood's role as the police officer who takes the law into his own violent hands was nothing more than a blueprint for fascist police actions. Others saw the film as a sincere, sympathetic treatment of one honest man's fight against the system.

Dirty Harry drew praise from some circles for Eastwood's performance, but other critics felt that Clint was letting loose all his political frustrations in the form of a movie. Eastwood denied that he's the least bit political, and he defended the film by saying, "I don't think *Dirty Harry* was a fascist film at all. It's just the story of one frustrated police officer in a frustrating situation. I think that's why police officers were attracted to the film. Most of the films that were coming out at that time, in 1972, were extremely anti-cop. . . . And this was a film that showed the frustrations of the job, but at the same time, it wasn't a glorification of police work."

One thing that everyone did agree on: *Dirty Harry* was the biggest hit of Clint Eastwood's career up to that time. Yet despite its enormous popularity, Eastwood and Siegel would not work together on another film until 1979, when they collaborated on *Escape from Alcatraz*.

1972 saw Eastwood slowing down a bit. He released only one film, the highly forgettable western *Joe Kidd*, which he filmed with director John Sturges. Part of the reason for Clint's relaxation of professional interests was a new, more important interest in his home life: His daughter Allison was born. Eastwood and Maggie devoted as much time as possible to being with their children, even though it meant that Clint was sacrificing millions of dollars by not seizing acting opportunities.

All this while, Eastwood insisted that his children and wife were not to be subjected to the scrutiny of the press and the resulting publicity. He has always felt that one of his key duties as a parent is to see to it that his family enjoys a normal lifestyle that leaves them free to choose their own paths. As a result, his children have rarely been photographed for the press.

A rare 1969 publicity shot for Paramount. Top row, left to right: Rock Hudson, John Wayne, Yves Montand. Bottom row: Lee Marvin, Robert Evans, Barbra Streisand, Clint Eastwood.

Eastwood clowns with Kyle on the set, 1972.

28

29

By 1973, Clint was ready to go to work again. In one of his most hectic periods, he starred in two films (one of which he directed) and directed, but did not star in, a third film. His first release in 1973 was *High Plains Drifter*, an eerie western with supernatural overtones and more than a coincidental flavor of the Leone westerns. Eastwood directed himself in this popular, off-beat epic, which proved another winner with his fans.

Eastwood's second project of the year was to direct a modestly budgeted love story called *Breezy*, which starred William Holden and Kay Lenz in a May-December romance. The film was attacked by many critics as hopelessly outdated and corny. Although this film failed to show a profit, Clint did gain quite a few good notices praising him for trying something different.

The failure of *Breezy* to find an audience frustrated Clint. For the first time, he appeared to be annoyed by critical reaction. He was also irritated when the Motion Picture Association of America tagged *Breezy* with an R rating, which restricted attendance by audiences under seventeen. Eastwood argued that this hurt the film's chance of making a profit because it was banned from the very audience he had hoped to appeal to. At least he could take solace in the fact that for the first time, no one could complain that a Clint Eastwood film was too violent. Although he did not star in it, Clint has often said that *Breezy* is the film he is most proud of.

Clint's disappointment was quickly soothed when Warner Bros. released his sequel to *Dirty Harry*. This film, *Magnum Force*, became a massive hit for Eastwood, although many critics stated that it had nowhere near the originality of its predecessor. Fans either felt otherwise or didn't care, and Eastwood found himself securely on top of the box-office ladder once more.

As previously mentioned, Eastwood is a very private man who does not easily grant interviews or promote his films. He simply doesn't have to. His audience is basically built in. The fans will see an Eastwood film regardless of whether he promotes it. Perhaps for this reason, he rarely appears on television. In the early seventies he would occasionally appear on his friend Merv Griffin's talk show, but even those appearances were few and far between. In late 1979 he appeared on a Tom Snyder interview special on NBC TV. During this program, film was shown of Eastwood directing *Bronco Billy*. Clint seemed to enjoy the flow of the interview. His only other major interview appearance in years has been on a Barbara Walters TV show, which ABC broadcast in 1980. The theme was sex symbols, and Eastwood, Paul Newman, and Burt Reynolds appeared in separate conversations. The interview was basically unenlightening but quite enjoyable.

One of Clint's earlier compromises on a TV program nearly turned out to be a disaster. The evening in question was the live telecast of the Academy Awards ceremony in 1973. Eastwood had been coerced into appearing on the show in order to present the award for best picture—an honor always reserved for the true giants of the industry. The opening of the show was to have featured Charlton Heston explaining the

Clint and Maggie attending a Frank Sinatra concert in 1971.

Clint making a rare appearance at the Academy Awards ceremony.

Eastwood throws out the first ball at a Los Angeles Dodgers game.

academy's voting rules through reading a witty script designed to spoof his image as the saviour-like hero he has portrayed in so many films. Moments before the show started, Clint found himself backstage with the show's producer, Howard Koch, who nervously informed Clint that Heston was stuck in a traffic jam and would be unable to make the scheduled appearance on time. With no one available to fill in, he begged Eastwood to take Heston's place and introduce the proceedings.

Never an extrovert, Clint immediately refused. However, Maggie felt sorry for Koch's predicament and convinced Clint that he could handle the assignment. Within the flash of a second, the glittery awards ceremony was being beamed into millions of homes throughout the world, and there, holding a manuscript of dialogue designed for the actor who had played Moses, stood Clint Eastwood. Clint decided that he would go on with the show exactly as written for Heston. He explained briefly what had happened and quipped that he was puzzled that the academy would choose for an "ad-libber" host "a guy who hasn't said ten words in his last fifteen pictures."

On the Warner Bros. back lot, 1973.

The audience loved it and gave Clint solid support by laughing in all the right places. Suddenly, and in his true screen image, Charlton Heston arrived onstage to rescue Clint. The academy members roared their enthusiasm and applause, and the following day's reviews claimed that it was one of the few genuinely funny moments in Oscar history. Clint received the lion's share of the praise and caused Rex Reed to write in astonishment "We learned Clint Eastwood can be funny!"

Eastwood has long been a believer in developing new talent, in addition to offering employment to members of his so-called stock company. Friends like Bill McKinney and Geoffrey Lewis, as well as his then-current romantic interest, Sondra Locke, had been offered more than steady employment because of Clint's loyalty. They had also gained a great deal of notoriety from being in so many box-office hits. This led to far more lucrative careers than many of them might have suspected they would have, had not Clint given them the chance to display their talents.

One major talent that Eastwood was fundamental in giving a break to was Michael Cimino. The future director had co-scripted *Magnum Force*, and Clint was so pleased with his work that he hired Cimino to write the screenplay for his 1974 adventure *Thunderbolt and Lightfoot*. When he read the completed script, Eastwood saw so much promise in the young man that he decided to go out on a limb and hire Cimino to direct *Thunderbolt and Lightfoot* as well. With Malpaso producing, Eastwood had enough authority to make such a choice and United Artists, the company releasing the film, said little to object.

Eastwood's gamble paid off handsomely. Not only was the film a hit at the box office, but it also generated far kinder reviews than Clint had been accustomed to. Although Cimino was dormant in Hollywood following this film, he resurfaced in 1978 to win the best-director Oscar for *The Deer Hunter*. In late 1980, Cimino's name would become a household word because of the failure of his film *Heaven's Gate* (reputed to be the most expensive film ever made). Nevertheless, he has emerged as a driving force in Hollywood, and his career owes a great deal to the experience he gained on Eastwood's film.

1975 saw the release of another film that Clint directed—*The Eiger Sanction*, a spy thriller done so realistically that it required Clint to climb some deadly mountain terrain to give the film the proper look of authenticity. It was a hazardous assignment, and studio brass often wondered if their major star would survive the location work. Yet at no time did Eastwood allow a stuntman to substitute for him. This is in keeping with his belief that a film suffers if a stuntman is used. Eastwood maintains that the audience can usually tell whether the actor is really doing his own stunts.

In order to maintain realism at all times, Clint has been subjected to the kind of rigorous action that most superstars would never even consider. In addition to his work on *The Eiger Sanction*, Eastwood has jumped from a bridge onto a speeding schoolbus (*Dirty Harry*), been dragged by a rope across the Rio Grande (*Hang 'Em High*), found himself

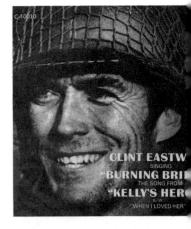

Rare picture sleeve from unreleased 1970 record with Clint singing the theme from Kelly's Heroes.

Posing with Burt Reynolds for the cover of Time.

clinging to a runaway car *(Magnum Force)*, and driven over explosions *(Kelly's Heroes)*. Fortunately, he has survived all this with but a few scrapes and bruises. He feels the risks are worthwhile, and the audience apparently agrees. Unlike the days when the moviegoing public had to settle for observing their favorite actors facing deadly situations while running in front of a back-screen projection, audiences are more sophisticated today. They want real thrills, and Eastwood never disappoints. His films might not always be considered works of art, but not even his severest critics have ever called them dull.

The mid-seventies were not the most appropriate time for Hollywood to invest its money in westerns. This genre had long been considered dead, although a few brave stars and directors had hoped to revive this traditional form of Americana on screen. In 1976, a series of highly publicized westerns flooded the nation's screens, with mostly disastrous results. Audiences stayed away in droves, and even a star like Paul Newman could not draw audiences to see his film for Robert Altman, *Buffalo Bill and the Indians*.

One western that did make an impact was Don Siegel's *The Shootist*, a superbly crafted film that offered John Wayne his last and perhaps best performance. The only other profitable western of the year was Eastwood's epic *The Outlaw Josey Wales*, which played to packed theaters throughout the summer. Many critics had predicted that the market had been lost even for Clint Eastwood westerns, but he soon proved them wrong.

Behind the camera for High Plains Drifter.

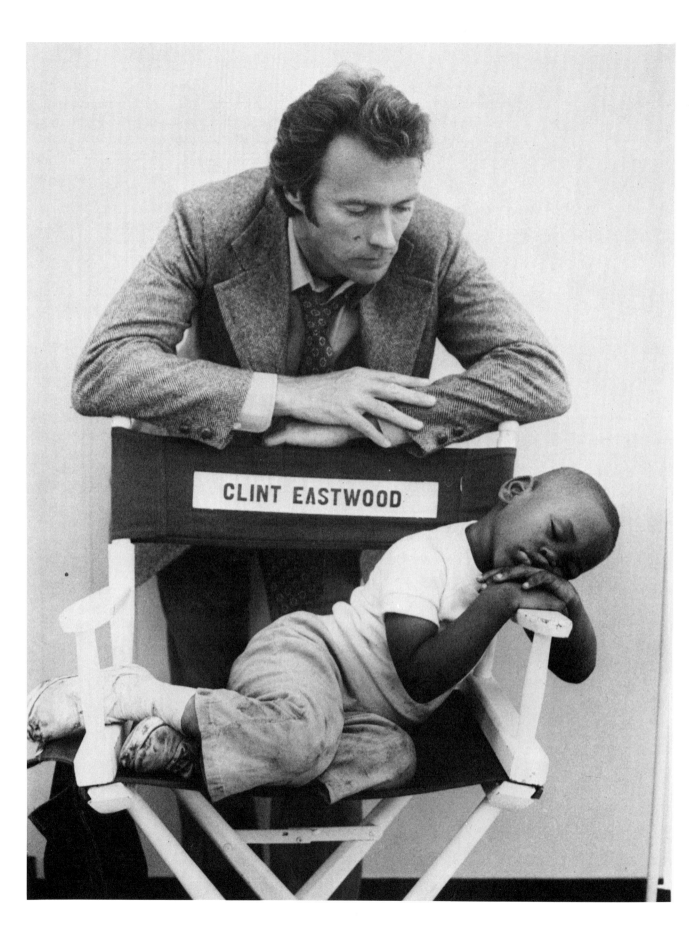

*Sneaking up on a visitor
on the set of* Magnum
Force.

This was Eastwood's highest-grossing western to that point and one of his more controversial films. Critics argued over whether the wholesale bloodletting on screen was excessive. Eastwood defended the film, and in doing so, he stated his position on gun control. He claimed that Americans should have the right to keep guns in their houses, but he did advocate much stricter gun-control laws. "All guns should be registered. I don't think legitimate gun owners would mind that kind of legislation. Right now the furor against a gun law is by gun owners who are overreacting. They're worried that all guns are going to be recalled. It's impossible to take guns out of circulation, and that's why firearms should be registered and mail-order delivery of guns halted." These views may have been surprising in their moderation for many of Eastwood's audience, but they reinforce the fact that Eastwood is not a carbon copy of the man he portrays on screen.

Throughout the late seventies, Eastwood continued to dominate the top place in the annual listings of box-office attractions. This was due, in large part, to his appearing in his traditional action-adventure vehicles, which garnered little support from critics but massive enthusiasm from his fans. In 1976, his third Dirty Harry film, *The Enforcer*, outgrossed the previous films of the series by a wide margin.

In 1977, Eastwood starred in and directed *The Gauntlet*, a successful but uninteresting detective thriller in which Eastwood was impressive in a change-of-character role as an alcoholic cop. The film marked his second on-screen appearance with Sondra Locke, the first having been in *The Outlaw Josey Wales*.

As Eastwood has matured as a director, he has desired to do so as an actor as well. Although many of his films contained broad elements of humor, none of them could have been considered an outright comedy. At this point in his career, with many years of successful filmmaking behind him, Eastwood decided he could afford to take the biggest gamble of his cinematic career—starring in a broad slapstick comedy entitled *Every Which Way but Loose*. Clint has said that every person in his private and professional lives advised him against doing this film. It was an uncertain medium for him to gamble with. He was sorely reminded that his last such gambles with new genres (*The Beguiled, Paint Your Wagon*, and *Breezy*) had been the only financial failures of his career.

Yet Eastwood saw something in this mild comedy that he felt would lead audiences into enthusiastic responses. This time, his inclinations proved correct. To the amazement of everyone—perhaps even Eastwood—*Every Which Way but Loose* was the biggest moneymaker of his long career. It also proved, as *Variety* noted, that if his fans stood in line for this film, they would stand in line for anything with Eastwood's name on it. With the success of this film, Eastwood was fully accepted as not only the reigning star of action films, but also a proven draw in the comedy market.

Much of *Loose* concerns Eastwood's onscreen romance with Sondra Locke. Rumors had circulated for some time that the two had become quite close off screen as well. Eastwood and Locke graciously refused to comment on these theories, contending that their private lives—and the state of Eastwood's marriage—were not for public consumption.

The rumors continued, however, even when Eastwood received high praise for his 1979 film *Escape from Alcatraz* (which reunited him with Don Siegel), a film that conspicuously lacked participation by any of his "stock-company players." Locke was not cast in the film, primarily because there were no roles for women. However, she did appear in Clint's 1980 summer release *Bronco Billy*.

By this time, Eastwood admitted publicly that he and his wife had filed for divorce. Eastwood said little more on the subject, and he remained particularly silent or noncommittal when asked to elaborate on his relationship with Locke. He would only comment on her in a professional way. There was little doubt, however, that Sondra Locke had become the leading lady in Clint Eastwood's life.

Eastwood's divorce case received a good deal of public attention. Although neither he nor Maggie ever courted the press to downgrade one another, it was reported that she had won a decision granting her the settlement sum of twenty-five million dollars—a staggering amount even for someone of Eastwood's wealth.

Eastwood next made the news with an unusual type of court appearance. His 1976 thriller *The Enforcer* was the subject of a well publicized court dispute in Manhattan in 1980. The claimant was a writer who had accused Malpaso and Warner Bros. of plagiarizing the title *The Enforcer* from one of his works. Eastwood appeared in court to testify that he had been inspired to use the title after having seen an old Humphrey Bogart film of the same name. Eastwood maintained that even this did not constitute plagiarism because Warner Bros., which had produced the 1976 *Enforcer*, also owned the title rights to the Bogart film. The judge quickly sided with Clint and dismissed the case.

By this point, Clint's growing legions of defenders were frustrated by the industry's failure to nominate him for an Oscar. However, he was not without recognition in Tinseltown. In 1980, the People's Choice Award—an annual tribute to those chosen the most populate actors in America on the basis of massive telephone surveys—honored him with its first Life Achievement Award. Many cynics said Eastwood would never appear to accept it, but they were wrong. He appeared on stage following a superbly edited compilation of his film career, to gratefully accept the award. Few could doubt that he was moved by the honor. He appeared the following year on the same program to accept the award for the most popular actor in America, having won over such competition as Burt Reynolds and Robert Redford. Sondra Locke presented the award to him.

Probably one of the most distinguished honors Eastwood has received has been the tribute given him by the Department of Film for the Museum of Modern Art in December 1980. On that occasion, the Museum held a day-long festival of Eastwood's films. Audiences at the sold-out festival got a rare chance to see the unedited version of *A Fistful of Dollars* (which, like most Eastwood films, has been severely edited for television) as well as *Escape from Alcatraz*. Later in the evening,

Eastwood himself appeared twice in front of an enthusiastic, standing-room-only audience comprised, not of giggling teenagers, but rather, of sincere and learned film scholars whose presence proved that Eastwood was now being considered as a real talent among not only actors, but directors as well. The museum was quick to point out that they were honoring Eastwood's achievements in those fields, as well as his talent in making exceptional films of such varying subject matter.

The Museum screened *Play Misty for Me*, after which Eastwood appeared to answer questions about his techniques as both director and actor. He later appeared, to preface a screening of *Bronco Billy* with some insight into how the film was made. In the course of the evening Eastwood displayed great wit and a good sense of humor. He proved well that his knowledge of filmmaking is quite extensive, and the audience followed both of his sessions with standing ovations.

Most actors might have used such an evening to promote a current film, but Eastwood chose not to do so, even though his sequel to *Every Which Way but Loose*, entitled *Any Which Way You Can*, had just opened around the country. Instead, he spoke strictly of his experiences in filmmaking and his gratitude for having been honored that evening.

On the Any Which Way You Can *set with producer Fritz Manes.*

Among Clint's remarks: he announced the screen "retirement" of the now-famous Dirty Harry character (a prediction rendered premature by 1988's *The Dead Pool*; Eastwood's favorite film in which he

37

has starred is *The Outlaw Josey Wales* ("I thought I did a pretty good job with that one"); when asked about his relationship with Sondra Locke, he once again limited his remarks to praising her for her talents as a professional actress; and he expressed his feelings at having been overlooked for an Oscar after so many years of providing Hollywood with some of its biggest-grossing films. On the latter subject matter, he stated that although he would always desire an Oscar, he felt that an honor such as the museum's—which gave him no physical award or plaque— was far more meaningful and humbling because it was given to him by the people that matter most, his public.

Since the tribute at the Museum of Modern Art, it has become quite fashionable in the international film industry to honor Eastwood in various ways. He has continued to win the People's Choice Award for Favorite Actor, and in 1988 he was voted All-Time Favorite Movie Star. In 1985, he was honored at the Cinematheque in Paris and was awarded a decoration by the Minister of Culture. Not bad for a guy who was once dismissed by a studio executive because his prominent Adam's apple precluded a career in films. (The same hapless executive also told Burt Reynolds he had no future in show business).

There has been a re-evaluation of Eastwood's talents by the critical establishment as well, with many reviewers grudgingly acknowledging Eastwood's skills both in front of and behind the camera. His films *Pale Rider* and *Bird* were both shown in competition at the Cannes Film Festival; *Newsweek* labeled him "An American Icon"; and Vincent Canby of *The New York Times* wrote with admirable candor: "I'm just now beginning to realize that, though Mr. Eastwood may have been improving over the years, it's also taken all these years for most of us to recognize his very consistent grace and wit as a filmmaker."

Eastwood's new-found respect can be attributed to his determination to take chances, and make films that are widely differentiated by their storylines. In 1982, for instance, he starred in the big-budget thriller *Firefox*, which appealed to his core group of fans. Later that year, however, he directed and starred in *Honky Tonk Man*, a low-key Depression-era drama that died at the box-office, but gained acclaim as a major career achievement.

Eastwood continues to maintain a reputation as a no-nonsene, cost-efficient filmmaker. In an age when most studios and stars quarrel endlessly about projects, salaries, and stars' egos, Eastwood has proven time and again that he will deliver a film under budget and ahead of schedule. This he accomplishes through working with a stock company of actors and technicians upon whom he knows he can rely. A cynic once complained that Eastwood was cheap, and probably had never paid more than $50,000 for a screenplay. Eastwood has countered that if this were the case he wouldn't be able to attract his "stock company" back for each succeeding film with such ease.

Throughout the eighties, Eastwood remained one of the most consistent box-office draws in the world. He also became less reluctant to deal with the press—both on favorable and unfavorable terms. He appeared

With Dave Turner of the Clint Eastwood Appreciation Society, 1987.

The Guest of Honor speaks at the "All Star Party for Clint Eastwood," a tribute from the Variety Club, 1986.

on more talk shows, and seemed more relaxed and humorous. However, he successfully sued the *National Enquirer* when the tabloid incorrectly linked him romantically with country singer Tanya Tucker. He began to publicly grumble about what he felt were harmful governmental policies in his beloved hometown of Carmel, and felt the township should ease its virtual ban on certain types of development. Eastwood groused that the present mayor even forbade the town from opening an ice-cream parlor.

No one thought much of these complaints from the Hollywood icon, until Eastwood made the stunning announcement that he would run for mayor of Carmel in the April 1986 elections. Citing differences with the current administration's "killjoy mentality," Eastwood claimed that, if elected, he would do away with local laws which many felt were archaic in their suppression of tourism and development. His opponent was 62-year-old Charlotte Townsend, and the prospect of Dirty Harry squaring off against an elderly female adversary proved to be a windfall for the press. Reporters from all over the world converged on the tiny hamlet until Eastwood himself began to grow weary of the attention.

Yet, he campaigned in a traditional way, and underplayed his public popularity by attending coffee klatches, kissing babies and ringing doorbells. Unsurprisingly, Eastwood won a landslide election in April, 1986. True to his word, he made the promised reforms and proved to be a popular and respected public official. The publicity, however, failed to wane. President Reagan joked "What makes him think that a middle-aged movie actor who played with a chimp could possibly have a future in politics?", and Carmel was rapidly becoming "Clintville" as merchants sought to exploit Eastwood's prominence. (One T shirt capitalized on Eastwood's meeting with the Pope by showing the two men shaking hands under the caption "Thou hast made my day!")

Despite his accomplishments and rewarding moments as mayor, Eastwood announced that he would not seek reelection to another two-year term in 1988. He cited infringement on his personal time and his career as the reason for his retirement from politics, although he did not exclude a return to the field in the future.

Eastwood's work in recent years has been among the most diversified and interesting of his career. He has made clear that at this point in his career, he is placing artistic satisfaction above box-office certainty. His long standing relationship with Warner Brothers has proven to be mutually beneficial. The studio has backed some of Clint's more prestigious films although there was little doubt these projects would have limited popular appeal. In return, through his Malpaso Productions, Clint regularly provides a film to please his core audience. Since the mid-eighties, he has won public and critical acclaim for his superb performance as the haunted detective in *Tightrope*, as well as give the ailing Western genre a boost with the well received *Pale Rider*. There have been misfires along the way as well. *Pink Cadillac* seemed to be an outdated nod an audience that evaporated with the *Smokey and the Bandit* sequels, and *The Rookie* was a misguided "buddy" film which failed to ignite any sparks.

Recording the soundtrack for Every Which Way But Loose.

Clint with young Kyle and Allison visit Leonard Nimoy and William Shatner on the set of Star Trek—The Motion Picture *(1979).*

Curiously, two of Eastwood's most acclaimed films have not been commercial successes. *Bird*, his 1988 directorial effort chronicling the short, troubled life of jazz legend Charlie Parker, received the kind of international acclaim Clint could only have dreamed about a few years before. A bold, innovative film in a completely unique directorial style, the movie was a dream come true for Eastwood, who had idolized Parker since his youth. Clint followed *Bird*—after the release of *Pink Cadillac*—with *White Hunter, Black Heart*, a mesmerizing semifactual recounting of the filming of *The African Queen*. Again, audiences stayed away, but Eastwood continued to fine-tune his acting and directorial skills. Like *Bird*, the movie was a critical success, particularly in Europe.

Although some felt Eastwood's box-office clout had lessened, his defenders argued that he was merely making more mature films for discriminating audiences. He continued to receive industry accolades, most notably the Hollywood Foreign Press Association's Cecil B. DeMille Lifetime Achievement Award, which was presented to him at the 1988 Golden Globes ceremonies by Sir Richard Attenborough (who preceded Clint's appearance with effusive praise and a "roast" consisting of outtakes from Eastwood's lesser works).

By 1992, Clint Eastwood had gained an international reputation as a talented actor and filmmaker, even as evidence mounted that his box-office appeal might be in decline. The release of his highly praised *Unforgiven* in the summer of 1992 proved that such predictions were premature. With this film, many felt Clint had achieved a high water mark in his career. Unlike his previously acclaimed films of recent years, *Unforgiven* appealed both to critics and audiences alike. The film had a healthy U.S. box-office gross of over $95 million, and earned a large number awards from international film critics associations—and, of course, the Academy Award for Clint both as Best Director and producer of the Best Picture of the Year.

When the first edition of this book was published in 1982, several reviewers scoffed that the authors were treating Eastwood as an auteur and world-class filmmaker. To that we pleaded guilty. Today, however, there is little in the way of such cynicism. Clint has paid his dues and has earned the respect of his audience and peers. Happily, these accolades are coming at a point in his career when he can still enjoy them and capitalize on them. He remains more active than ever, and as this edition goes to press, is starring in a new thriller, *In the Line of Fire*, for director Wolfgang Petersen for mid-1993 release.

The dirtiest word for the screen's Dirty Harry seems to be "retirement." He recently wrote in *Parade* magazine,

Vintage Eastwood—mist, danger, and gunplay. From City Heat *(1984).*

I want to meet my own challenges. I don't think I'll ever retire. I love playing golf and skiing. I make time for those things, but I wouldn't want to get up every morning only to say, "Where am I going to tee off today?" That would be boring. Some people are obsessed with retirement, and when they actually make the move, they lose interest in everything, then fade away. I think that energy and the challenge and enjoyment of work are important. Human beings are not meant to sit still. I'd like to be a bigger and more knowledgeable person 10 years from now than I am today. I think that as we grow older we must discipline ourselves to continue expanding, broadening, learning, keeping our minds active and open. And that's the challenge each of us has earned.

One of Eastwood's famous lines from *Magnum Force* is: "A man's got to know his limitation." Fortunately, Clint never believed those who identified his limitation earlier in his life, or he might still be digging swimming pools. Hopefully, he will continue to expand his horizons and grace the screen with an expanding body of work that only seems to grow richer as he matures as actor and director.

These early photos of Eastwood in Revenge of the Creature *show his brief appearance as a bumbling lab assistant.*

THE EARLY FILMS

Revenge of the Creature, 1955, black-and-white, 82 minutes. Released by Universal Pictures. Directed by Jack Arnold. Starring John Agar, Lori Nelson, John Bromfield, Clint Eastwood.

Eastwood's first appearance on a motion-picture screen occurred in this sequel to *Creature from the Black Lagoon*, a horror film from Universal that had met with some mild success. Director Jack Arnold repeated the premise of a half-man, half-fish sea monster breaking loose from his captors and setting an entire city to fleeing in terror. A subplot had the creature falling in love with a woman ichthyologist.

Eastwood was on screen for only a few brief moments in the role of a lab technician who misplaces some white mice. He commented years later, "I had only three or four lines and can't remember a word of them." Yet the film was significant in getting Eastwood accustomed to the procedures of shooting a feature-length film.

Francis in the Navy, 1955, black-and-white, 80 minutes. Released by Universal Pictures. Directed by Arthur Lubin. Starring Donald O'Connor, Martha Hyer, Richard Erdman, Martin Milner, David Janssen, Clint Eastwood.

Eastwood's second film appearance was as unspectacular as his first, although it was significant for his career because he received screen credit. The film was part of a successful series revolving around the misadventures of a talking mule named Francis (the off-screen voice was that of Chill Wills) and his harried, dumb, but sincere owner, played by Donald O'Connor. In this film the mule is mistakenly drafted, and the resulting confusion provides the comedic premise. Eastwood's role was slightly larger than the one he was given in *Revenge of the Creature*.

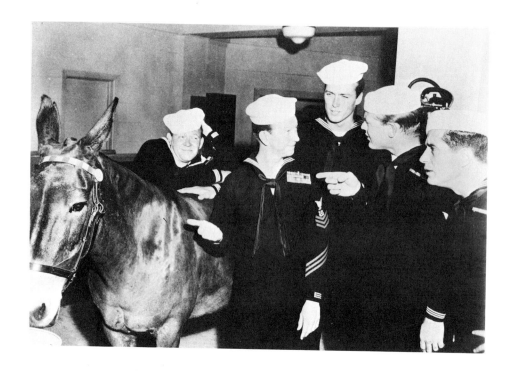

Clint Eastwood (center) with Donald O'Connor and Francis the talking Mule. Frank Jenks leans on the mule.

Lady Godiva, 1955, color, 85 minutes. Released by Universal Pictures. Directed by Arthur Lubin. Starring Maureen O'Hara, George Nader, Rex Reason, Victor McLaglen, Clint Eastwood.

The sole *raison d'être* for this forgettable failure was to exploit the legend of Lady Godiva, who in medieval times supposedly expressed her social protests by riding naked through the city on horseback. Not surprisingly, the film did less than deliver the titillating ride that many in the audience may have expected.

A paper-thin storyline revolving around a battle between the Saxons and the Normans was developed, with Eastwood taking a drop in screen credits from the fifth line in *Francis in the Navy* to near bottom for this low-budget adventure. He is listed simply as First Saxon, a minor distinction to be sure, but here it was somewhat better than having been cast in the title role, as he most often was in his later, more successful films.

Tarantula, 1955, black-and-white, 80 minutes. Released by Universal Pictures. Directed by Jack Arnold. Starring John Agar, Mara Corday, Leo G. Carroll.

This film continued the tradition of casting Eastwood in the smallest bit parts. Another low-budget Universal horror film, *Tarantula* presented the stale threat of a giant spider—created by exposure to an overdose of atomic radiation (the popular fear to exploit in the fifties)—menacing John Agar and Leo G. Carroll among others.

Eastwood's only appearance comes late in the film, when he shows up behind a mask, as an air-force pilot trying to napalm the spider.

TARANTULA

That's Eastwood behind the pilot's mask as he leads a squadron of fighters in an effort to bomb the monstrous creature into submission.

Never Say Goodbye, 1956, Technicolor, 96 minutes. Released by Universal Pictures. Directed by Jerry Hopper. Starring Rock Hudson, George Sanders, Ray Collins, David Janssen, Shelley Fabares.

Universal at this time was pushing Rock Hudson as their favorite glamour boy, and this film focused on a doctor who, through a misunderstanding, walks out on his wife, taking their young daughter with him. Reunited years later, they keep the mother's identity from the daughter until she can regain the child's love.

The Rock Hudson character dominated the screen, and Eastwood had the rather unchallenging role of the star's laboratory assistant, the second time he had played such a role. Following this film, Universal dropped Eastwood from his contract, leaving the actor depressed and unemployed.

The First Traveling Saleslady, 1956, color, 92 minutes. Released by RKO. Directed by Arthur Lubin. Starring Ginger Rogers, Barry Nelson, Carol Channing, James Arness, Clint Eastwood.

Recovering from having his contract terminated with Universal, Eastwood went to work for the ill-fated RKO Studios, the long-time haven for low-budget films. This film was no exception, but Eastwood was given his largest role up to that time, as well as more amiable treatment from his employers, who promised him a separate byline in the credits, "And introducing Clint Eastwood."

The film, set in 1897, dealt with a corset designer played by Ginger Rogers, who heads west with her secretary to sell barbed wire after a Broadway show is closed by police because of a number using her corsets.

The film displayed Eastwood's believability as a love interest, and his role in the film, while not important, was far better than any part Universal had given him.

Clint Eastwood, threatens Carol Channing.

Clint Eastwood finds the sheriff (Dan White) and his deputy tied up.

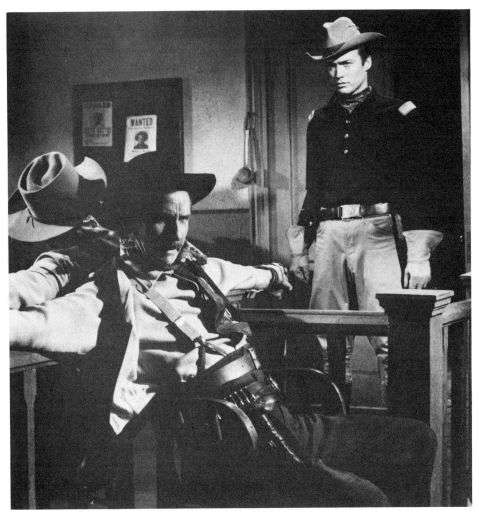

THE FIRST TRAVELING SALESLADY

With David Brian (left), Barry Nelson (hands in pockets), and Carol Channing.

Romance.

Star in the Dust, 1956, Technicolor, 80 minutes, Released by Universal Pictures. Directed by Charles Haas. Starring John Agar, Mamie Van Doren, Richard Boone, Leif Erickson, Coleen Gray, James Gleason, Clint Eastwood.

Released through Universal, *Star in the Dust* cast Eastwood, unbilled for the first time since *Revenge of the Creature*, in the very small role of a ranch hand. The storyline deals with a sheriff who finds himself battling a town to do his duty and handle a professional killer who has murdered three farmers. This was the third time Eastwood appeared in a starring vehicle for John Agar, the first having been *Revenge of the Creature* and the second, *Tarantula* the year before.

Escapade in Japan, 1957, color, 93 minutes. Released by RKO and Universal. Directed by Arthur Lubin. Starring Teresa Wright, Cameron Mitchell, Jon Provost, Roger Nakagawa, Clint Eastwood.

Primarily an adventure film for children, *Escapade in Japan* marked Eastwood's second film for RKO. This was also Eastwood's fourth stint under the direction of Arthur Lubin.

The story deals with the adventures of two youngsters, one American and one Japanese, as they search for the American boy's parents, whom he was on his way to meet when his plane was forced down. Eastwood had a minor role as a serviceman named Dumbo who inspires the two young boys to run away on a "thrilling" adventure in Japan.

Eastwood bit part in
Lafayette Escadrille.

Lafayette Escadrille, 1958, black-and-white, 93 minutes. Released by Warner Bros. Directed by William Wellman. Starring Tab Hunter, Etchika Choureau, Marcel Dalio, David Janssen, Jody McCrea, Bill Wellman, Jr., Clint Eastwood.

Lafayette Escadrille appeared, on paper at least, to be the most promising film in which Eastwood had yet appeared. Designed as a fast-moving action adventure about a heroic U.S. pilot in World War I, the film was directed by the eminent William Wellman, upon whose original story the screenplay is based. Wellman had also sat in the director's chair for *Wings*, the silent classic that became the first film ever to win an Oscar. *Lafayette* was another story, however. The film was bogged down with a slow-moving plot revolving around an independent troubleshooter (Tab Hunter) whose adventures find him first in France, fighting the Germans, and later in the U.S. air corps after America enters the war.

Eastwood's role was very minor. He was cast as a background fighter pilot and was given no dialogue, although his sheer physical presence managed to make him noticeable to audiences. The film turned out to be a disappointment to both critics and audiences, and William Wellman thereafter gracefully retired from the silver screen.

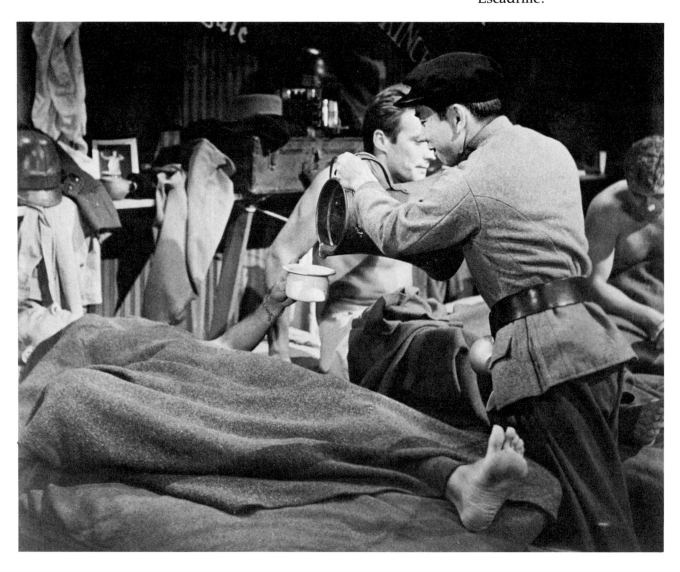

Clint Eastwood (in background) in a scene from Lafayette Escadrille.

Ambush at Cimarron Pass (1958)

CAST

Sergeant Matt Blake, Scott Brady; *Theresa,* Margia Dean; *Corbin,* Baynes Barron; *Henry,* William Vaughan; *Corporal Schwitzer,* Ken Mayer; *Private Zach,* John Manier; *Private Lasky,* Keith Richards; *Keith Williams,* Clint Eastwood; *Private Nathan,* John Merrick; *Sam Prescott,* Frank Grestle; *Johnny Willows,* Dirk London; *Stanfield,* Irving Bacon; *Cobb,* Desmond Slattery.

CREDITS

Produced by Herbert E. Mendelson. *Directed by* Jodie Copeland. *Screenplay by* Richard G. Taylor and John K. Butler. *Cinematography,* John M. Nickolaus. *Editor,* Carl L. Peirson. *Music by* Paul Sawtell and Bert Shefter. *Running time: 73 minutes.* A 20th Century-Fox release of a Regal Production.

SYNOPSIS

Sergeant Matt Blake (Scott Brady), a soldier in the Union army, is assigned to escort a prisoner named Corbin (Baynes Barron) to the command post where he will stand trial for selling arms to the Apaches. Enroute, Blake encounters Sam Prescott (Frank Grestle), a former Confederate-army officer, who is now a rancher taking his herd to a distant railroad. Both men ride together and, despite obvious political differences, manage to fight off a surprise Indian attack. Although the shaky relationship is enough to get them through the battle, it is bitterly opposed by two of Prescott's men: Keith Williams (Clint Eastwood) and "Judge" Stanfield (Irving Bacon). Williams detests the alliance because of the harsh feelings he still houses from the Civil War, and the cowardly Blake proposes buying the Indians' friendship by giving them Corbin's captured rifles.

As the group slowly progresses toward the fort, they encounter many hardships, including an Indian ruse that causes one of Prescott's men to be captured and tortured to death. Further complications occur when an Apache plan to drive off the horses succeeds, leaving the group with virtually no water and the burdensome task of carrying all the stolen rifles by hand.

One by one, members of the party are killed, and eventually Williams and Stanfield plot a mutiny. Before any action can be taken, the Indians mount an attack, during which another soldier is killed and Prescott is wounded. Williams vents his anger on Blake, and the two men have a bruising fight, which leaves Williams the loser. He quickly begins to change his attitudes, and as he becomes more willing to accept Blake, he

Clint Eastwood standing over his men.

also begins to see through Stanfield's cowardly nature.

A subsequent attack at a place called Cimarron Pass finds Stanfield releasing Corbin, only to be knifed to death by the prisoner. Corbin gains little. As he runs toward the Apaches for help, they shoot and kill him.

A full-scale battle erupts when Blake and his men sneak into the Apache camp to release the horses. Although they succeed, the horses are stampeded, leaving the group stranded and still a long distance from the fort.

Although safe from Apaches, Blake realizes that his men will never be able to reach the fort if burdened with the weight of the rifles. He commands that each gun be dismantled and destroyed, making it possible for the group to reach the fort safely.

Ambush at Cimarron Pass provided Eastwood with the most important and visible role of his career up to that time. The role of a lone, trouble-making confederate soldier may have provided little challenge for Eastwood, but he was seen on screen far more frequently than his other roles had allowed. Although Eastwood would later jokingly call this film the worst movie ever made, it was actually a good-natured, minor western.

Clint Eastwood (center) and soldiers bivouacked before coming to the aid of Margia Dean.

However, *Ambush at Cimarron Pass* was notable for gaining Eastwood his first favorable critical notices, modest though they may have been. The February 14, 1958, issue of *Variety* had this to say about the film;

Jodie Copeland's first directorial effort, *Ambush at Cimarron Pass*, moves rather well within the limitations of its low budget. . . . Top-liner Scott Brady, as a Union soldier who fights Apaches now that there are no more rebels, is sincere in his approach and quite believable in his performance. Fine portrayals also come from Margia Dean, Frank Grestle, Clint Eastwood and Dirk London.

Variety

A Fistful of Dollars (1964)

CAST

The Man with No Name, Clint Eastwood; *Marisol,* Marianne Koch; *Ramon Rojo,* John Wells; *John Baxter,* W. Lukschy; *Esteban Rojo,* S. Rupp; *Benito Rojo,* Antonio Prieto; *Silvanito,* José Calvo; *Consuelo Baxter,* Margherita Lozano; *Julian,* Daniel Martin.

CREDITS

Produced by Harry Colombo and George Papi. *Directed by* Sergio Leone. *Director of photography,* Jack Dalmas. *Music,* Ennio Morricone. *Screenplay by* Sergio Leone and Duccio Tessari, adapted from *Yojimbo,* by Akiro Kurosawa. Color by Technicolor and Scope. Released by United Artists. *Running time: 96 minutes.*

A Fistful of Dollars was the brainchild of Italian director Sergio Leone, who had long admired films about the American West. For years Leone had felt that the storyline for Japanese director Akiro Kurosawa's epic film *Yojimbo* could easily be adapted to a setting in the old West. This idea had worked a few years before, quite successfully, when director John Sturges adapted Kurosawa's *The Seven Samurai* and reworked it as the western classic *The Magnificent Seven*.

Leone financed the modestly budgeted film by raising the necessary two hundred thousand dollars from German, Spanish, and Italian interest groups. Of this total, Clint Eastwood received a fifteen-thousand-dollar salary and a chance to see Europe for free. His experiences were both humorous and frustrating, as he found himself the only person on the set who could speak English. Yet despite these problems, the film wrapped in a very short time, and Eastwood returned to America to continue filming *Rawhide* episodes.

In 1967, *A Fistful of Dollars* was released to eager audiences in the United States, having been a hit three years earlier in Europe. Although it was fashionable to scoff at the cheap look of the film at the time, as

*Eastwood prepares for
the showdown with
Rojo.*

well as its laughable dubbing, *A Fistful of Dollars* outgrossed some of the most famous westerns in history. Leone's style, while crude, was nevertheless effective. Unlike many films, *Dollars* becomes more interesting with each viewing. Leone proved to have the skill and talent required to fashion an exciting film that was often excessive in gore but never dull for a moment.

More importantly, it provided Clint Eastwood the chance to prove he was more than just a minor TV actor. If his acting here is not memorable, the general impression his character made is quite unforgettable. Critics had laughed that Eastwood was nothing more than a temporary fad with teenagers, but this film would prove them wrong. Eastwood was not only here to stay, but with *A Fistful of Dollars*, he was beginning to make some of the most influential changes in the film industry that Hollywood had ever seen.

Eastwood inspects the casualties of the graveyard battle.

SYNOPSIS

When a cigar-smoking, tight-lipped stranger with no name (Clint Eastwood) enters the Mexican border town of San Miguel, he is harassed and shot at by a group of men in the employ of Sheriff Baxter (W. Lukschy), the leader of a powerful gang of criminals who sell whiskey and guns to the Indians, as well as fight continuous battles with a rival gang led by a man named Rojo (John Wells).

In revenge, this man with no name guns down the entire group of men who have annoyed him, leaving several bystanders more than a little impressed by his lightning-fast draw. Rojo, also impressed, hires him as a member of his gang. The stranger feels no sense of loyalty to Rojo, however, and sees him as the cutthroat he is. This opinion is reaffirmed when he witnesses a spectacular ambush, orchestrated by Rojo, in which Rojo steals a fortune in gold from an army caravan.

As part of a plan to steal the gold for himself, the stranger stages a battle between the Rojo and Baxter gangs. He then locates the gold but not before being spotted by Marisol (Marianne Koch), a beautiful woman whom Rojo is holding captive. The stranger takes Marisol to the Baxters and leaves her with them. Baxter plans to exchange her for his son, whom Rojo is keeping prisoner at his ranch.

This infuriates Rojo and leads to another war between the two gangs. When the Rojo gang emerges victorious, the stranger comes out of hiding and slaughters all of Rojo's men. In a final showdown with Rojo, the stranger uses a makeshift bullet-proof shield to distract the gang leader long enough to gun him down.

The stranger then rides nonchalantly out of town, leaving a path of destruction behind him.

REVIEWS

The cheapjack production . . . misses both awfulness and mediocrity: It is pure manufacture. Mr. Eastwood shows a talent for squinting and

Eastwood and an accomplice stare down the villains.

mouthing a cigarillo.

Judith Crist, *New York World Journal Tribune*

Clint Eastwood is tall, lean and hard looking. He should be good for many a year of hero. . . . This is a splendid experience to share.

Archer Winsten, *New York Post*

50 million Italians can't be wrong, or can they? Nearly that many. . . have taken to this movie like pasta. The Man with No Name [is] played by a nameless, true-to-western type bidding to become a name, Clint Eastwood. Eastwood has the deadpan detachment that the role demands. Word has it that [he] will someday outdraw James Bond. That remains to be seen.

Kathleen Carroll, *New York Daily News*

A pensive gaze from the Man with No Name.

Eastwood puts his grisly double-cross into effect.

Baxter's gang learns the danger of insulting Eastwood's "mule."

Eastwood discusses his plans with a friendly cantina *owner.*

A bullet-proof vest saves Eastwood from the blast of Rojo's gun.

Successful promotional poster.

For a Few Dollars More (1965)

CAST

The Stranger, Clint Eastwood; *Colonel Mortimer*, Lee Van Cleef; *Indio*, Gian Maria Volonte; *Colonel's sister*, Rosemary Dexter; *Hotel manager's wife*, Mara Krup; *Hunchback*, Klaus Kinski; *First man*, Mario Brega; *Second man*, Aldo Sambrel

CREDITS

Producer, Alberto Grimaldi. *Director*, Sergio Leone. *Screenplay*, Luciano Vincenzoni. *Music*, Ennio Morricone. *Director of photography*, Jack Dalmas. *Screenplay by* Sergio Leone. Color by Technicolor. *Running time: 125 minutes*. Released by United Artists.

If the success of *A Fistful of Dollars* caught its creators and the world at large by surprise, *For a Few Dollars More* did not. Leone was fully aware that he had stumbled onto a good thing, which moviegoing audiences were quite enthusiastic about. This sequel was given a budget of six hundred thousand dollars, three times the budget of its predecessor. Eastwood's salary increased accordingly. For his second appearance as the Man with No Name, he received fifty thousand dollars, a modest sum by his standards today but thirty-five thousand dollars more than he received for *A Fistful of Dollars*.

Like the former film, *For a Few Dollars More* was filmed in Spain, one year after Eastwood had finished his first spaghetti western. Upon release, it, too, was greeted with horrendous critical notices, but reassuringly, it accumulated the same astronomical grosses around the world.

Eastwood's rendezvous with Indio and his gang.

SYNOPSIS

Triple-crossed by the colonel (Lee Van Cleef).

In the Southwest, shortly after the Civil War, two bounty hunters find themselves on the track of the same criminal. Both men, a steely-eyed young man called the Stranger (Clint Eastwood) and his older peer, a former Confederate officer known as Colonel Mortimer (Lee Van Cleef), decide to band together and hunt their quarry, agreeing to split any rewards.

The quarry is a criminal named Indio (Gian Maria Volonte), a vicious bankrobber who has been convicted of killing Mortimer's sister. They track down Indio, and the Stranger gains his confidence by helping one of his henchmen escape from jail, an action that results in his becoming a member of Indio's gang. Along with three other men, the Stranger is assigned the job of creating a distraction large enough to enable Indio and his other conspirators to rob the town bank.

Once alone with his "partners," the Stranger kills them all, but he cannot move quickly enough to prevent the robbery from taking place. While the colonel waits for the Stranger to lead Indio into a planned ambush, the Stranger talks Indio into traveling in a direction opposite from that which he and the colonel had agreed upon. The Stranger's plan to enact a double-cross at the colonel's expense is prevented when the colonel, not a man to be taken so easily, suspects the deception and confronts the Stranger when he arrives at his destination. The two men decide to rejoin forces and continue with the quest to collect the bounty money.

The bounty hunters talk Indio into helping them rob a safe, then attempt to steal it from him. The plan backfires, however, when Indio captures them, but not before they have hidden the gold. When torture fails to make the men reveal where they have hidden the money, Indio pretends to release them, only to have them followed. A violent battle ensues, during which the Stranger and the colonel annihilate Indio's army. The climax comes when the colonel confronts Indio and kills him in revenge for his sister's death. Satisfied with vengeance, the colonel allows the Stranger to keep the reward money. The Stranger quickly agrees and leaves town with a gruesome cargo, the bodies of dozens of wanted men, on the back of his wagon.

REVIEWS

The gunman of Mr. Eastwood is a fearless killing machine. . . . Mr. Leone piles violence upon violence and charges the screen with hideous fantasies of sudden death.

Bosley Crowther, *New York Times*

A treat for necrophiliacs. The rest of us can get our kicks for free at the butcher store.

Juidth Crist, NBC *Today Show*

[The] script generally manages to avoid the cliché pitfalls traditional to the western and the dialogue is literate and satisfying to the ear. But it is thanks to Leone's bigger-than-life style, which combines upfront and closeup details in a hard hitting pace reminiscent of the Bond pix, that his acquires it's credible and impactful diversion. Clint Eastwood is fine in a tailor-made role for the squint-eyed opportunist.

"Hawk.," *Variety*

Van Cleef (left) and Eastwood discuss plans over Indio's (Gian Maria Volonte's) body.

Armed to the teeth, Eastwood makes his point quite effectively.

Eastwood arrives in town—and inevitable danger.

Preparing for a showdown with some reluctant adversaries.

Lee Van Cleef (left) and Eastwood stage plans for Indio's capture.

Eastwood is put on the spot at Indio's hideout.

Eastwood orchestrates the final showdown.

Eastwood talks things over with the sheriff.

The inimitable stare that confronts enemies of the Man with No Name.

The Good, the Bad, and the Ugly (1966)

CAST

The Stranger, Clint Eastwood; *Tuco*, Eli Wallach; *Setenza*, Lee Van Cleef; with Aldo Giuffre, Mario Brega, Luigi Pistilli, Rada Rassimony, Enzo Petito.

CREDITS

Produced by Alberto Grimaldi. *Directed by* Sergio Leone. *Screenplay by* Luciano Vincenzon and Sergio Leone. *Music by* Ennio Morricone. *Film editors*, Nino Baragli and Eugenio Alabiso. *Director of photography*, Tonnio Delli Colli. *Running time: 161 minutes*. Techniscope and Technicolor. Released by United Artists.

By the time this third and last episode in the Eastwood-Leone school of offbeat westerns went before the cameras in 1965, everyone knew that its success was inevitable. Leone succeeded in securing a budget of a million dollars—far more than had been spent on the two previous *Dollars* westerns put together. Eastwood received two hundred fifty thousand dollars for his efforts and for the first time found himself regarded as one of the highest-paid actors around.

Leone showed that he had the skill to use his budget wisely, and *The Good, the Bad, and the Ugly* often appears to be an enormously expensive film. Leone fashioned an incredibly tense and engrossing film that far surpassed his earlier efforts in both technical achievements and directorial style. At times the film, running close to three hours, appears to be a virtual epic, with scenes of hundreds of men engaged in raging battles; extremely realistic art decoration and sets; and a wide use of varied locations, used to the utmost benefit.

Critics treated *The Good, the Bad, and the Ugly* slightly better than its two forerunners, although most reaction was still very negative. The usual arguments about excessive violence and unnecessary gore were brought out again. While some of these criticisms may have been justified, *The Good, the Bad, and the Ugly* contains far too many positive qualities to be dismissed as just another blood-and-guts western.

The film has many haunting and memorable moments. Among them: a nerveracking scene in which Eastwood frantically tries to load an empty pistol before a team of assassins break into his room; the torturous walk across the desert in a sun so strong that you can feel the sweat pour from your face; an epic battle that more than ably demonstrates Leone's skill at effectively handling even the most difficult of sequences; the suspense-filled final showdown that makes the viewer cringe on the edge of her or his seat; and perhaps most effective of all, a stunning scene in which Confederate prisoners of war are forced into a makeshift band in order to drown out the screams of their comrades being tortured. As a young man plays sweet love songs on his harmonica, the camera captures an unforgettable moment in which we see the tears of his disgrace and sorrow stream down his face.

Eastwood performed well in this film, although the acting requirements were not much more difficult than those of the earlier films. He perfectly invoked the personification of cool, and there was even a brief moment of humanity demonstrated by the Man with No Name, as he is briefly shown bemoaning the futility of war.

Eastwood received first-rate support from Lee Van Cleef, who managed to make his character one of the more memorable screen villains of recent years. The scene-stealing trophy, however, must go to Eli Wallach, who gives an outrageously hammy, yet admittedly delightful performance as the back-stabbing Tuco.

The Good, the Bad, and the Ugly may not have been a masterpiece, but it was a very fine film that scorches the memory. It is one of the finest films Eastwood has appeared in.

Tuco (Eli Wallach) brutally threatens Eastwood on the grueling desert march.

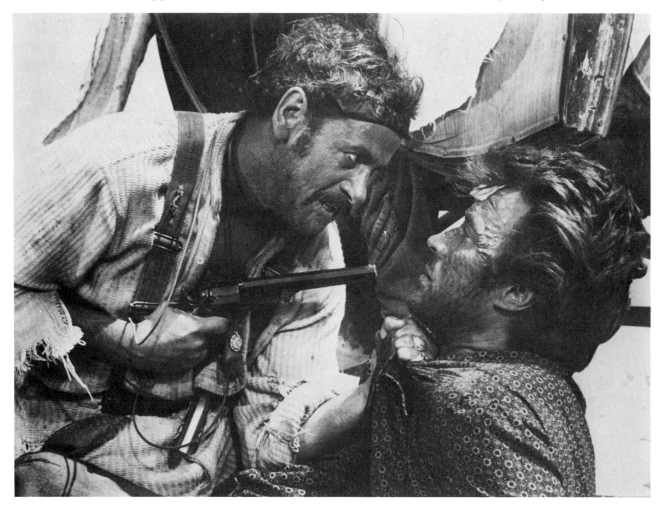

SYNOPSIS

At the height of the Civil War, a Mexican bandit named Tuco (Eli Wallach) is nearly captured by two bounty hunters. His life is saved by a mysterious stranger (Clint Eastwood), who kills both bounty hunters.

It is soon clear why this stranger, whom Tuco nicknames Joe, has saved the life of the Mexican. He wants to form a partnership in which he will collect the reward money for capturing Tuco and then rescue him before he can be hanged. The plan works, and the act is repeated over and over, with Tuco's head becoming more profitable each day.

At the same time, a terrifying bounty hunter named Setenzo (Lee Van Cleef) is following up on information that he hopes will lead him to a fortune in buried Confederate gold. Setenzo recruits a band of devoted followers and begins to menace and torture all who have come into contact with the money.

Meanwhile, Tuco and Joe have ended their partnership violently. Tuco captures Joe and drags him on a torturous walk across the desert. Just as he is about to die, Joe stumbles across a deserted stagecoach filled with dead bodies. The last survivor, a Confederate soldier, whispers to Joe the secret of the gold's location.

Joe and Tuco's partnership is reinstated when it is discovered that each man knows a necessary part of the gold's secret location.

While posing as Confederate soldiers, Tuco and Joe are captured by Union troops and sent to a prison camp run by Setenzo, who has become an army sergeant in hopes that it will lead him closer to the gold. When his torture methods fail to make his pisoners give away their secret, the three men form an uneasy alliance.

Eventually they reach a cemetery where the gold is hidden. It becomes clear upon its discovery that only a showdown will decide who will take the riches. As the three men stare each other down, Setenzo draws. Joe guns him down. Tuco looks on incredulously as he realizes that the gun he is attempting to fire has been previously emptied by his "trusting" partner.

Joe spares Tuco's life, but not before humiliating him in a dangerous way. He ties Tuco up and places him on a shaky wooden cross with a noose tied around his neck, the noose being attached to a tree. As Tuco begs for mercy, precariously keeping himself upright for dear life, Joe fires a long-distance rifle shot that knocks Tuco safely to the ground. As the Mexican fruitlessly runs after him, swearing, Joe unemotionally rides away with the gold.

REVIEWS

The Good, the Bad, and the Ugly might serve as the film's own capsule review. The good lies in Sergio Leone's skillfull camera work. Bad is the word for the wooden acting . . . and Ugly is his insatiable appetite for beatings.

Time

Eastwood finds himself again in a precarious situation at the hands of Tuco.

Crammed with sadism and a distaste for human values that would make the ordinary misanthrope seem like Pollyanna. [Its] only possible excuse for existence [is to] make money. Somehow that isn't enough.

Arthur Knight, *Saturday Review*

[The film] must be the most expensive, pious, and repellent movie in the history of its peculiar genre. . . . There is scarcely a moment's respite from the pain. [Eastwood's] face and voice are expressionless throughout. Sometimes it all tries to pass for fun.

Renata Adler, *New York Times*

With Tuco at his mercy, Eastwood manages a rare look of amusement.

The tables turned, Tuco is now humiliated by Eastwood.

At the graveyard showdown, Eastwood outguns "Angel Eyes."

Eastwood's search for gold leads him to the bed of a Mexican prostitute, in a scene shown only in European versions of the film.

Eastwood prepares to shoot a rope from around Tuco's neck for the last time.

The Witches (1967)

PART ONE

"The Witch Burned Alive"

Starring Silvana Mangano, Anne Girardot, Francisco Rabal, Elsa Albani. *Directed by* Luchino Visconti. *Story and screenplay by* Giuseppe Patroni Griffi.

PART TWO

"Civic Sense"

Starring Silvana Mangano, Alberto Sordi. *Directed by* Mauro Bolognini. *Story and screenplay by* Bernardino Zapponi.

PART THREE

"The Earth As Seen from the Moon"

Starring Silvana Mangano, Toto, Ninetto Davoli. *Directed and written by* Pier Pasolini.

PART FOUR

"The Girl from Sicily"

Starring Silvana Mangano, Pietro Rossi.
Directed by Franco Rossi, *Screenplay by* Franco Rossi, Luigi Mani.

A straitlaced Eastwood peruses a newspaper with wife Silvana Mangano.

PART FIVE

"A Night Like Any Other"

Starring Silvana Mangano, Clint Eastwood, Armando Bottin, Gianni Gori. *Directed by* Vittorio De Sica. *Screenplay by* Cesare Zavattini, Fabio Carpi, Enzio Muzzii.

The Witches is Eastwood's most bizarre film to date, if it can be called a Clint Eastwood film at all. The movie is basically a showcase for producer Dino De Laurentiis's wife, Silvana Mangano, who, having been absent from the screen for several years, had hoped to make a striking comeback in this fantasy filmed in Italy.

Eastwood plays a conservative, modern role as the husband of Magnano in the last of five different short stories that constitute the film. His episode, titled "A Night Like Any Other," was shot in Italy in 1965 by director Vittorio De Sica, who had earlier triumphed with some neorealistic masterpieces like *The Bicycle Thief. The Witches*, however, proved to be too offbeat to find an audience.

De Sica had called Eastwood "the new Gary Cooper," on the basis of his success in Italy with the two *Dollars* films, and hoped to bring the actor to superstardom in his native country with this film. This did not prove to be the case, however. Eastwood's role was dull and forgettable, and the film, though actually filmed in 1966, did not even find an American distributor until 1967, when United Artists released it sporadically to a few art houses and then shelved it.

Clint Eastwood with Silvana Mangano.

Clint Eastwood with Silvana Mangano.

Hang 'Em High (1968)

CAST

Jed Cooper, Clint Eastwood; *Rachel*, Inger Stevens; *Captain Wilson*, Ed Begley; *Judge Adam Fenton*, Pat Hingle; *Jennifer*, Arlene Golonka; *Preacher*, James MacArthur; *Madam Peaches Sophie*, Ruth White; *Sheriff Dave Bliss*, Ben Johnson; *Miller*, Bruce Dern; *The Prophet*, Dennis Hopper; *Stone*, Alan Hale, Jr.; *Jenkins*, Bob Steele; *Sheriff Ray Calhoun*, Charles McGraw; *Loomis*, L.W. Jones; *Marshal Hays*, Jack Ging.

CREDITS

Producer, Leonard Freeman, *Director*, Ted Post. *Screenplay*, Leonard Freeman and Mel Goldberg. *Associate producer*, Irving Leonard. *Photography*, Richard Kline and Leonard South. *Art director*, John B. Goodman; *Editor*, Gene Fowler, Jr.; *Music*, Dominic Frontiere. A Co-production of Leonard Freeman Productions and Malpaso Company. Released by United Artists. Color by DeLuxe. *Running time: 101 minutes.*

Hang 'Em High was Eastwood's first major American film, following the *Dollar* trilogy. Anxious to remind audiences that they were viewing a genuine American film, the producers cast many well-known American actors in supporting roles. The violence was frequent, and well done, but *Hang 'Em High* broke no new ground for Eastwood. Eastwood's salary rose to four hundred thousand dollars plus a percentage of the profits. His price was justified, for the film quickly showed a handsome profit.

Eastwood was persuasive in having former *Rawhide* director Ted Post helm *Hang 'Em High*. Post's work on the film was impressive, if not overly creative. The movie relied totally on Eastwood's mystique to keep the audience's interest. To this end, Eastwood helped make the action sequences seem as exciting as possible by performing his own stunts. At one point, he allowed himself to be dragged across the Rio Grande with a rope tied around his neck, to give the scene a realistic look. His actions were not in vain. The best sequence in the film features this stunt work by Eastwood, and the actor has continued to do his own stunts work as often as possible.

SYNOPSIS

Jed Cooper (Clint Eastwood) has just purchased a herd of cattle from a local rancher and is driving them across the Rio Grande enroute to his own land. He is attacked by a group of vigilantes, who inform him that they have just found the cattle baron dead. Since Cooper has the herd, he is the prime suspect in the murder. Struggling bitterly, Cooper cannot save himself from being lynched and left for dead.

He is rescued just in time by a passing lawman (Ben Johnson) and

Saved from a lynch mob, Eastwood is immediately arrested.

taken to Judge Fenton (Pat Hingle), the local magistrate. Fenton deputizes Cooper and authorizes him to track down the vigilantes, first warning him that all the men are to be taken alive for trial. Cooper ignores these rules and begins to track the members of the gang down and kill them one by one. He prefaces one gun battle with the ominous warning, "You made two mistakes: You hung the wrong man, and you didn't finish the job."

Cooper also finds himself involved with two women of opposite extremes: Rachel (Inger Stevens), a local businesswoman, and Jennifer (Arlene Golonka), a fun-loving prostitute. Caught off-guard one day, Cooper is gunned down by the hired hands of the head of the lynching party, a man named Wilson (Ed Begley), who is determined to kill Cooper before the lawman can get to him

Miraculously, Cooper once again survives Wilson's murderous plans, thanks in part to the tender nursing of Rachel. When he recovers, Cooper traces Wilson and his men back to Wilson's sprawling ranch house. A blazing gunfight ensues, and only Wilson and Cooper survive. As Cooper gains entrance to the house, he finds that the terrified Wilson has committed suicide—ironically through hanging.

REVIEWS

A western of quality, courage, danger and excitement which places itself squarely in the procession of old fashioned westerns made with the latest techniques. . . . The one whose fate becomes your strongest participation is Clint Eastwood. His good-looking tranquility in the midst of life and death issues may really be nothing but the limitation of a strong, silent hero, but it looks good on him. You're with him all the way, and that's what makes this one of the tenser western experiences of the current film month.

Archer Winsten, *New York Post*

Hang 'Em High has its moments. . . . It even has a point, unlike the previous sado-masochistic exercises on foreign prairies where the grizzled Mr. Eastwood stalked around in a filthy serape, holster-deep in corpses. Hollywood [has] thrust him into a cold-hearted western that not only makes sense, but actually promotes good old fashioned law abidance, for all its granite facade. The best thing about this picture . . . is a mass execution on that big platform. Ted Post has directed this scene brilliantly. Most unfortunate of all, Mr. Eastwood, with his glum sincerity, isn't much of an actor. Even so, *Hang 'Em High* attains more altitude than any of Mr. Eastwood's previous jaunts far from home.

Howard Thompson, *New York Times*

Hang 'Em High is one of the best western fims of this year.

Film Weekly

*Hopelessly outnumbered,
Eastwood can do little to
prevent being lynched.*

*Now deputized,
Eastwood deals out swift
justice to a vigilante.*

A publicity pose with
Inger Stevens.

A roll in the hay with
"bad girl" Arlene
Golonka.

Eastwood gets some
much-needed care from
Inger Stevens.

76

*In a filthy cell,
Eastwood recuperates
from near death.*

*After being dragged
across a river, Eastwood
is humiliated by
vigilantes.*

With Inger Stevens.

Bruce Dern finally succumbs to Eastwood's fists.

Saved from certain death by Ben Johnson.

Bruce Dern and Eastwood battle it out.

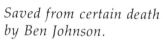

A tense moment in a struggle with prisoner Bruce Dern.

Eastwood rescues a calf
he will soon be accused
of having stolen.

A moment of serenity
with Inger Stevens.

A publicity shot with
(left to right) Inger
Stevens, Pat Hingle, Ed
Begley, and Arlene
Golonka.

Eastwood on the set of
Hang 'Em High.

Coogan's Bluff (1968)

CAST

Coogan, Clint Eastwood; *Sheriff McElroy*, Lee. J. Cobb; *Julie*, Susan Clark; *Linny Raven*, Tisha Sterling; *Ringerman*, Don Stroud; *Mrs. Ringerman*, Betty Field; *Sheriff McCrea*, Tom Tully; *Millie*, Melodie Johnson; *Jackson*, James Edwards; *Running Bear*, Rudy Diaz; *Pushie*, David F. Doyle; *Taxi driver*, Louis Zorich; *Ferguson*, James Gavin

CREDITS

Executive producer, Richard E. Lyons. *Producer-director*, Donald Siegel. *Associate producer*, Irving Leonard. *Screenplay*, Herman Miller, Dean Riesner, Howard Rodman. *Story*, Herman Miller. *Photography*, Bud Thackery. *Music*, Lalo Schifrin. *Costumes*, Helen Colvig. *Assistant director*, Joe Cavalier. Released by Universal. Color by Technicolor. *Running time: 94 minutes.*

At this point in his career, Eastwood wanted to expand into new territory. Universal, which had been unable to find use for the actor in the prior decade, now offered him the opportunity to star in an unusual film about the adventures of a modern Arizona lawman who encounters a sort of culture shock while in New York to extradite a criminal. The script was unfinished at the time, and no director had been set, although Alex Segal had at one time been accepted, then rejected. The company and Eastwood finally settled on Don Siegel as director. Siegel had made a name for himself by directing some very well-received films on low budgets, such as *Riot in Cell Block 11* and the original version of *Invasion of the Bodysnatchers*.

Coogan's Bluff was not an easy film to get off the ground. In addition to the difficulties in finding a suitable director, the script had gone through ten drafts, all of which had been unacceptable to someone with veto power. Siegel argued with Eastwood incessantly and was about to withdraw from the film, when he and Clint—with the aid of writer Dean Riesner—took the best elements of all ten drafts and came up with a satisfactory screenplay for everyone. The resolution of this problem led to the first cinematic teaming of Eastwood and Siegel, and this film remains one of their finest achievements.

The script is tight and fast moving. Siegel displayed an amazing talent for creating inventive camera setups during fight sequences. The pool-room brawl is nearly the finest action scene one could imagine, and Siegel directed it stunningly. He also filmed an exciting motorcycle chase at the Cloisters, in New York, which was aided immeasurably by Eastwood's doing most of his own stunt work.

As for Clint, his performance was again cited as wooden by most critics. However, they were quick to compliment him on his very deft

Coogan arrives at his New York quarters—a flophouse.

Eastwood helps stage a camera angle for the pool-room fight.

handling of the witty confrontations between himself and Lee J. Cobb. These debates do provide some very watchable moments. Eastwood delivered a tough, exciting action hit of the kind that makes audiences stand in line and cash registers jingle around the world.

SYNOPSIS

Eastwood as Arizona Deputy Sheriff Walt Coogan.

Arizona deputy Walt Coogan (Clint Eastwood) is sent to New York to extradite James Ringerman (Don Stroud), wanted for murder in Arizona. When he arrives in the big city it is immediately apparent that Coogan feels out of place. He is soon at odds with Detective Lieutenant McElroy (Lee J. Cobb) after McElroy informs him that his stay in New York has been extended owing to Ringerman's having taking an overdose of LSD.

While waiting for the doctors to release Ringerman to him, Coogan flirts with Julie Roth (Susan Clark), an attractive social worker and probation officer. Restless, Coogan bluffs the hospital staff into releasing Ringerman in his custody, but not before he sees Ringerman whisper a message to his visiting girlfriend, Linny Raven (Tisha Sterling). Coogan cannot overhear the conversation, but its significance becomes clear when he is attacked at the heliport and knocked unconscious by Ringerman's gang.

Coogan is seriously hurt and hospitalized. To make matters worse, he is ordered off the case. Julie tries to ease Coogan's damaged ego by inviting him over to her apartment. While there, he finds out that one of her probation cases is none other than Linny Raven. Coogan runs out on the stunned Julie and makes his way over to Linny's apartment, where he seduces her and evokes a promise that she will lead him to Ringerman.

Linny brings Coogan to a run-down pool room, where he is confronted by Ringerman's gang. Trapped, Coogan is hopelessly outnumbered but puts up an incredible fight. Jumping from pool table to pool table, he smashes billiard balls and cue sticks into his adversaries, knocking several of them unconscious and wounding the others before being savagely beaten himself. He escapes moments before the police arrive, and returns to Linny's apartment. This time, he beats her until she takes him to Ringerman's hideout, the famous monastery called the Cloisters. Coogan confronts Ringerman in a high-speed motorcycle chase climaxed by Coogan's successfully leaping onto Ringerman's motorcycle, knocking him helpless.

The next day Coogan leaves New York with his man and bids farewell to Julie and Lieutenant McElroy, who admits respect for the Arizona lawman despite his unorthodox methods.

REVIEWS

Coogan's Bluff is probably the worst happening of the year.
Judith Crist, The New Yorker

If James Dean had lived to grow a few inches taller and attain a lean, graceful movie middle age . . . and if he and been tranquilized beyond all emotion the result would have been Clint Eastwood. . . . He is constantly upstaged by more colorful minor characters and the restless scenery of the big city.

Vincent Canby, *New York Times*

Clint Eastwood stars in a role that is more like a change of clothes, instead of pace . . . well produced and directed by Don Siegel. With its bare breasts and buttocks nudity, and bone cracking, lip splitting brutality, the film will find its own market. . . . Eastwood projects a likable image even when his actions on screen are not so. Overall, film sags under its sex and violence emphasis.

"Murf.," *Variety*

Fast and tough and so well made that it seems to have evolved naturally. Some of the best American moviemaking of the year. Clint Eastwood performs with a measure of real feeling in the first role that fits him comfortably as his tooled leather boots.

Time

Eastwood gives director Siegel a hand by helping choreograph the pool-room fight.

Coogan's Bluff is a simple lesson in cultural cross-fertilization. Remarkable fellow, that Eastwood, and a pleasure to watch. You have absolute confidence that he will not only get himself into trouble, but out of it, too. The first is due to his nature. The second is due to the script. . . . As directed by Don Siegel it comes out entertaining in all the usual ways. . . . There are no surprises. The action is steady, rough and organized.

Archer Winsten, *New York Post*

. . . A fine idea, and for a while it is presented by producer-director Donald Siegel in a smooth, amusing manner. . . . The showdown, a chase on motorcycles, is so wild it creates laughs instead of suspense. Eastwood and Lee J. Cobb are good together, each man measuring the other's strength, ability and nerve.

Wanda Hale, *New York Daily News*

Director Siegel (left) watches Eastwood prepare for a scene on the Universal lot.

Eastwood searches for Ringerman's whereabouts in the Pigeon-toed Orange Peel disco.

Hopelessly outnumbered, Eastwood nevertheless puts up a gallant fight in the pool hall.

Rehearsing a sequence with Tisha Sterling.

Eastwood gets rough with Linny Raven (Tisha Sterling).

Lee J. Cobb (right) exchanges words with Eastwood.

Eastwood with prisoner (Don Stroud).

Poster art.

Eastwood and friend.

Where Eagles Dare (1969)

CAST

John Smith, Richard Burton; *Lieutenant Morris Schaffer*, Clint Eastwood; *Mary Ellison*, Mary Ure; *Vice-admiral Rolland*, Michael Hordern; *Colonel Wyatt Turner*, Patrick Wymark; *Cartwright Jones*, Robert Beatty; *Colonel Kramer*, Anton Diffring; *Olaf Christiansen*, Donald Houston; *Reichsmarshall*, Ferdy Mayne; *Torrance-Smythe*, Neil McCarthy; *Edward Carraciola*, Peter Barkworth; *Lee Thomas*, William Squire; *Sergent Harrod*, Brook Williams; *Heidi*, Ingrid Pitt

CREDITS

Produced by Elliott Kastner. *Directed by* Brian Hutton. *Story and screenplay*, Alistair MacLean. *Photography*, Arthur Ibbetson, B.S.C. *Music composed and conducted by* Ron Goodwin. *Film editor*, John Jympson. *Second-unit director*, Yakima Canutt. *Sound editor*, Jonathan Bates. A Jerry-Elliot Kastner Picture. Color by Metro and in Panavision. Released by MGM. *Running time: 155 minutes.*

Where Eagles Dare is an epic adventure indeed. It took a great deal of time, energy, money, and endurance to get this MGM production off the ground. MGM sources claim that the project stemmed from actor Richard Burton's anxiousness to find an old-fashioned adventure story he could make for the entertainment of his two sons. Burton approached his friend producer Elliot Kastner, and Kastner in turn approached famed adventure novelist Alistair MacLean, who had previously written, among others, *The Guns of Navarone*.

With Ingrid Pitt.

MacLean told Kastner that all his novels had either been filmed already or were being filmed. Kastner suggested that his friend try something new, writing a story directly for the screen and then turning it into a novel. MacLean was at first leery about this but eventually accepted, writing the screenplay for *Where Eagles Dare* in six weeks.

Kastner signed Eastwood to play Burton's sidekick, a move that forced Eastwood's name into second place. MGM soothed any blows to his ego, however, by paying him eight hundred thousand dollars for his efforts. (Burton reportedly received one million dollars for his role.) Kastner and his co-producer Jerry Gershwin then hired a virtual unknown, Brian G. Hutton, to direct the film. This move was a considerable gamble, placing such a large-budgeted film in the hands of a young director who had previously made only two other films, *The Pad and How to Use It* and a detective film called *Sol Madrid*.

Once the filming started, however, Hutton proved he could handle his assignment with admirable professionalism. The problems of shooting *Where Eagles Dare* were enormous. The producers needed to find an authentic castle in the Bavarian Alps to use as the Nazi stronghold. They

Eastwood blasts the Nazis in the fierce battle within the castle.

Burton (left) and Eastwood map strategy for their escape.

secured the right to shoot in Schloss Hohenwerfen, an eleventh-century architectural masterpiece in Austria. At the time of the filming the castle was a training school for police officers.

The biggest difficulty for the crew was transporting the incredible amount of cameras, food, and equipment safely to the mountain peak via a long, twisting road so narrow that traffic could proceed in only one direction at any time. Once filming began, the producers were faced with new obstacles: howling blizzards that left four-foot snowdrifts; subzero temperatures that caused machinery to break and crew members to be victimized by frostbite; avalanches that threatened everyone's lives; and enough other difficulties to rival those of the screenplay.

Concern for realism did not end with the sets. The action sequences, coordinated by famed stuntman Yakima Canutt, were among the most authentic and hair raising ever filmed. So many explosions were set off that even Hutton and Kastner were caught off-guard at one point and had their clothing almost singed from their bodies. One memorable scene finds Burton in a hand-to-hand struggle to the death with a Nazi soldier atop a moving cable car. Still another stunt found Eastwood driving a speeding motorcycle and sidecar through a blinding snowstorm while on a terrifying mountain road.

These efforts paid off handsomely, however. *Eagles* generated the best reviews of any Eastwood film up to that time. It was also quite successful at the box office. Eastwood worked well with Burton, although the latter easily stole most of the better lines of dialogue. Although the screenplay itself is pure tongue-in-cheek escapism of the James Bond order, the

Eastwood in action during the getaway.

individual action scenes are both suspenseful and convincing. Although this is a film of virtually nonstop violence, most critics felt the humor in it compensated for the bloodletting and gave *Where Eagles Dare* favorable reviews.

SYNOPSIS

British officer John Smith (Richard Burton) is summoned by the Allied High Command for a top-secret assignment. His superior, Colonel Turner (Patrick Wymark), informs him that an important American general is being held captive by the Nazis in a seemingly impenetrable fortress high in the Bavarian Alps. The mission assigned to Smith, who will lead a commando squad, is to parachute behind enemy lines, gain access to the fortress, and rescue the general before he can be tortured into revealing the plans for the impending D-Day invasion of Europe.

Smith's right-hand man is American Lieutenant Schaffer (Clint Eastwood), a tight-lipped but fast-thinking officer who seems to fear nothing. Aided by five other commandos, Smith makes the daring parachute drop into enemy territory. Although they are undetected, the jump has cost the life of one man who presumably died in the fall. Smith, however, quietly suspects that the death may have been the work of a double agent in his ranks.

With Richard Burton, posing as Nazi officers.

Eastwood plants a diversionary bomb.

While the men organize their plans, Smith slips away to a meeting with intelligence operative Mary Ellison (Mary Ure), whose presence is a secret to the other men. Smith and his men then make the ascent to the mountains, where they discover that the fortress is accessible only by a lengthy cable-car ride.

With time quickly running out, the commandos disguise themselves as Germans and move about town undetected. Mary Ellison arrives and aids the men by posing as a maid in the castle. Before the plan can be carried out, however, another of the party is found dead. Smith and Schaffer are then discovered and captured in a pub. The commandos make a narrow escape after managing to set fire to a railway station.

The two men penetrate the castle and battle it out with the Nazis. They succeed in rescuing the general, but it is discovered that he is no more than an actor who has played a part in a plot to expose spies within the Allied High Command, including a member of Smith's party. Smith himself is first exposed as a double agent and later as a triple agent, loyal in the end to the Allied cause. A fiery battle to the death within the castle and a fierce struggle involving Smith and a Nazi soldier atop a cable car precede a harrowing escape from the castle.

Smith commandeers a bus and, with the Nazis in hot pursuit, steers a course for the airport to meet with a rescue plane.

On board the craft, the commandos are greeted by Turner. To everyone's amazement, Smith exposes him as the top traitor in the espionage ring and gives him a simple choice: a scandalous death after court-martial or a more honorable end by leaping from the plane without a parachute. Seeking to preserve his family from humiliation, Turner chooses the latter. The weary commando team, safe at last, returns home.

Burton (right) and Eastwood give instructions to the commando squad.

REVIEWS

If you can stop being so serious and sophisticated . . . you can have a wonderful time at *Where Eagles Dare.* Genuinely entertaining . . . chockfull of equal doses of suspense, action, and well-timed anxiety. Burton and Eastwood . . . single handedly knock off half the German army, and all they get is one slight flesh wound on Burton's hand, no bigger than a bite from Elizabeth Taylor. . . . *Where Eagles Dare* has brilliant acting, good sound effects, and beautiful photography. . . .

It's damn good to have around.

Rex Reed, *Women's Wear Daily*

Where Eagles Dare is so good for its genre that one must go back to *The Great Escape* for a worthy comparison.

Variety

Richard Burton and Clint Eastwood balance out the savage and sardonic elements of the movie into an inconsistent but generally engrossing entertainment.

Village Voice

Eastwood escapes with (left to right) Robert Barksworth, Robert Beatty, and Mary Ure.

Silencing a Nazi guard.

*With Richard Burton
and Mary Ure.*

*Richard Burton and
Eastwood observe Nazi
movements.*

Paint Your Wagon (1969)

CAST

Ben Rumson, Lee Marvin; *"Pardner,"* Clint Eastwood; *Elizabeth*, Jean Seberg; *"Rotten Luck Willie,"* Harve Presnell; *"Mad Jack" Duncan*, Ray Walston; *Horton Fenty*, Tom Ligon; *Parson*, Alan Dexter; *Horace Tabor*, William O'Connell; *Haywood Holbrook*, Ben Baker; *Mr. Fenty*, Alan Baxter; *Mrs. Fenty*, Paula Trueman; *Atwell*, Robert Easton; *Foster*, Geoffrey Norman; *Steve Bull*, H. B. Haggerty; *Joe Mooney*, Terry Jenkins; *Schermerhorn*, Karl Bruck; *Jacob Woodling*, John Mitchum; *Sarah Woodling*, Sue Casey; *Indian*, Eddie Little Sky; *Higgins*, Harvey Parry; *Wong*, H. W. Gim; *Frock-coated man*, William Mims; *Hennessey*, Roy Jenson; *Clendennon*, Pat Hawley

With Lee Marvin (left).

CREDITS

Produced by Alan Jay Lerner. *Directed by* Joshua Logan. *Screenplay and lyrics by* Alan Jay Lerner. *Adaptation by* Paddy Chayefsky. *Music by* Frederick Loewe. *Music for additional songs by* André Previn. *Based upon the musical play* Paint Your Wagon, *presented on the stage by* Cheryl Crawford. *Choral music conducted by* Roger Wagner. *Orchestral music scored and conducted by* Nelson Riddle. *Choral arrangements and music, assistant to the producer,* Joseph J. Lilley. *Associate producer,* Tom Shaw. *Director of photography,* William A. Fraker, A.S.C. *Costumes and production designed by* John Truscott. *Film editor,* Robert Jones. *Second-unit direction,* Tom Shaw and Fred Lemoine. *Second-unit photography,* Loyal Griggs. *Aerial photography,* Nelson Tyler. *Choreography of "Gold Fever" and "Best Things,"* Jack Baker. *Production managers,* Carl Beringer and Fred Lemoine. *First assistant director,* Jack Roe. *First assistant director, second unit,* Al Murphy. *Script supervisor,* Marshall Wolins. *Dialogue coach,* Joseph Curtis. *Production coordinator,* Gene Levy. *Titles designed by* David Stone Martin. *Assistant to the producer,* Jonas Halperin. *Art director,* Carl Braunger. *Set decorator,* James I. Berkey. *Costume coordinator,* Anne Laune. *Costume supervisor,* Bill Jobe. *Makeup,* Frank McCoy. *Hairdresser,* Vivian Zavitz. *Special effects,* Maurice Ayres and Larry Hampton. *Camera operator,* David Walsh. *Camera assistant,* Bob Byrne. *Sound mixer,* William Randall. *Stereophonic rerecording supervisor,* Fred Hynes. *Gaffer,* Joe Smith. *Key grip,* Tom May. *Property,* Tom Eaton.

Eastwood helps save some disaster-stricken travelers.

Paint Your Wagon (1969)
MUSICAL SYNOPSIS

ACT I

"I'm on My Way"
(opening and main titles)
"I'm on My Way"
(Maestoso version)
"I Still See Elisa"
"The First Thing You Know"*
"Hand Me Down That Can o' Beans"
"They Call the Wind Maria"
"A Million Miles Away Behind the Door"*
"I Talk to the Trees"
"There's a Coach Comin' In"

ACT II

"The Gospel of No Name City"*
"Best Things"*
"Wand'rin' Star"
"Gold Fever"*
"I'm on My Way"
(Finale)

*Additional material with Lyrics by Alan Jay Lerner and Music by André Previn.

Paint Your Wagon, by Alan Jay Lerner and Frederick Loewe, was originally presented on Broadway in 1951.

If *Where Eagles Dare* proved to be a difficult task, that experience almost paled for Eastwood in comparison to the pressures he felt shooting his next project, the filming of the hit Broadway musical *Paint Your Wagon*. By the time the play was purchased for the film rights, it seemed outdated. A more suitable storyline was created centering on a *ménage-à-trois* situation among the principals. A fourteen-million-dollar budget was originally assigned to the film, and even that huge sum was easily surpassed when the film went far over budget. It seemed that from the start every conceivable wrong decision had been made.

The change in the storyline could not prevent the film from failing to interest young people in this plodding, actionless tale. Expanding the dullness on screen made it even more apparent how unsuitable *Wagon* seemed as an epic musical film. Paramount, which financed and released the picture, then cast two of Hollywood's best-known strong, silent types, Lee Marvin and Clint Eastwood, as the leads.

Most of the five-month shooting schedule found the cast and crew filming in Baker, Oregon, a tiny town in the mountains that seemed to be the worst place in the world to shoot a large-budget film. Virtually everyone and everything had to be flown in by plane or helicopter at great expense. Eastwood later made public his contempt for the wastefulness he observed as he related witnessing helicopter flights assigned to people who wanted to go on shopping sprees or other frivolous errands. The boredom was frightful for everyone, and the cast and crew grew restless to see the last day's shooting.

The director, Joshua Logan, who had previously filmed *South Pacific*, *Fanny*, and *Camelot*, found himself unable to prevent the budget from skyrocketing to twenty million dollars. Tempers flared, the location grew tougher, and for a while it appeared that no progress was being made on the film.

Eastwood could do little to help matters. He rented a forty-acre farm in Baker and passed the days away barbecuing with Lee Marvin and slopping pigs. Occasionally his wife, Maggie, and newborn son, Kyle, who was delivered when Eastwood was in Austria shooting *Where Eagles Dare*, would fly in and visit the restless actor.

Eventually, the film was finished, and it was released late in 1969. Yet *Paint Your Wagon* is not the terrible movie many people believe it to be. The cinematography, sets, and large-scale musical numbers are quite impressive.

Eastwood has some heated words with Lee Marvin, as Jean Seberg looks on.

Eastwood's singing came off better than that of his co-stars, if for no other reason than that he "talked" most of the songs in a soft voice. His two numbers were basically well received by critics, although Eastwood fans could not relate to their hero in this type of role. The film undeniably has its share of good moments, but when one realizes how much money was wasted and not even reflected on the screen, *Paint Your Wagon* somehow deserved its fate.

98

SYNOPSIS

A publicity shot with Lee Marvin and Jean Seberg.

The time is the era of the California gold rush. Ben Rumson (Lee Marvin), a tough, boozing prospector, joins forces with another fortune seeker named Pardner (Clint Eastwood). The two men live opposite lifestyles, Rumson being cantankerous and hard fighting, Pardner quiet and soft-spoken.

As the search for gold drags on, Rumson can no longer contain his desire to have a wife. He arranges with a local Mormon to purchase one of his two wives, Elizabeth (Jean Seberg), for eight hundred dollars. The fact that Rumson has one of the few women in the territory makes it inevitable that other men will try to charm her away. Rumson, violently jealous, is talked into satiating their desires by hijacking a wagon full of ladies of ill repute and bringing them back to the prospectors. The plan is a success, and the women are housed in the prospector's favorite haven, the Grizzly Bear Saloon.

While Rumson is away, however, Elizabeth and Pardner discover that they are in love. Upon learning this when he returns, Rumson is furious and wants to break up with Pardner. This is avoided when Elizabeth explains that she doesn't want either man for a husband; rather, she wants them both.

Uncertain of the chance of a successful *ménage à trois*, the men both agree to give the situation a try. Everything is peaceful until a family is rescued from a blizzard-stricken wagon train and brought to recuperate with the trio. Among those rescued is Mr. Fenty (Alan Baxter), a family patriarch, and his wife, both of whom are conservative and modest-living people. They are appalled to learn of the group marriage around them, and they protest even more when their son Horton (Tom Ligon) begins to idolize Rumson and follow his wayward lifestyle.

While this crisis grows within the household, a greater one is threatening the town: The gold is petering out, and the place will soon become a ghost town. Elizabeth and her husbands are steadfast in their determination not to move from their home. Rumson devises a plan whereby he, Pardner, and some other conspirators will tunnel under the Grizzly Bear Saloon and collect all the gold dust that prospectors have spilled through the cracks in the floors over the years.

The elaborate plan is successful, and the team charts out plans to search out more gold under the floors of every popular entertainment center in town. The result is a vast subterranean network of tunnels and passageways. Before the team can strike it rich, however, there is an upset in Ben's and Pardner's personal lives. Elizabeth, having been influenced by the Fentys is overcome with guilt about her lifestyle and throws Ben and Pardner out. To add insult to injury, all the underground caverns collapse, owing to slipshod construction.

Before long, there is no reason for the populace to stay in town, and they begin a mass exodus. Only a handful of the original settlers remain. They are determined to make a go of it in the land they have grown to love. Rumson decides to go on in search of more adventures, leaving

Pardner and Elizabeth to work out their personal problems and face the hardships of survival.

REVIEWS

Paint Your Wagon is a big, bawdy, rip-roaring Western musical of the gold rush in California.

New York Daily News

Paint Your Wagon will have an uphill fight to be a blockbusting boxoffice hit.

Variety

Though it is overproduced and sometimes a little weird, the movie is pretty interesting, especially once you get past the slow first half.

Women's Wear Daily

Paint Your Wagon is a monument to unparalleled incompetence. First they bought an expensive musical property and hired actors who can't dance or sing. Then they took a score that is an American institution and cut out most of the songs. It was nose-dripping closeups that destroyed *Camelot*. You'd think Alan Jay Lerner would have learned his lesson from that fiasco. Instead, he has once again hired [*Camelot* director] Joshua Logan and thereby compounded the error. *Camelot* was only a fifteen-million-dollar disaster; *Wagon* cost twenty. An interminable film . . . Absolutely nothing happens. Everyone is so busy overacting around Clint Eastwood, they make it easy for him to walk away with what little there is of the shambles. . . . He has a casual, soft elegance that instantly makes him a friend to the audience. . . . I found myself looking forward to his one dimensional underplaying out of sheer gratitude.

Rex Reed, *Holiday*

Eastwood, as Pardner, quietly sings a song.

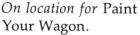

On location for Paint Your Wagon.

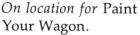

Lee Marvin is restrained by Eastwood in an exciting moment.

Eastwood strikes a more comfortable pose.

With Lee Marvin (left).

On the set with Jean Seberg and director Joshua Logan.

Alan Jay Lerner and Clint Eastwood.

Clint Eastwood, Alan Jay Lerner, Joshua Logan, Lee Marvin, and Jean Seberg.

Kelly's Heroes (1970)

CAST

Kelly, Clint Eastwood; *Big Joe,* Telly Savalas; *Crap Game,* Don Rickles; *General Colt,* Carroll O'Connor; *Oddball,* Donald Sutherland; *Moriarty,* Gavin MacLeod; *Mulligan,* George Savalas; *Maitland,* Hal Buckley; *Colonel Dankhopf,* David Hurst; *German Lieutenant,* John Heller.

CREDITS

Director, Brian G. Hutton. *Screenplay,* Troy Kennedy Martin. *Camera,* Gabriel Figuerou. *Editor,* John Jympason. *Music,* Lalo Schifrin. *Sound,* Cyril Swern, Harry W. Tetrick. A Gabriel Katzka, Sidney Beckerman Production. Metro Color and Panavision. *Running time: 146 minutes.* Released by MGM.

Returning to a World War II backdrop for the second time in two years, Eastwood found himself in Yugoslavia shooting *Kelly's Heroes.* Originally titled *The Warriors,* this film showed several parallels with *Where Eagles Dare.* For one, both were directed by Brian G. Hutton. Also, both were large-budgeted war films produced by MGM, and both were tongue-in-cheek adventures that mixed a good deal of humor with explosive action.

The Yugoslavian locations were not particularly difficult, but they were very boring. Eastwood's co-stars consisted of quite a few well-known American actors, among them Telly Savalas, Donald Sutherland, Carroll O'Connor, and Don Rickles. With a crew like that surrounding him, Eastwood found the isolation a great deal more bearable.

Certain marvelous touches in *Kelly's Heroes* stand out: a blazing battle led by Oddball's tanks, complete with "inspiring" music ("I've been Working on the Railroad" is heard as a train station is demolished), a very suspenseful finale that makes the audience tingle with the fear that the soldiers' plan will not be successful, the title song, "Burning Bridges," which perfectly fits the mood of the film, and a hilarious parody of *The Good, the Bad, and the Ugly,* with Eastwood, Sutherland, and Savalas in a showdown with a Panzer tank set to the accompaniment of western music.

Despite favorable audience reaction, Eastwood expressed frustration with the completed film. He charged that it could have been a classic if MGM boss James Aubrey had not ordered final-cut privileges taken away from director Hutton. Eastwood pleaded to let Hutton edit the film himself, but his cries fell on deaf ears. Whether the potential for a classic war film had been there, only Eastwood and the people concerned will ever know. What remains, however, is a very entertaining adventure that provides more than its share of laughs and excitement.

*Eastwood and Donald
Sutherland (with beard)
lead their men into
action.*

*Eastwood enjoys a joke
on the set.*

The Leone-type
showdown with
Eastwood (center),
Donald Sutherland (left),
and Telly Savalas
(right).

Eastwood approaches
black-market operator
Crap Game (Don
Rickles).

SYNOPSIS

In World War II Europe, a squad of Americans capture a German general. The interrogation is disrupted by a dangerous artillery barrage. Private Kelly (Clint Eastwood), however, gets the general drunk and learns that he is on a mission to deliver sixteen million dollars' worth of gold to a secret German treasury in France. When Kelly arrives back at headquarters, he is informed that the company captain has left for three days and has given the men a pass for the same length of time. Kelly suggests to the men that they strike behind enemy lines on their free time, secretly steal the gold, bury it, and return after the war to divide it.

The top sergeant, Big Joe (Telly Savalas), initially vetoes the move, but he relents when it becomes clear that he cannot stop his men from going. Kelly enlists the help of a soldier named Crap Game (Don Rickles), a hustler who can seemingly provide just about any weapon. For armored support, Kelly recruits Oddball (Donald Sutherland), the bizarre leader of a Sherman-tank squad, whose lifestyle consists of getting high on drugs and meditating to unorthodox music. When his squad is completed, Kelly has assembled his own secret little army.

The group moves swiftly through enemy lines, scoring a number of incredible victories that reach the top of the U.S. brass. General Colt (Carroll O'Connor), an egotist who sees the move as nothing more than a group of dedicated soldiers taking the war into their own hands, is delighted at their progress and plans a way to gain credit for the victories when the men arrive in Claremont, the town in which the gold is hidden.

After numerous battles and the loss of several lives, Kelly's men manage to capture Claremont, only to be faced with new obstacles: the arrival of General Colt on the other side of town and a devoted Panzer commander whose tank is guarding the bank vault that contains the gold.

Colt is mistaken for Eisenhower by the French populace, and his ego doesn't allow him to tell them differently. The ensuing celebration gains Kelly enough time to convince the Panzer commander that a share of the gold would be worth more to him than protecting it for his doomed cause.

As General Colt relishes the appreciation of the French people, Kelly and his men successfully load their truck with gold and carry away their fortune.

REVIEWS

Kelly's Heroes is not without its problems. But it is very visibly without solutions to them. Clint Eastwood, who is not generally a funny man, plays with a thin-lipped determination of such withdrawn ferocity . . . that you would expect his goal to be murder rather than money.

Roger Greenspun, *New York Times*

By punctuating his film with continual bombings and skirmishes, director Brian Hutton has assured himself of a wide-awake audience, even though the war theme is tiresome. Those who want action will find plenty of it here.

Ann Guarino, *New York Daily News*

It's obvious that dumb-dumb venality, with lack of taste and/or wit and an opportunity to use the Yugoslav army at cut-rate prices, motivated the making of *Kelly's Heroes*. . . . It's a noisy film with only boom-boom to keep you awake. . . . Eastwood manages not to change expressions once during the 146 minutes of this nonsense.

Judith Crist, *New York*

Let yourself coast with the action, of which there is plenty, and I think you're in for a chuckling time.

Bob Salmaggi, *Group W Radio*

Jumps at a pace matched only by slapstick comedy of the great days!

Archer Winsten, *New York Post*

Kelly's Heroes abounds with brilliance! It's a superbly acted, exquisitely photographed, howling spoof of wartime heroics.

Argosy

The biggest hunk of gut-grabbing adventure since that "Dozen" got "Dirty." . . . An intriguing robbery caper with the unexpected bonus of some genuine hilarity.

Newton North, *City East*

Very commercial WWII comedy drama. Big general audience prospects. Eastwood's performance remains in his traditional low-keyed groove. Hutton's direction is professionally routine, and that's without a knock, either. [He] is most satisfactory.

"Murf.," *Variety*

Eastwood and his men set off on their mission impossible.

With Don Rickles (right).

Eastwood is trapped by Nazis in a mine field.

With Don Rickles (left) and Donald Sutherland (top).

Crap Game (Don Rickles) gripes to Eastwood about being strafed by Nazi planes.

Kelly's heroes role into action.

Eastwood slays a Nazi in the battle for the town's gold.

111

Two Mules for Sister Sara (1970)

CAST

Hogan, Clint Eastwood; *Sister Sara*, Shirley MacLaine; *Colonel Beltran*, Manolo Gabregas; *General LeClaire*, Alberto Morin; *First American*, Armando Sivestre; *Second American*, John Kelly; *Third American*, Enrique Lucero; *Juan*, David Estuardo; *Juan's mother*, Ada Carrasco; *Juan's father*, Pancho Cordova.

CREDITS

Producer, Martin Rackin. *Director*, Don Siegel. *Screenplay*, Albert Maltz, from a story by Budd Boetticher. *Photography*, Gabriel Figueroa. *Editor*, Robert Shugrue. *Music*, Ennio Morricone. *Stunt Coordinator*, Buddy Van Horn. Released by Universal. Color by Technicolor and Panavision. *Running time: 105 minutes.*

Clint Eastwood initially discovered the script of *Two Mules for Sister Sara* while on location for *Where Eagles Dare*. When Richard Burton introduced Eastwood to his then wife, Elizabeth Taylor, both Taylor and Eastwood expressed a desire to do a film together. Liz had been sent the script for *Sara* and thought of it as a possible property for them both.

Eastwood tossed around the idea for a while, but when Universal, which purchased the property, balked at supplying Taylor's high salary and accompanying benefits, the project was temporarily shelved. After Eastwood filmed *Paint Your Wagon*, *Sara* was brought to life again, this time with Don Siegel directing and Shirley MacLaine filling the female lead.

On the set with Shirley MacLaine.

Eastwood uses dynamite to aid the guerrillas.

The film was shot in Mexico over a period of four months, and the location proved to be a very difficult one. Within days, every member of the cast and crew became victimized by Montezuma's Revenge, except Eastwood, who attributed his good fortune to his steady diet of fresh fruits. Other tensions brewed, with MacLaine and Siegel often having to overcome a nervous working relationship.

MacLaine proved to be a professional, reporting for work despite her stomach sickness. On screen, she and Eastwood registered quite well together, and Eastwood was happy with the resulting film. (He has stated that his drunk scene, in which MacLaine liquors him up in order to remove an arrow, was his best acting to date.) Siegel, however, was disappointed in the film and looked forward to its finish.

Despite the pitfalls in production, *Two Mules for Sister Sara* overcame its horrendous title and showed the expected large profits that had become synonymous with an Eastwood film. The action sequences are well done, and the two stars gave amusing and very endearing performances.

Sister Sara (Shirley MacLaine) is almost raped by bandits.

SYNOPSIS

The setting is Mexico in the days of the old West. Mexican guerrillas known as Juaristas are trying to rid their country of what they feel is exploitation by the French. A plan is drawn up to attack a French army post in Chihuahua. Hogan (Clint Eastwood), an American mercenary, happens upon a group of bandits about to rape a woman (Shirley Mac-Laine). In a fast gun battle, Hogan kills the assailants. He learns that this is no ordinary woman, but a nun who is being pursued by the French for giving aid to the Juaristas.

Hogan is talked into bringing the woman to a place of safety, mostly because he is fascinated with her personality and charm. Along the way, however, Sister Sara proves to be a not-so-ordinary nun. Hogan is shocked to hear her swear, and even more shocked to find that she can drink excessively. Her spellbinding ways influence Hogan to take part in guerrilla activities against the French. The two form a plan to sabotage a French supply train by climbing high up on a bridge to plant dynamite. When Hogan is wounded by an Indian arrow, Sister Sara completes the task successfully.

As the awkward relationship continues, Sara convinces Hogan to help her join a group of Juaristas and plan an attack on a French fort. Along the way, they take refuge in a bordello, where it is revealed that Sister Sara is herself a prostitute disguised as a nun. Hogan's ego is bruised, but he remains steadfast in his desire to help the Juaristas.

The plan works well. Sara and Hogan join the Juaristas and lead a victorious battle for the fort. When the smoke of gunfire clears, Hogan and Sara finally make love and ride peacefully into the sunset.

REVIEWS

. . . the realization of a movie lover's dream. I'm not sure it's a great movie, but it is very good and it stays and grows in the mind the way only movies of exciting narrative intelligence do. Good performances by Eastwood and MacLaine.

Roger Greenspun, *New York Times*

Eastwood is letter-perfect in his familiar role. It's a picture too familiar to be praised highly, but too professionally competent . . . to be damned out of hand.

Archer Winsten, *New York Post*

What the film lacks in original humor, it makes up for in excitement. Eastwood acts with greater naturalness than he has in the past.

Howard Kissel, *Women's Wear Daily*

Eastwood simply does not act (in this film, anyway). The film lacks a single genuine moment. Miss MacLaine and Mr. Eastwood don't generate any chemistry together and Siegel does little or nothing to fill the vacuum.

Variety

Ad-campaign artwork for the Sister Sara *poster.*

Shirley MacLaine and Eastwood plot strategy with the rebels.

Eastwood as Hogan observes Sister Sara in a troubled situation.

The Beguiled (1971)

CAST

John McBurney, Clint Eastwood; *Martha*, Geraldine Page; *Edwina*, Elizabeth Hartman; *Carol*, Jo Ann Harris; *Doris*, Darleen Carr; *Hallie*, Mae Mercer; *Amy*, Pamelyn Ferdin; *Abigail*, Melody Thomas; *Lizzie*, Peggy Drier; *Janie*, Pattie Mattick.

CREDITS

Producer and director, Don Siegel. *Screenplay*, John B. Sherry and Grimes Grice, from the novel by Thomas Culliman. *Camera*, Bruce Surtees. *Art director*, Alexander Cavalier. *Music*, Lalo Schifrin. Color by Technicolor and Panavision. *Running time: 105 minutes*. Released by Universal.

While he was on location shooting *Two Mules for Sister Sara*, Universal gave Eastwood the script to *The Beguiled*, a novel the company owned. It was a bizarre story, practically a Gothic horror tale without the supernatural, and Eastwood had never been offered anything quite like it. He showed the script to Don Siegel, and both men agreed it would be a promising, if risky film venture.

Production went smoothly, since most of the scenes were interiors. Siegel gave cinematographer Bruce Surtees his first job on the film, and the results were staggering. Surtees took elaborate steps to photograph the actors from seemingly impossible angles, often in almost total darkness.

The one major obstacle in shooting the film came from Universal boss Jennings Lang, who became enraged when he learned that Eastwood's character was to be killed off. Lang argued that this had never been done to Clint before and that audiences simply wouldn't buy the death of their hero, particularly at the hands of a group of women. Siegel argued that this was a new side of Eastwood that could not be measured or confined by his past cinematic images. Siegel and Eastwood persisted in their belief that Eastwood's character should be killed, and eventually they won their way.

The Beguiled is a masterful, extraordinary film that is somewhat ambiguous; its very nature combines beauty and horror. The entire atmosphere of the film is that of a decayed culture symbolized by the "living dead" inhabitants of a school. Eastwood's character invades that atmosphere like a breeze, which first comforts the women and finally chills them to the point where his presence is no longer bearable.

Eastwood gives a forceful, dynamic performance that ranks among the finest work he or any actor can be expected to do. Siegel's direction was simply superb, and the music and set decoration were excellent.

For all its qualities, however, *The Beguiled* did poorly at the box office, probably because Universal advertised it as though it were a standard Eastwood western. Fans felt cheated and stayed away in droves. The

Eastwood prepares to dynamite a French structure.

117

puzzling title did not help matters any, although it was substantially better than a few Universal had contemplated using (including *Pussy-footing Down at the Old Plantation* and *On One I Walked*).

Although Eastwood and Siegel were extremely disappointed over the reception and handling of their film, European critics were ecstatic over it. It was hailed as a masterpiece in Europe and is considered by some foreign critics as one of the great films of the seventies.

With Elizabeth Hartman.

As Johnny McB.

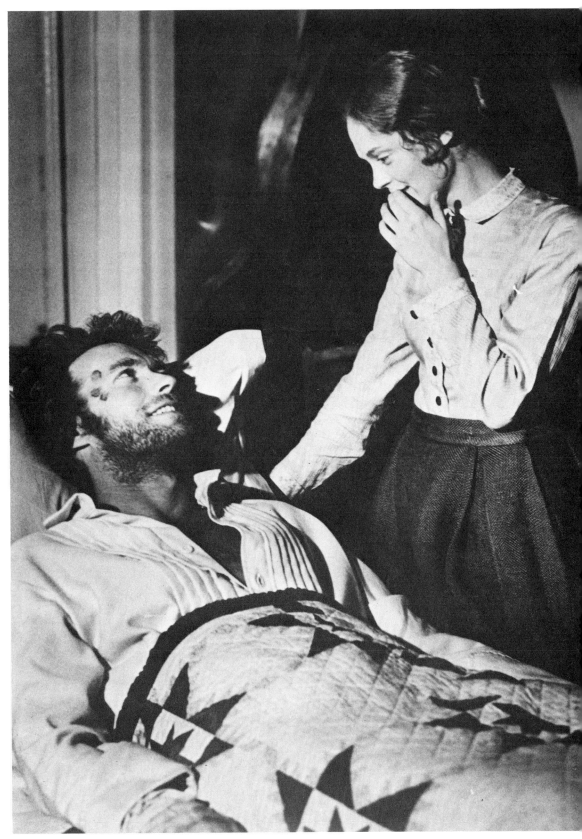

Eastwood is comforted by Elizabeth Hartman.

SYNOPSIS

Amid the horror of the South, torn by the Civil War, a once-fashionable school for young ladies still stands, a crumbling relic of a bygone era of glory. Amy (Pamelyn Ferdin), a ten-year-old student at the school, is picking mushrooms one day, when she discovers a severely wounded Union soldier named John McBurney (Clint Eastwood) lying in agony with a broken leg. Amy takes an immediate liking to Mr. McB, as she calls him, and manages to get him back to her school.

The arrival of the man causes great confusion and consternation at the school. The headmistress, Martha Farnsworth (Geraldine Page), decides to shelter McB after a teenaged student named Edwina (Elizabeth Hartman) convinces her that his arrest would result in his certain death.

McB is pampered and catered to by the ladies, and it becomes clear that he is the object of their repressed sexual desires. He takes advantage of the situation by charming several of the women, including Martha, into bed. Edwina, however, becomes extremely possessive and brings herself to believe that he is madly in love with her.

Continuing with his "beguiling" of the young ladies, McB is observed by Edwina making love to one of the girls. Enraged with jealousy, Edwina pushes McB down a long flight of stairs, resulting in severe damage to his recently healed leg. Martha decides to amputate the leg with a hacksaw, ostensibly because she feels it will save his life. However, there are indications that this act, too, is a result of her suppressed jealousy.

Eastwood enjoys a rare moment of levity with Geraldine Page (left) and Elizabeth Hartman.

Upon awakening, McB is horrified to learn of the amputation. He accuses the girls of doing the operation needlessly in order to keep him among them. His true nature comes out as he announces that in compensation he will live like a king at the school and pick and choose his bed partners as he pleases. Even Amy is turned against her former idol when he kills her pet turtle.

Now the women are afraid of this new side of McB. They send Amy out to pick poison mushrooms and feed them to him at dinner. While he is eating, however, McB shocks the women by apologizing for his attitude and turning over a new leaf. He announces his intentions to marry Edwina, who, overcome with shock, becomes horrified. McB stares incredulously with the realization of what must have happened. Seconds later, he falls over dead.

The final irony comes the next day, when it is discovered that Amy did not, after all, pick poisonous mushrooms. McB must have died of a heart attack. The schoolgirls set to work on a shroud to honor McB, whose brief presence with them has left an indelible impression on all their lives.

Eastwood stares in horror as he realizes that Geraldine Page (right) has amputated his leg.

121

REVIEWS

The Beguiled is stunningly adapted and directed.

Los Angeles Times

The grand amputation scene certainly proves that Lenny Bruce was underestimating public taste when he predicted that we only pay admission to see small children get run over by automobiles. The film was rated "R" so that the family that like to vomit together can do it at the movies.

Judith Crist, *New York*

A remarkably beguiling film.

London Times

The performances are uniformly excellent, with Clint Eastwood being the most impressive, particularly in the second half of the film, in which he is called upon to break with the more passive dimensions of the role and demonstrate a greater versatility and range than his best past work has indicated.

Hollywood Reporter

Eastwood gives . . . an astonishing, though certainly not great, performance.

Motion Picture Exhibitor

Don Siegel directing Eastwood and Pamelyn Ferdin.

Play Misty for Me (1971)

CAST

Dave, Clint Eastwood; *Evelyn*, Jessica Walter; *Tobie*, Donna Mills; *Detective*, John Larch; *Birdie*, Clarice Taylor; *Madge*, Irene Hervey; *Doctor*, Jack Ging; *Al Monte*, James McEachin; *Bartender*, Donald Siegel; *Jay Jay*, Duke Everts.

CREDITS

Producer, Robert Daley. *Director*, Clint Eastwood. *Screenplay*, Jo Heims and Dean Riesner. *Photography*, Bruce Surtees. *Art direction*, Alexander Golitzen. *Sound*, Robert Martin, Robert L. Hoyt. *Editor*, Carl Pingitore. *Music*, Dee Barton. *Songs* "Misty," composed and performed by Erroll Garner; "The First Time Ever I Saw Your Face," sung by Roberta Flack. Released by Universal. A Malpaso Production. Color by Technicolor. *Running time: 102 minutes.*

With *Play Misty for Me*, Clint Eastwood reached a milestone in his cinematic career. It was the first film in which he was both star and director. *Misty* came to Eastwood as an untitled sixty-page manuscript from a former secretary from Malpaso, who was aspiring to be a screenwriter. Eastwood was immediately intrigued by the storyline. He optioned the story but could find no studio interested enough to finance it.

Eventually, Universal bought the rights. Eastwood convinced the studio to back the project, with his own company, Malpaso, producing. Universal agreed, providing that Eastwood star, direct, and take a percentage of the profits rather than a straight salary. Eastwood did not mind acting in the film, but was quite nervous about directing it as well. Don Siegel convinced him to try his hand and signed Eastwood's membership card in the Director's Guild. Eastwood then began the search for an actress to portray the pivotal role of the maniacal Evelyn, around whom the entire story revolves. While watching *The Group*, he became impressed with Jessica Walter, and although the studio wanted to hold out for a better-known name for marquee value, Eastwood got his way and cast Walter as Evelyn. Then, in a bizarre move, he talked Siegel into playing a supporting role as a bartender. Siegel was as nervous in his new role in front of the camera as Clint was behind it. Eastwood enjoyed joking with the nervous Siegel, and at one point he made the harried director act his scene eleven times. Finally, after Siegel was told he had it right, Eastwood told the cameraman to put film in the camera!

Play Misty for Me is a perfect example of Eastwood's tight economy in filmmaking. The entire movie was shot in four and a half weeks, without a single studio shot. Yet the total budget came out to only $750,000.

Misty was photographed in the Carmel–Monterey Peninsula area of

Evelyn (Jessica Walter) makes Eastwood an offer he can't refuse.

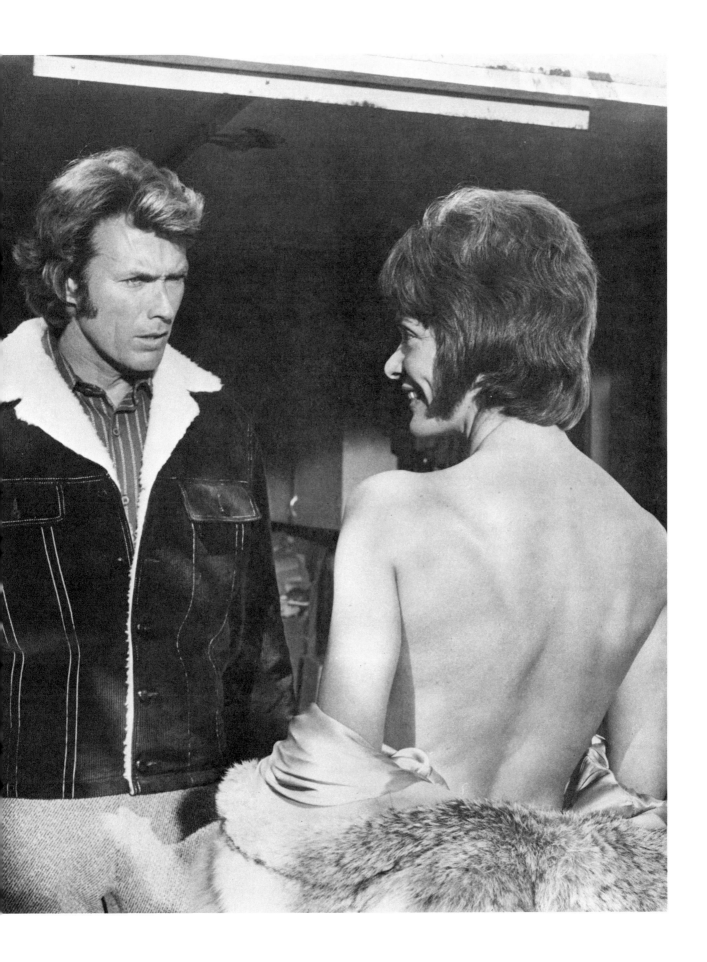

California, where Eastwood had lived for several years. Some sequences were shot live at the Monterey Jazz Festival.

Misty is, indeed, an effective shocker. Although the Hitchock-like inspirations are often too obvious (the scissor stabbing of Sergeant McCallum is a direct steal from Martin Balsam's staircase murder in *Psycho*), Eastwood crafted an often remarkably tense, occasionally terrifying film that audiences took to immediately. Eastwood's use of fast editing and helicopter shots over the Peninsula at sundown give the film an atmosphere of both beauty and terror. The dialogue is crisp and realistic as well.

Although Walter stole the show with a performance that should have been Oscar nominated, Eastwood delivered one of his finest characterizations. His portrait of a quiet man pushed to the breaking point by a bizarre relationship was letter perfect. He also proved that his talents were definitely not limited to acting. His direction of *Misty*—despite a few slow points—is extremely impressive, and he fashioned a film that was a deserved success.

Eastwood reunites with former flame Donna Mills.

126

SYNOPSIS

The most popular disc jockey in the Carmel-Monterey area of California, Dave Garver (Clint Eastwood), finds himself at loose ends because his girl, Tobie (Donna Mills), has broken their relationship and moved away. Garver is therefore an easy pickup at the Sardine Factory, a bar he frequents and mentions often on his show. Among the numerous phone calls he gets at the station are those from a woman who calls each night and asks him, "Play 'Misty' for me." The voice belongs to fan Evelyn Draper (Jessica Walter), who encounters Dave at the bar and persuades him to sleep with her with no strings attached.

It does not turn out that simple, however. Soon Evelyn is dropping in on Dave unexpectedly, which causes Dave a great deal of inconvenience. When Tobie returns to town and Dave resumes his courtship, Evelyn—in a paranoid fit—knifes Dave's cleaning woman (Clarice Taylor) and destroys all his possessions. Police Sergeant McCallum (John Larch) informs Dave that Evelyn has been sent to a mental institution.

Sometime later, she calls Dave with her nightly request for "Misty." She explains that she has been cured and released and is calling to say goodbye, since she is leaving for a new life in Hawaii. Dave sympathetically tells her that there are no hard feelings. Later that night, however, Dave awakens in his bedroom to the sound of "Misty" being played on his phonograph. He suddenly sees Evelyn above him ready to stab him with a butcher knife. Dave's quick actions save his life, but Evelyn makes good her escape. Although worried, Dave reports for work and goes on the air the following night.

Concerned for Tobie's safety, Dave asks McCallum to look in on her. Dave later discovers that Tobie's recently acquired roommate is none other than Evelyn. He rushes to her house, but it is too late. McCallum has been stabbed to death with a pair of scissors, and Tobie is tied up in the dark house, to be used as bait to get Dave inside. As he roams the rooms, Dave is suddenly attacked and badly wounded by the knife-wielding Evelyn. Time and time again she slashes Dave, until he finally manages to grab her and land a solid punch to her face, sending her crashing through the balcony to the ocean below. As Dave comforts Tobie, the radio ironically plays a tape of Dave honoring Evelyn's previous request to play her favorite song, "Misty."

REVIEWS

Clint Eastwood makes his directorial debut in *Play Misty for Me*. After a slow start, he proves he can handle both sides of the camera ably. The contemporary thriller holds interest for the most part. Jessica Walter . . . is so good as the possessive and obsessive woman that the viewer will want to strangle her. In fact, when the much-put-upon Eastwood finally punches her in the jaw as she tries to stab him, this viewer wanted to cheer. . . . Eastwood is best when he picks up the threads of the story and carries it on to its violent climax. The thriller stands out as a study of psychotic obsession.

Ann Guarino, *New York Daily News*

Eastwood displays a vigorous talent for sequences of violence and tension. He has obviously seen *Psycho* and *Repulsion* more than once, but those are excellent texts and he has learned his lessons well.

Time

An often fascinating suspenser . . . Excellent casting, handsome production and stretches of good direction by Eastwood are the assets. . . . Suffers from frequent digressions into landscape; the effect of the latter on pacing is murderous.

"Murf.," *Variety*

Play Misty for Me marks a surprisingly auspicious directorial debut for Clint Eastwood.

Village Voice

Play Misty for Me is about the best thriller I've seen in a long time.

Chicago Sun-Times

Psycho in mothballs . . . As for Eastwood's directorial debut, he should be credited for making up in helicopter shots what the movie lacks in plot, motivation and script. Then, to guarantee commercial success, he even throws in a nude scene, a visit to the Monterey Jazz Festival, and his best friend is black. You can't have everything but you sure can try.

Rex Reed, *New York Daily News*

Play Misty for Me suggests strongly that Clint Eastwood is more than a multitalented actor, producer and gunman. He is also a director who, at least in this picture, shows a good sense of what it takes to make an audience get goose pimples.

Archer Winsten, *New York Post*

Eastwood's first encounter with Jessica Walter at bartender Don Siegel's pub.

Eastwood and Don Siegel share some encouraging news on the set.

On the job as disc jockey Dave Garver.

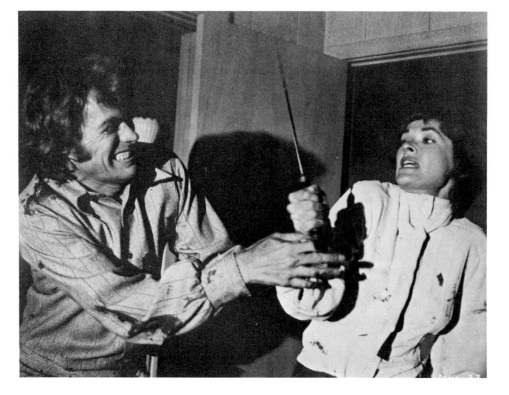

Enjoying the surf with Donna Mills.

Eastwood and Jessica Walter.

The director.

130

Dirty Harry (1971)

CAST

Detective Harry Callahan, Clint Eastwood; *Bressler*, Harry Guardino; *Chico*, Reni Santoni; *Scorpio*, Andy Robinson; *Chief*, John Larch; *DeGeorgio*, John Mitchum; *Mrs. Russell*, Mae Mercer; *Norma*, Lyn Edgington; *bus driver*, Ruth Kobart; *Mr. Jaffe*, Woodrow Parfey; *Rothko*, Josef Sommer; *Bannerman*, William Paterson; *liquor-store proprietor*, James Nolan; *Sid Kleinman*, Maurice S. Argent; *Miss Willis*, Jo De Winter; *Sergeant Reineke*, Craig G. Kelly; *mayor*, John Vernon.

CREDITS

Produced and directed by Don Siegel. *Executive producer*, Robert Daley. *Screenplay by* Harry Julian Fink and R. M. Fink and Dean Riesner. *Story by* Harry Julian Fink and R. M. Fink. *Director of photography*, Bruce Surtees. *Art director*, Dale Hennesy. *Film editor*, Carl Pingitore. *Sound by* William Randall. *Music by* Lalo Schifrin. *Set Decorator*, Robert DeVestel. *Assistant Director*, Robert Rubin. Panavision and Technicolor. *Running time: 103 minutes.* Released by Warner Bros.-Seven Arts.

When Don Siegel stumbled across a story about a right-wing detective in an age of peace protests and anti-police sentiment, the director thought it was tailor-made for Eastwood. Warner Bros. agreed, and the cameras started rolling. *Dirty Harry* was filmed on location (the only studio shot was the opening bank-robbery sequence) in San Francisco. The film came in on a relatively low budget and under schedule. For once, the locations did not prove to be a hassle, although Siegel did complain that they put enormous physical strain on him. One problem occurred when the crew prepared to shoot night sequences. Filming was limited to a few hours, owing to complaints from neighborhood residents that all the activity was keeping them awake.

Eastwood blasts a bank robber. (Note the attraction on the theater marquee.)

Siegel was also concerned about Clint's insistence upon doing his own stunts, most notably his now-famous leap from a railroad trestle onto a speeding schoolbus. Eastwood maintained that there was no way a double could have done the scene as effectively, and he was right. The stunt worked marvelously well on screen.

Don Siegel first rejected the notion of casting Andrew Robinson in the first of his psycho killer roles. Robinson in real life is a gentle, peace-loving man with good looks and a charming personality. However, Siegel changed his conception of the villain and decided that it would be more effective and terrifying if the maniac proved to be just like the average man in the street. The choice was a wise one. Robinson's performance ranks with the most memorable of screen villains.

The filming of *Dirty Harry* was relatively low key, but its reception upon release certainly was not. It shortly became one of the most controversial films in recent memory, with one school of critics arguing that it condoned fascism and police power while others argued that it was about time the screen reflected a sympathetic look at a police officer's frustrations rather than always painting them as dishonest extortionists.

Dirty Harry was not only a financial success, but it could better be termed a "phenomenal success." It quickly outgrossed any of Eastwood's previous films and jumped high on *Variety's* list of the top moneymaking films of all time. If the critics were divided, audiences weren't. They stood in line by the droves to see Eastwood as *Dirty Harry*.

For once, Eastwood was playing a character with some substance. His role, originally offered to Frank Sinatra and John Wayne, proved to be one of the best of his career. Critics were mostly complimentary toward his acting, which, under Don Siegel's superb direction, was letter perfect.

A stand-off with Scorpio.

Eastwood examines the switchblade that will eventually save his life.

Behind the camera polishing his directorial met

SYNOPSIS

When a sadistic, maniacal killer (Andy Robinson) stalks San Francisco, Detective Harry Callahan (Clint Eastwood) is called in on the case by his superior, Lieutenant Bressler (Harry Guardino) and the mayor (John Vernon). The object of the killer's game is clear: He intends to hold the city in terror until a ransom of a hundred thousand dollars is paid. Bressler and the mayor decide that the safest way to pacify the killer, who identifies himself as Scorpio, is to meet his demand, a proposal that gets immediate flack from Callahan, a man of few words but violent actions.

Harry is reluctant to accept the assignment of a young partner named Chico (Reni Santoni), but the two eventually begin to respect each other. The killer announces that he has buried a fourteen-year-old girl alive and will let her die unless paid two hundred thousand dollars. Harry gets the assignment to deliver the money and is backed up by Chico, who remains hidden from the killer's view. Harry is run all over town by the killer's demands and eventually confronts him in a park late at night.

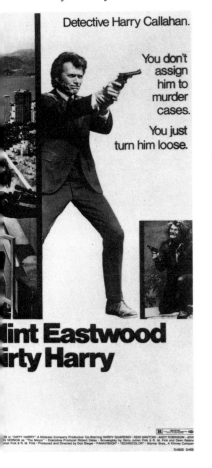

Advertising poster for Dirty Harry.

Scorpio immediately takes the money and, after announcing that he intends to let the girl die, hits Harry over the head and knocks him to the ground. As his vicious kicks rack Harry with pain, Chico dashes from the woods, only to be wounded by submachine-gun fire from Scorpio. In the confusion, however, Harry manages to jam a long switchblade into the killer's thigh, sending him limping through the woods in agonized panic.

Harry traces Scorpio to a closed football stadium and pursues him onto the field. He captures the killer and begins to torture him in order to find the whereabouts of the girl. Scorpio confesses where he has hidden her, and the girl is soon found—dead. Harry's troubles are only beginning, however. The DA severely criticizes him for torturing the suspect, and because his civil rights have been abused, Scorpio is released from police custody.

The killer quickly arranges for a muscleman to beat him mercilessly, then tells the news media that the beating was Harry's doing. This brings Harry more abuse from his own brass about being too brutal in his police methods.

Harry predicts that Scorpio will kill again. Like clockwork, the killer kidnaps a schoolbus at gunpoint and terrifies the children and driver. His demands this time include ransom money and a fueled plane for an escape.

Against orders, Harry takes off after the killer on his own. As the bus passes under a railroad trestle, Harry leaps onto the roof and plays a deadly cat-and-mouse game as Scorpio desperately tries to shoot him by firing into the roof. The bus goes out of control near a quarry plant, and Harry relentlessly pursues his prey through the winding passageways and conveyor belts of the plant.

When he can't escape Harry any longer, Scorpio grabs a young boy who is fishing by the bay and holds a gun to his head, demanding that

133

Harry throw down his .44 Magnum. Harry coolly pretends to do so, but suddenly his gun hand springs upward and he fires, hitting Scorpio and seriously wounding him. Harry gives Scorpio a choice: He can surrender or gamble that Harry is out of ammunition and grab for a nearby pistol. Scorpio takes the gamble, but before he can fire, Harry's gun blasts him into the water, dead.

As the police cars begin to arrive, Harry stands on the dock and disgustedly throws his badge into the water.

REVIEWS

A bluntly violent, very well made suspense thriller.

Los Angeles Times

Dirty Harry is very effective at the level of a thriller.

Chicago Sun-Times

A fast-paced detective story. Eastwood is excellent.

New York Daily News

One of the year's ten best.

Time

Don Siegel gives advice in the opening sequence.

On the set with Don Siegel.

*Eastwood helps film
Andy Robinson's ordeal
at the football stadium.*

*Eastwood performs one
of his most hazardous
stunts.*

As Harry Callahan.

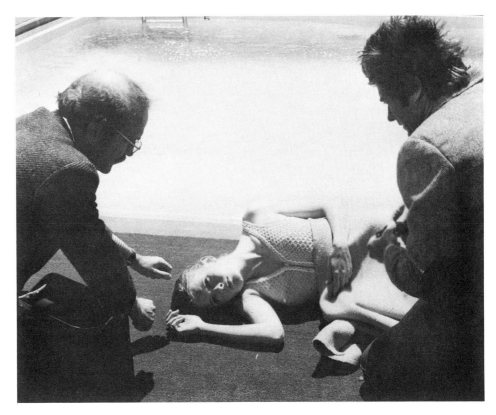

Investigating a murdered young woman's senseless death.

*Eastwood's fast draw
wounds Scorpio (Andy
Robinson).*

*With Harry Guardino
(left) and John Larch.*

Eastwood confronts Andy Robinson on the football field.

Preparing for a shot at Scorpio.

Eastwood receives a warning from boss Harry Guardino.

Eastwood pursues his man through the empty football stadium.

Eastwood receives a
brutal kick from Scorpio
(Andy Robinson).

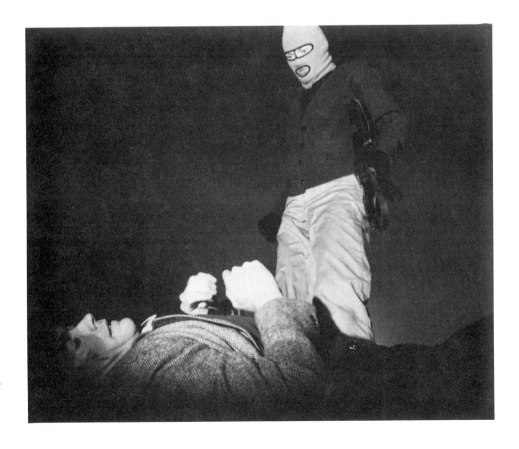

Eastwood lies helpless at
the hands of Andy
Robinson.

Joe Kidd (1972)

CAST

Joe Kidd, Clint Eastwood; *Frank Harlan*, Robert Duvall; *Luís Chama*, John Saxon; *Lamarr*, Don Stroud; *Helen Sanchez*, Stella García; *Mingo*, James Wainwright; *Roy*, Paul Koslo; *Sheriff Mitchell*, Gregory Walcott; *Elma*, Lynne Marta.

Eastwood and a companion ride into a small town.

CREDITS

Executive producer, Robert Daley. *Producer*, Sidney Beckerman. *Director*, John Sturges. *Original screenplay by* Elmore Leonard. *Photography by* Bruce Surtees. *Music by* Lalo Schifrin. *Editor*, Ferris Webster. A Malpaso Company Production. Color by Technicolor and Panavision. *Running time: 88 minutes*. Released by Universal Pictures.

Joe Kidd is one of Eastwood's least-talked-about films. This is because it came hot on the heels of Dirty Harry and was released while the other film was still deeply ingrained in the minds of the public. For although this is a serviceable, often quite interesting western, there is nothing the least bit remarkable or memorable about it.

The property was shown to Eastwood as an original screenplay by Elmore Leonard called *Sinola*. Leonard's writing seemed to have a real feel for atmosphere and characterization that intrigued Eastwood. Universal backed the film for Malpaso Productions, and Eastwood found

Eastwood in the title role of Joe Kidd.

himself working with a first-rate director, John Sturges, whose accomplishments included such films as *Bad Day at Black Rock*, *The Magnificent Seven*, and *The Great Escape*.

Even with all this talent, the film is often sluggish and dull. Eastwood's character never becomes interesting enough to identify with, and the way in which he changes sides is reminiscent of The Man with No Name. The action scenes do work well, the most spectacular being Eastwood's use of a train to crash through a building housing the villains. Although the acting was uniformly unimpressive, there is a certain amount of chemistry that registers when Eastwood is on screen with Robert Duvall (who can make even the dullest dialogue seem fascinating), but these moments are few and far between.

Although no one much talks about *Joe Kidd*, it can be placed in the ranks of Eastwood's more successful films, having outgrossed many of his better-known efforts.

Eastwood helps snipe at Harlan's men.

SYNOPSIS

The story is set on the Mexican-American border in the old West. Mexicans living on the U.S. side find themselves being exploited and persecuted by American landholders, most notably land baron Frank Harlan (Robert Duvall). The Mexicans find a charismatic leader in Luís Chama (John Saxon), and he takes them before a biased judge to defend their land rights.

Upon learning the judge's nature, the Mexicans turn to violence and nearly kill the judge, whose life is saved by Joe Kidd (Clint Eastwood), a prisoner jailed for drunkenness. This action endears Kidd to Harlan, who recruits him as a tracker for the army of gunmen he has hired to annihilate the Mexicans who oppose him.

Kidd seems convinced that he is on the wrong side when he has several run-ins with Harlan. The final straw comes when Harlan lures Chama into a trap, an action that Kidd considers cowardly. Kidd decides to change sides and join Chama's forces.

The action leads to a heated range war, which the Mexicans eventually win with the aid of Kidd, who, in a dramatic and daring move, drives a locomotive off the track and into the buildings housing Harlan's men.

The range war is over, but Kidd is not entirely approving of Chama's methods. He forces the guerrilla leader into surrendering and facing a fair trial.

REVIEWS

What puts *Joe Kidd* fatally out of balance is the surpassing excellence of western performances by Clint Eastwood, Robert Duvall and John Saxon. In a sense, they are diamonds set in dung. As for Eastwood and Duvall, it's a pleasure to watch them work. They really go further than the picture permits them, and it may even be that they successfully counteract and cover the picture's flaws.

Archer Winsten, *New York Post*

The great value of Clint Eastwood is that he guards his virtue very cannily, and in the society of *Joe Kidd,* where men still manage to tip their hats to the ladies, but just barely, all the Eastwood effects and mannerisms suggest a carefully preserved authenticity. I think it's a very good performance in context. Ultimately, it is the only real point of interest to *Joe Kidd,* and it is especially interesting because in recent years the Eastwood point of view has appeared mostly as analogy to the larger vision of the director. What emerges here is a kind of authoritative normalcy, an actor's gift to an ordinary film that at least gives him reasonable room to breathe.

Roger Greenspun, *New York Times*

Just another Clint Eastwood movie . . . tacky, aimless western. Eastwood is one of the most limited actors on screen. *Joe Kidd* will undoubtedly be of interest to the multitude of Eastwood fans. Others are advised to find another way to spend an hour and a half.

Dennis Hunt, *San Francisco Chronicle*

A concise and solidly crafted western that attests to the continuing flexibility of its durable genre . . . strikes a note of contemporary awareness without seeming to strain for relevance. Well written . . . [it] manages to be a satisfying, traditional-style adventure. *Joe Kidd* is a film of all-around high quality.

Kevin Thomas, *Los Angeles Times*

Confronting Luís Chama (John Saxon).

Eastwood in action at a trap set for Chama.

High Plains Drifter (1973)

CAST

The Stranger, Clint Eastwood; *Sarah Belding*, Verna Bloom; *Callie Travers*, Marianna Hill; *Dave Drake*, Mitchell Ryan; *Morgan Allen*, Jack Ging; *Mayor Jason Hobart*, Stefan Gierasch; *Lewis Belding*, Ted Hartley; *Mordecai*, Billy Curtis; *Stacey Bridges*, Geoffrey Lewis; *Bill Borders*, Scott Walker; *Sheriff Sam Shaw*, Walter Barnes.

CREDITS

Producer, Robert Daley. *Director*, Clint Eastwood. *Executive producer*, Jennings Lang. *Screenplay by* Ernest Tidyman. *Photography by* Bruce Surtees. *Art Director*, Henry Bumstead. *Editor*, Ferris Webster. *Music by* Dee Barton. *Assistant director*, Jim Fargo. A Malpaso Film. Color by Technicolor and Panavision. *Running time: 105 minutes*. Released by Universal Pictures.

Eastwood receives a not-so-welcome reception from the citizens of Lago.

Eastwood was attracted by *High Plains Drifter* when he read a nine-page idea for the screenplay at Universal. He immediately felt it would make a memorable, offbeat western, and he found the right man to do the script, Ernest Tidyman, who had recently won an Oscar for his brilliant screenplay for *The French Connection*. This time it was Eastwood who approached Universal with the idea of directing, instead of the reverse situation, which had occurred with *Play Misty for Me*.

Universal tried unsuccessfully to persuade Eastwood to shoot the film on the studio lot. Instead, Clint had an entire western town built in the desert near Lake Mono in the California Sierras. It took a large crew nearly eighteen days to construct the town, which was to be burned to the ground in the film's chilling climax. Professional house painters were called in to paint each building red when the day came to film that particularly bizarre sequence wherein Eastwood orders the town to be made into a replica of hell.

Once again, Eastwood shot his story in sequence, and once again he came in under budget and under schedule, much to Universal's delight.

The drifter arrives in town.

High Plains Drifter is every bit the offbeat western Eastwood had hoped it would be. It is unlike any other western in that it has a tantalizing mystery that suggests the supernatural. Although Eastwood denies there is anything supernatural about the nature of the film (he has gone on record stating that his intention was to insinuate that the identity of the mysterious drifter is that of the murdered sheriff's brother), the eeriness of the music, cinematography, and actions of the stranger make the film not only entertaining, but thought provoking as well.

As well made as it is, *High Plains Drifter* is not a likable film. There isn't one single character who is not either a killer or a sniveling coward. Audiences root for the Eastwood character not because he is morally sound, but simply because he disposes of so many despicable people. Eastwood once again shows a remarkable directorial flair for atmosphere and terror. The action sequences are excellently staged and are greatly helped by the tight, fast editing.

Little was required of Eastwood in the acting department, but he is totally convincing in what he does. If he did not win any new fans for his performance, he did continue to prove that he was a talented director. Not surprisingly, *High Plains Drifter* became another link in an almost unbroken chain of box-office hits.

With Billy Curtis.

With Marianna Hill.

With sidekick Billy Curtis.

SYNOPSIS

Studying script changes.

A mysterious stranger (Clint Eastwood) arrives in the isolated desert town of Lago in the 1870s. The silent drifter arouses instant suspicion and uneasiness among the populace. Almost immediately upon his arrival, he is harassed and goaded into a gunfight by three bullies. The stranger astonishes everyone by outdrawing them and killing them without showing any emotion.

The only clue to this man's past is a recurring nightmare that haunts the stranger as he sleeps in the town hotel. The gruesome dream depicts a helpless man who is whipped to death by three shrouded men, while a cowardly crowd of citizens refuses to help.

The scene switches to a town-council meeting where some prominent and equally spineless townspeople are frantically discussing how to deal with an unavoidable problem: the impending arrival of a group of escaped convicts who are enroute to Lago to destroy the town.

In desperation, the townspeople beg the stranger to protect them from the convicts. The stranger, obviously relishing the knowledge that he has this town of cowards at his mercy, agrees to help them. His preparations seem absurd to the people of the town, but everyone is too afraid to question his logic or ability. When all his orders for the arrangement of an ambush are carried out, he demands that the entire town be painted red. This is done, and Lago becomes a menacing, nightmarish vision under the desert sky. The stranger also renames the town Hell.

When the convicts arrive, however, the ambush fails. The stranger has apparently vanished, and the convicts take over the town, killing and looting. When they begin to burn down the town, one of them is suddenly snared around the neck by a bullwhip. A second killer is found hanged. In panic, the leader runs into the street, only to be shot to death by the man responsible for these actions: the stranger.

The town is saved from the killers, but the citizens must face something more terrifying. The events have led them all to revive their memories of the night these criminals whipped Sheriff Duncan to death while the townspeople stood by, too afraid to aid him. No one is sure why the stranger's presence has brought these memories to life; yet when a citizen asks timidly who he is, he replies, "You know who I am." As he rides away as mysteriously as he arrived, he seems to vanish into thin air. There is more than a little suspicion on the part of the citizens that they have encountered the vengeful ghost of Sheriff Jim Duncan.

REVIEWS

Even Clint Eastwood makes fun of Clint Eastwood's pitifully narrow range as an actor. *High Plains Drifter* should put an end to those jokes . . . because Eastwood the director gives notice of a solid and exciting talent. There are already traces of a distinctive Eastwood style. [His] performance is redeemed by his work on the other side of the camera. [It's] a movie to build a future on.

Jerry Oster, *New York Daily News*

One of the year's most hysterical comedies. The acting is a riot, the direction (by Eastwood) is as interesting (and as mobile) as the rear end of Eastwood's horse. I've seen better westerns at the Pepsi Cola Saloon at Disneyland.

Rex Reed, *New York Daily News*

Part ghost story, part revenge western, more than a little silly, and often quite entertaining. Neither Ernest Tidyman (who wrote the screenplay) nor Eastwood are taking themselves too seriously.

Vincent Canby, *New York Times*

Shows Clint Eastwood to be a genuinely talented filmmaker. . . . Not at all a likable film, but an impressive one.

London Observer

Breezy (1973)

CAST

Frank Harmon, William Holden; *Breezy*, Kay Lenz; *Bob Henderson*, Roger C. Carmel; *Betty Tobin*, Marj Dusay; *Paula Harmon*, Joan Hotchkiss; *Marcy*, Jamie Smith Jackson; *Man in Car*, Norman Bartold; *Harmon's date*, Lynn Dorden; *Nancy*, Shelley Morrison; *Bruno*, Dennis Olivieri; *Charlie*, Eugene Peterson.

CREDITS

Producer, Robert Daley. *Executive producer*, Jennings Lang. *Director*, Clint Eastwood. *Screenplay*, Jo Heims. *Photography*, Frank Stanley. *Editor*, Ferris Webster. *Music*, Michel Legrand. *Sound*, James R. Alexander. *Assistant director*, Jim Fargo. Released by Universal. Color by Technicolor. *Running time: 106 minutes.*

With *Misty* and *Drifter* successfully behind him, and with critical acclaim toward his directing talents more favorable with each film, Eastwood decided to go out on a limb and direct a film in which he would not appear.

To go further against his image, he selected a script called *Breezy*, a low-key, sentimental tale of a May-December romance. Eastwood had a difficult time selling the studios on the story, but his string of successes at Universal led the studio to take a chance on the modestly budgeted film. Shooting took place in and around Los Angeles, and the film was completed for the remarkably low cost of $750,000.

Eastwood very much enjoyed directing *Breezy*, and had stated at the time it was the film of which he was the proudest. The cast had nothing but compliments for his skills as director, and he received high praise from old pro William Holden, who raved that he would work with Clint again any time.

The film was released to harsh reviews, with most critics calling it hopelessly outdated. Although Eastwood's fans would probably have disregarded these notices had he starred in the film, this time the reviews seemed to take their toll. Hurting matters even further was the R rating, which excluded the teenagers to whom Eastwood had hoped to appeal.

Eastwood was hurt and upset by reaction to the film, and for the first time he seemed annoyed by critical response. Nevertheless, *Breezy* is an often touching and consistently well-acted film. Clint elicited an electrifying performance from Kay Lenz as Breezy, and William Holden is seen here at his best. If *Breezy* is often corny, it is nonetheless thoughtful and well meaning. It is an entertaining, engrossing film totally undeserving of its fate. In short, it is a movie of which Clint Eastwood can justifiably be proud.

Giving direction to William Holden and Kay Lenz.

Eastwood has a laugh on the set with Kay Lenz.

William Holden and Kay Lenz enjoy a day in the park.

156

SYNOPSIS

Frank Harmon (William Holden), a successful, aging divorced real estate executive, is annoyed to find a free-spirited teenage girl (Kay Lenz) wandering aimlessly around the grounds of his house. In order to get rid of her, he gives her a ride off the property. His conversation with the girl is strained and annoying to Harmon. Unknown to him, the girl, named Breezy, is suspicious of her driver because she has been accosted by another motorist shortly before.

Although Harmon's business is successful, he has become a virtual hermit, wanting neither to date nor to socialize with his peers. Later that evening, Harmon is shocked to find Breezy at his front door. She states that she has come to recover a guitar she left in his car, and in short order she talks him into inviting her into the house and letting her take a bath. Breezy asks if she might spend the night, but Harmon refuses and sends her away.

The next night, two police officers bring Breezy to Harmon's house and ask him to confirm the story she has told them about Harmon's being her uncle. Knowing she'll be arrested for vagrancy if he denies the tale, he plays alone. Breezy spends the night, and against his better judgment, Harmon finds himself becoming more and more involved with the young woman.

The following evening, Frank succumbs to his desires and makes love to Breezy. The affair blossoms, and both Breezy and Harmon find a great deal of happiness.

Happier times for Frank (William Holden) and Breezy (Kay Lenz).

157

Harmon, however, is beginning to look at the affair in a new perspective. He is embarrassed by friends and threatened by Breezy's growing interest in people her own age. He reluctantly tells her that they must not see each other again. Not long afterward, a woman Harmon is very close with informs him that her husband has been killed in a car crash. Seeing closely what loneliness is, now that this woman has to face her life alone, Harmon decides he will not be subjected to the same fate, particularly when there is someone who wants his love very badly. Harmon searches out Breezy and locates her in the park. The affair resumes, with Harmon courageously putting aside social taboos for the inner comfort of finding true love.

William Holden delights in taking Kay Lenz on a shopping spree.

REVIEWS

So perfectly awful that it's almost good enough for laughs.

Judith Crist, *New York*

Clint Eastwood continues to rise as a director in *Breezy*. He proved what he could do with *Play Misty for Me*, conquered the western form of film with *High Plains Drifter*, and now hits the bullseye with a sentimental April-November romance that could have been awful, but isn't.

Archer Winsten, *New York Post*

Fine work [from] William Holden and low keyed direction by Clint Eastwood sustain the narrative flow and mood in this film

Howard Thompson, *New York Times*

Clint Eastwood's most accomplished directorial job so far . . . a love story in which almost everything works.

Molly Haskell, *Village Voice*

William Holden and Kay Lenz discuss differences in their lifestyles.

Magnum Force (1973)

CAST

Harry Callahan, Clint Eastwood; *Lieutenant Briggs,* Hal Holbrook; *Early Smith,* Felton Perry; *Charlie McCoy,* Mitchell Ryan; *Davis,* David Soul; *Sweet,* Tim Matheson; *Grimmes,* Robert Urich; *Astrachan,* Kip Niven; *Carol McCoy,* Christine White; *Sunny,* Adele Yoshioka.

CREDITS

Producer, Robert Daley. *Director,* Ted Post. *Screenplay,* John Milius, Michael Cimino. *Based on a story by* John Milius, *from original material by* Harry Julian Fink, R. M. Fink. *Photography,* Frank Stanley. *Editor,* Ferris Webster. *Music,* Lalo Schifrin. *Art director,* Jack Collis. *Assistant director,* Wes McAfee. Released by Warner Bros. Color by Technicolor and in Panavision. *Running time: 124 minutes.*

Magnum Force was a follow-up to Eastwood's 1971 smash hit *Dirty Harry*. That film, while being hailed by many and panned by just as many, had become Eastwood's most successful movie. He now felt it time to return to the screen as Dirty Harry, and audiences were only too eager to prove his hunch correct.

In *Magnum Force,* the Harry character is undeniably more subdued than in the original film, although he is quite definitely still a man who shoots first and asks questions later. "Shooting is all right," he tells a group of Nazi-like policemen, "as long as the right people get shot." This was all too obviously to alert audiences that this was still the same tough guy Eastwood had played before, although a bit mellower when it came to upholding the traditions of the system.

Critics were quick to scoff at the softening of the Harry character. In fact, some reviewers saw it as a means to bribe their supposedly liberal instincts into giving the film a more favorable notice by playing up to liberal politics. There was no controversy, at least at the box office, in terms of the public. This film far outgrossed its predecessor and proved that the old addage about sequels being poor imitations was simply not true in this case.

Magnum Force lacked the impact and originality of *Dirty Harry,* but under Ted Post's capable direction, it remained an engrossing, fast-paced thriller. There are countless shoot-outs to keep the audience on the edge of their seats, and once again, Eastwood is plainly visible doing most of his own stunts, which greatly benefits the authenticity of the action sequences.

Clint seemed less enthusiastic about his character than he appeared to be the first time around. His performance is solid enough but not as penetrating as it was in *Dirty Harry.* This is a minor criticism, however, of a first-rate action thriller that remains one of Eastwood's biggest successes.

A moment of rapture.

With Adele Yoshioka.

SYNOPSIS

When an old partner is killed during an apparently routine investigation, Detective Harry Callahan (Clint Eastwood) takes charge of the case both on and off-duty. At the same time, San Francisco is being swept with a series of mysterious, vigilante-type slayings of suspected criminals. Lieutenant Briggs (Hal Holbrook), to whom Harry reports, assigns a young detective named Smith (Felton Perry) to act as Callahan's partner.

Poster artwork for Magnum Force.

The trail of evidence suggest to Harry that his friend had stumbled onto the vigilantes and had been killed to prevent him from arresting them. This hunch proves correct when he eventually finds that a group of young police officers are acting on their own in killing criminals. Callahan is asked to join them, but he angers them with his refusal on the grounds that they are just as criminal as the people they have murdered. Callahan suspects correctly that he is now marked for death.

Harry upsets Briggs with his accusations about his fellow officers, and Briggs tries to convince him that his theories are incorrect, despite evidence to the contrary. As a further warning, Harry receives news that Smith has been killed by a bomb in his mailbox. Harry avoids falling prey to a similar setup.

Before he can act, Harry is taken for a ride by Briggs, ostensibly to discuss the case. However, Briggs draws a gun on Harry and admits to being the head of the vigilante squad. Harry disarms Briggs in a tense struggle and is pursued to a waterfront pier by Briggs's men. A high-speed motorcycle chase ends with Harry killing his adversaries. A final confrontation with Briggs ends when Harry tosses a bomb into his superior's getaway car.

REVIEWS

Mr. Eastwood's unshakable cool makes me miss Richard Widmark's style in playing this kind of part. All that Eastwood can manage is a frown that suggests tension. The excitement is mainly in the camera-work, which is stunning.

Nora Sayre, *New York Times*

Magnum Force is another cop opera with a decent twist to its story but a slow motion style. . . . It eventually leaves one not caring how much it turns out. [It's] a picture that needs to crack along if it is to work. As it is, it picks its way so carefully that we tire of it as we would tire of watching an uninspired ant negotiate a maze.

Variety

The story is simple one, rather far fetched, but capable of supplying large outbursts of violent action that gives Eastwood the opportunity to exemplify absolute equanimity under the most extreme pressure. Afterwards, he's still as calm as before. He makes a wonderful hero, as practically everyone in the country has already noticed.

Archer Winsten, *New York Post*

Publicity shot for Magnum Force.

Eastwood takes cover from the vigilante cops.

Preparing for the final confrontation.

Another lethal pose for a theater poster.

Eastwood examines the aftermath of a shootout in a supermarket.

Inside an old ship, Eastwood is pursued by his enemies.

With Felton Perry.

*Eastwood enjoys a rare
moment of relaxation.*

*Eastwood confronts
Lieutenant Briggs (Hal
Holbrook) with some
incriminating evidence.*

With Felton Perry (left) and Hal Holbrook.

Eastwood dismantles a bomb placed in his mailbox.

Lieutenant Briggs (Hal Holbrook) gets the drop on Eastwood.

Eastwood finds himself at the mercy of a skyjacker.

Thunderbolt and Lightfoot (1974)

CAST

Thunderbolt, Clint Eastwood; *Lightfoot*, Jeff Bridges; *Goody*, Geoffrey Lewis; *Melody*, Catherine Bach; *Curly*, Gary Busey; *Red Leary*, George Kennedy; *vault manager*, Jack Dodson; *tourist*, Gene Elman; *welder*, Burton Gilliam; *Dunlop*, Roy Jenson; *secretary*, Claudia Lennear; *crazy driver*, Bill McKinney; *Mario*, Vic Tayback.

CREDITS

Produced by Robert Daley. *Direction and screenplay*, Michael Cimino. *Photography*, Frank Stanley. *Art director*, Tambi Larsen. *Editor*, Ferris Webster. *Music*, Dee Barton. Released by United Artists. A Malpaso Company Film. Color by DeLuxe and Panavision. *Running time; 115 minutes.*

Michael Cimino, with whom Eastwood was impressed after Cimino had co-authored the screenplay for *Magnum Force*, was given not only the writing but the directorial reins of Clint's next film, *Thunderbolt and Lightfoot*.

Filming was basically uneventful. Eastwood worked well with Cimino, who made a very impressive debut as a director. The real fun of the film comes in watching the chemistry generated between Eastwood as the aging con man and his young, aspiring sidekick played by Jeff Bridges. For once, Eastwood had some interesting actors in well-written roles to play opposite. The film benefited from crisp dialogue and a minimum of physical violence. The result here was for the better. *Thunderbolt and Lightfoot* is a film about people, and it did not need excessive gore to keep it interesting.

Critics were far kinder to this Eastwood effort than they had been to most of his earlier films. He was praised for trying a change of role and for letting his co-star handle most of the scene-stealing dialogue. Jeff Bridges received the lion's share of the critical acclaims (enough to win him an Oscar nomination for Best Supporting Actor). The film also proved to be a substantial hit with audiences.

Director Cimino also gained praise, although he would not have another movie released until 1978, when his film *The Deer Hunter* earned him not only the Academy Award for best director, but also the satisfaction of seeing his film honored as best picture of the year.

Eastwood demonstrates the use of a Howitzer cannon to Jeff Bridges (left), George Kennedy (center), and Geoffrey Lewis (right).

Eastwood prepares to use a cannon in his daring robbery.

Eastwood gets rough with a local troublemaker.

173

SYNOPSIS

A retired thief named Thunderbolt (Clint Eastwood) is posing as a minister, when he is chased out of his pulpit by a former confederate who recognizes him. Fleeing across a field, he is rescued by a young trouble-shooter named Lightfoot (Jeff Bridges). The two men become immediate friends, with the younger man trying to prove he is as tough as Thunderbolt was in his prime.

When it becomes apparent that Thunderbolt is constantly being pursued by two irate men, he confides that some time ago he was part of a robbery of a government vault. He had hidden the cache of stolen money behind a blackboard in an old one-room schoolhouse in the middle of an obscure field, and only he knows its location. The two men try to make it to the schoolhouse before Thunderbolt's former partners catch up with them. They soon find to their dismay that the old school has been replaced by a modern one.

They are overcome by their two pursuers—Red (George Kennedy), a hot tempered, violent man, and Goody (Geoffrey Lewis), his slow-thinking follower. Thunderbolt convinces the men that he has no knowledge of the whereabouts of their stolen money. Lightfoot then suggests the foursome pull off an identical robbery—an idea greeted first with laughter and then with gradual acceptance. An elaborate scheme is devised to make the plot succeed. With the aid of a Howitzer cannon, the four men blast open the vault and steal the money.

With the police in hot pursuit, Goody is killed, and Thunderbolt and Lightfoot attempt to escape by posing as lovers at a drive-in movie (with Lightfoot in makeshift drag). They succeed, only to confront Red, who is violently angry because the police have closed in. He knocks Thunderbolt out and gives Lightfoot a severe beating before trying to escape the police in a high-speed chase. Red loses control of his car and crashes through the window of a department store, where he dies a brutal death when unleashed guard dogs tear out his throat.

Thunderbolt and the badly hurt Lightfoot make good their escape without any of the money. However, they chance upon the old schoolhouse, which has been restored as a monument and placed in a new location. Thunderbolt enters the building and finds the original money still hidden behind the blackboard. He immediately takes Lightfoot to town and celebrates by buying him the one item he has always wanted —a new white convertible. As the two men drive down a lonesome highway, Lightfoot manages to joke through his intense pain. Suddenly he closes his eyes, and Thunderbolt realizes his one friend has died, leaving him with a fortune that cannot fill the emptiness inside him.

REVIEWS

A demented exercise in Hollywood hackery . . . lame gags that would have been rejected by the Three Stooges. A no talent Michael Cimino, about whom you are unlikely to hear more, scribbled the smarmy

Eastwood takes a belt at Red (George Kennedy).

dialogue and bravely took credit for the illiterate direction. Clint Eastwood, Jeff Bridges and George Kennedy are some of the occasional professionals who limp through the staggeringly silly situations in search of a paycheck. Cheap potboilers like this shouldn't be released. They should be recycled and used to catch droppings on the floors of chicken coops.

Rex Reed, *New York Daily News*

Good acting by Eastwood and Bridges; watch out for new director Cimino.

Film Weekly

Eastwood with his "girlfriend" (Jeff Bridges in drag).

The Eiger Sanction (1975)

CAST

Jonathan Hemlock, Clint Eastwood; *Ben Bowman,* George Kennedy; *Jemima Brown,* Vonetta McGee; *Miles Mellough,* Jack Cassidy; *Mrs. Montaigne,* Heidi Bruhl; *Dragon,* Thayer David; *Fretag,* Reiner Schene; *Meyer,* Michael Grimm; *Montaigne,* Jean-Pierre Bernard; *George,* Brenda Venus; *Pope,* Gregory Walcott.

CREDITS

Produced by Robert Daley, Richard D. Zanuck, David Brown. *Directed by* Clint Eastwood. *Screenplay by* Hal Dresner, Warren B. Murphy, Rod Whitaker, *based on novel by* Trevanian. *Camera,* Frank Stanley. *Editor,* Ferris Webster. *Music,* John Williams. *Art Direction,* George Wedd, Aurelio Crugnola. *Sound,* James R. Alexander. *Assistant director,* Jim Fargo. Released by Universal. *Running time: 125 minutes.* Color by Technicolor and Panavision.

Universal offered Eastwood the script to *The Eiger Sanction,* a James Bond–type adventure based on a bestseller. While the company discussed who should direct the film, Eastwood decided he would have to get into shape for the hazardous climbing sequences on the Eiger mountain, a foreboding Swiss monolith rising thousands of feet. While training for the film at Yosemite National Park, Eastwood realized that for the film to be truly exciting, there could be no studio shots of the climb. He also knew that he would have to do all his own stunt work in order to keep the authenticity intact. The more he studied the production schedule, the more he knew that there would be no logical way the director and the main star could work effectively together on the mountain while enduring rock slides and high winds. Therefore, Eastwood knew that the film would require his directing skills as well.

Universal did not object to this idea, although there was more than a little concern over the safety of the world's number-one box-office attraction as he would dangle precariously off the side of a mountain. Eastwood was now a middle-aged man with no climbing experience. Could a few more weeks of training actually enable him to meet the demands of the location? On the second day of shooting, British stuntman David Knowles was killed by a runaway boulder. For Eastwood, the death cast a pall over the entire production. Yet not wanting Knowles's death to be in vain, he became determined to finish the film.

The location was more hazardous than anyone had anticipated. Eastwood has admitted to being terrified on several occasions, especially when ceaseless rock slides brough down pellets that "struck my helmet like shots from a .22."

For all the work that went into it, *The Eiger Sanction* was not a great

176

success, although it did perform satisfactorily at the box office. Critics hailed the stunt work but saw the film as a 007 takeoff with Eastwood totally miscast in his role as an art professor who reluctantly returns to being a professional assassin.

The storyline was admittedly predictable and not very involving. Yet to dismiss *The Eiger Sanction* as a dull film is unjust. Eastwood's direction flounders in some of the overtalkative sequences, which seem boring and uninspired. However, on the face of the Eiger, his directorial work ranks with some of the most impressive action sequences ever to appear in a major film. There is not one phony backdrop or papier mâché rock. When Eastwood dangles precariously above the Eiger, it is really him doing the stunts, and the effect is thrilling.

Eastwood and George Kennedy (also kneeling) on a not-very-enviable location in Arizona.

SYNOPSIS

Cameraman Mike Hoover shoots a dummy of Eastwood while Clint looks on.

Former professional assassin Jonathan Hemlock (Clint Eastwood) is comfortable in his new occupation as an art teacher at a prestigious college. One day he is summoned by a secret U.S. intelligence agency to perform another "sanction"—an agency term for a killing. Hemlock agrees solely because he sees it as another way to finance his valuable collection of art masterpieces.

After performing the sanction, however, it becomes apparent that he will not be allowed to go home. The agency blackmails him into agreeing to perform an even more dangerous sanction that will require him to scale the Eiger Mountain in Switzerland, unmask an enemy agent in an international mountain-climbing party, where he will be a guest, and kill the spy while on the mountain.

Eastwood is coerced into performing the sanction by Dragon (Thayer David).

Hemlock is aided by old friend Ben Bowman (George Kennedy), whose help and expertise prove extremely valuable. He also romances and beds a beautiful woman named Jemima Brown (Vonetta McGee). Finally, the ascent of the Eiger begins. The climb almost kills each member of the team at some point, and everyone acts like a suspect. As a series of deaths narrows down the list of suspects, Hemlock finds out that the agent he is trying to unmask is none other than Ben Bowman.

An ironic series of circumstances leads to Hemlock's realization that Bowman knows he has been uncovered. Before he can get down the mountain, however, Hemlock finds himself dangling from a precipice, facing certain death. A rescue party appears, headed by none other than Bowman. Helpless and unable to move, Hemlock is powerless to stop what he feels are merely makeshift rescue attempts by Bowman to convince other members of the party that he is trying to save Hemlock's life. To Hemlock's astonishment, Bowman does save him.

With both men back on the ground, Bowman justifies the actions of his past enough to convince Hemlock to refuse to carry out the sanction and return home. Hemlock deludes his blackmailers at the agency into thinking that the real assassin has been killed.

Eastwood prepares for a climbing sequence.

REVIEWS

Eastwood, who also directs and according to the studio, did his own mountain climbing without doubles, manages fine suspense both in the Swiss and Monument Valley climbs, as well as a strong delineation of character. His direction displays a knowledge that permits rugged action.

Variety

A good film to sleep to.

Film Weekly.

Enjoying a laugh with George Kennedy and a very homely admirer.

Hemlock (Eastwood) performs the Zurich sanction.

Eastwood (top) and professional climber Doug Halston perform a dangerous stunt.

182

*Eastwood dangles
helplessly while his
would-be killer holds his
lifeline.*

On the set with Vonetta McGee.

Eastwood is about to exterminate assassin Jack Cassidy.

Eastwood fights it out with Walter Krauss, the target of the Zurich sanction.

Eastwood prepares for another climb on the location.

185

Eastwood as Jonathan Hemlock begins the ascent up the Eiger.

Eastwood directs the location sequences in Zurich.

Clowning around with George Kennedy on location in Switzerland.

Eastwood on a tough location for The Eiger Sanction.

The Outlaw Josey Wales
(1976)

CAST

Josey Wales, Clint Eastwood; *Lone Wolf*, Chief Dan George; *Laura Lee*, Sondra Locke; *Terrill*, Bill McKinney; *Fletcher*, John Vernon; *Grandma Sarah*, Paula Trueman; *Jamie*, Sam Bottoms; *Little Moonlight*, Geraldine Keams; *Carpetbagger*, Woodrow Parfrey; *Rose*, Joyce Jameson; *Cobb*, Sheb Wooley; *Kelly*, Matt Clarke; *Chato*, John Verros; *Ten Bears*, Will Sampson; *Carstairs*, William O'Connell; *Comanchero leader*, John Quade.

CREDITS

Producer, Robert Daley. *Director*, Clint Eastwood. *Screenplay*, Phil Kaufman and Sonia Chernus, *based on the book* Gone to Texas *by* Forrest Carter. *Cinematography by* Bruce Surtees. *Production design*, Tambi Larsen. *Editor*, Ferris Webster. *Music*, Jerry Fielding. *Sound*, Tex Rudloff, Bert Hallberg. *Set decoration*, Chuck Pierce. *Assistant director*, Jim Fargo. *Stunt coordinator*, Walter Scott. A Warner Bros. Release. Color by DeLuxe. *Running time: 135 minutes.*

The idea for *The Outlaw Josey Wales* first came to Eastwood's Malpaso Productions through producer Bob Daley. Forest Carter, a middle-aged half-Cherokee Indian, had submitted a little-known book he had written, asking Daley to give Eastwood the story for consideration as a film. Daley was immediately enthusiastic about the property, and when Eastwood shared his enthusiasm, they purchased the screen rights for Malpaso, with Warner Bros. contracting to release the film.

Eastwood agreed to star in *Josey* providing someone else would direct. Clint had been impressed with the work of director Phil Kaufman *(The Great Northfield Minnesota Raid)* and hired him to direct *The Outlaw Josey Wales*. Kaufman did several rewrites of the script and managed to shoot a week's worth of footage. At this point, however, Clint decided that Kaufman's version of the film was far from the epic he had envisioned. Reluctantly, and with all respect, Eastwood removed Kaufman from the film and decided to take on directing it as well as starring.

The film was shot in Utah, Arizona, and California in eight and a half weeks. The shooting took its toll on Eastwood, who was still exhausted from his *Eiger Sanction* chores; yet there were no major problems on any of the locations.

The film contains a great deal of violence and some very impressive camera work from Clint's usual cinematographer, Bruce Surtees. Jerry Fielding's music was another plus, and it earned an Oscar nomination for best original score.

The movie is one of Eastwood's most popular and profitable films, having been successfully reissued several times.

SYNOPSIS

The farm of Josey Wales (Clint Eastwood), along the Missouri-Kansas border, is raided by Union renegades just before the Civil War. Josey's wife and son are killed, and he is left for dead. His quest for revenge leads him into the Confederate army, where Commander Fletcher (John Vernon) dupes his men into a "peaceful" surrender to the Union. Union leader Terrill (Billy McKinney), responsible for the deaths of Eastwood's family, executes most of the confederate troops.

Josey escapes and rescues a friend named Jamie (Sam Bottoms), who, although wounded, has managed to survive the massacre. The two men form a close bond, and Josey is deeply hurt when the younger man dies.

Continuing his sad life alone, Josey tries to escape Terrill's band of vengeful pursuers by heading into the Indian nation. Here he meets Lone Wolf (Chief Dan George), an elderly Cherokee who, like Josey, has been victimized by many hardships in his life. The two decide to head for Mexico but in the interim allow a young Navajo girl (Geraldine Keams) to join them when they find she has been unjustly outcast from her tribe. Still enroute to their destination, the group rescues an old woman (Paula Trueman) and her granddaughter (Sondra Locke) from the hands of a gang of bandits dressed as Indians.

Upon arriving in Texas, Josey decides that this is where he will stop running and face his hunters. The group settles on a farm formerly owned by the old woman's son, who has died in the war. With the aid of a friendly Commanche chief, the group bands together and miraculously defeats Terrill's group of cutthroats when they eventually arrive to kill Josey. With this revenge, Josey relaxes and looks forward to finding some of the joy in life he has not known since his family's death.

REVIEWS

Formula Clint Eastwood slaughter film for regular market . . . About the only difference between [the film] and other formula Clint Eastwood vengeance-violence thrillers is that, with a mortality rate of one corpse every 90 seconds over its interminable 135 minutes' length, [it] stretches to the breaking point the credulity of the PG rating. . . . It's nothing more than a prairie *Death Wish*.

"Murf.,"*Variety*

Seems to last two days. Never before . . . has so much time been devoted to such trivia. On the interminable journey [Eastwood] is accompanied by a stock company of ferocious hams. Either they are terrible actors or it just looks like overacting when you move your eyebrows on the same screen with Eastwood. . . . Eastwood manages a grunt, a mumble and an occasional "I reckon so." So much for his performance.

Rex Reed, *New York Daily News*

One of the year's ten best.

Time

Eastwood directs a shootout (inset).

Eastwood holds Chief Dan George at bay.

Ad-campaign artwork for The Outlaw Josey Wale[s]

After seeing his family massacred, Eastwood vows vengeance.

Eastwood gives his enemies a double-barreled dose of gunfire.

Unused ad campaign for Josey—this artwork was used overseas, however.

Josey gets his justly deserved revenge.

With Sondra Locke.

Eastwood in the pose that makes his fans shout for action.

193

The Enforcer (1976)

CAST

Harry Callahan, Clint Eastwood; *Kate Moore,* Tyne Daly; *Lieutenant Bressler,* Harry Guardino; *Captain McKay,* Bradford Dillman; *DiGeorgio,* John Mitchum; *Bobby Maxwell,* DeVeren Brookwalter; *mayor,* John Crawford.

CREDITS

Produced by Robert Daley. *Directed by* James Fargo. *Screenplay,* Stirling Silliphant, Dean Reisner, based on characters created by Harry Julian Fink and R. M. Fink. *Camera,* Charles W. Short. *Editors,* Ferris Webster, Joel Cox. *Music,* Jerry Fielding. *Art director,* Allen E. Smith. *Stunt coordinator,* Wayne Van Horn. Color by Technicolor. *Running time: 96 minutes.* Released by Warner Bros.

With *Josey Wales* still ringing up theater cash registers all over the world, Eastwood was not in any hurry to start another project. However, two enterprising young men had written a screenplay for a detective film that they thought might interest Eastwood. With no way to contact him personally, the aspiring writers dropped off their script at the Hog's Breath Inn, a restaurant Eastwood owns in Carmel. The maître d' saw to it that Clint got the manuscript, and the result was sudden interest on Eastwood's part in developing the script into a possible vehicle.

Sterling Silliphant and Dean Reisner, two of Eastwood's favorite screenwriters, went to work on the story and developed it into another *Dirty Harry* sequel. Originally titled *Dirty Harry III,* the film was later entitled *The Enforcer*—a definite improvement in terms of marquee value.

The film marked the first time James Fargo had directed an Eastwood picture himself, although he had been assistant director of earlier Eastwood films. Fargo seemed adept enough at directing the action sequences, but the film suffered in the less lively scenes. No originality was shown in making Harry Callahan a more interesting character, and critics who complained that Harry seemed boring in *Magnum Force* were struggling to stay awake during *The Enforcer.*

The film received nearly unanimous pans, with virtually all reviewers indicating that the film would have seemed far better on a TV screen.

However, although *The Enforcer* was not an important film for Eastwood, it was not deserving of the roasting it received. The worst that could be said of the film was that it was predictable and unimaginative. There are good elements, such as the exciting opening sequence in which Harry crashes a car through a store window, a fast-moving and exciting climax filmed on Alcatraz, Eastwood's tangle in a massage parlor, and a delightful performance from Tyne Daly. Eastwood had nothing to work with except the shell of the original character of Harry Calla-

Eastwood as Josey Wales—an "army of one."

han, and there was no way he could make it interesting.

Audiences didn't seem to mind, however; *The Enforcer* is one of the biggest money makers in Eastwood's career.

A publicity shot for The Enforcer.

SYNOPSIS

San Francisco detective Harry Callahan (Clint Eastwood) is called to the scene when a group of gunmen hold up a liquor store and savagely abuse their hostages. Callahan responds to the gunmen's demands by crashing a car through the window of the store and single-handedly killing all the criminals with a quick draw of his .44 Magnum.

Meanwhile, a group of terrorists kill two Public Service gas men and use their uniforms as part of their plot to rob an arms company. The plan is nearly foiled when Harry's longtime friend and fellow policeman ''Fatso'' (John Mitchum) stumbles onto the plot and shoots it out with the criminals. Fatso is mortally wounded in the gun battle, and Harry takes a personal interest in the case.

However, because of his past reprimands about violence from the police brass, Harry is assigned a novice partner, Kate Moore (Tyne Daly), who is to act as his watchdog. The two bicker at first, but Harry finds his partner more than capable when the going gets rough. Eventually, Harry finds himself falling in love with the woman he first despised.

As the dragnet tightens around the terrorists, the criminals kidnap the mayor (John Crawford) and take him as a hostage to the abandoned prison at Alcatraz. Harry and Kate trace the group there and engage in a wild shootout, during which Kate is mortally wounded and dies in Harry's arms. Crazed with a desire for revenge, Harry confronts the terrorist leader, who has positioned himself in the island lighthouse. Using one of the terrorists' bazookas, Harry blasts his opponent to oblivion and rescues the mayor. His victory is hollow, however, because it has cost him the life of the only woman he has ever really cared for.

Eastwood blasts it out in a rooftop chase with an adversary.

REVIEWS

The action is reasonably fast and competently photographed. The picture doesn't exactly drag, but it is maggoty with non-ideas.

Richard Eder, *New York Times*

Taking the picture for what it tries to be, a crime thriller with Eastwood going beyond the law to protect the public, one must admit that both in audience participation and lethal excitement, the entertainment level is wildly explosive.

Archer Winsten, *New York Post*

One might wish that *The Enforcer* had the cinematic smarts imparted by director Don Siegel to the original *Dirty Harry,* a tenser, tauter piece of work. But *The Enforcer* is fairish fun, and certainly no threat to liberal democracy.

Richard Shickel, *Time*

The Enforcer . . . uses the same basic plot strategy as *The Outlaw Josey Wales*. It sets up a collection of villains so disgustingly cruel and inhuman that Eastwood can spend the rest of the movie killing them with a perfect conscience.

Pauline Kael, *The New Yorker*

The Enforcer is the third or fourth Dirty Harry movie with Clint Eastwood blowing people's heads off and creating the kind of havoc Batman would find juvenile. . . . It all went out of style years ago with Clint Eastwood's mumbling. . . . Save your money, it'll be on TV by Easter.

Rex Reed, *New York Daily News*

Worn out copy of *Dirty Harry* . . . the format seems to be falling apart at the seams. However . . . there is enough explicit violence to satisfy the target audience. The spitball script lurches along through 96 minutes, stopping periodically for blood and assorted running and jumping and chasing stuff. The next project from this particular mold had better shape up or give up.

"Murf.," *Variety*

Eastwood in an unused sequence for The Enforcer.

198

*Eastwood is at odds with
superiors Bradford
Dillman (left) and Harry
Guardino.*

*Eastwood has a
confrontation with the
owner of a massage
parlor.*

The Gauntlet (1977)

CAST

Ben Shockley, Clint Eastwood; *Gus Mally*, Sondra Locke; *Josephson*, Pat Hingle; *Blakelock*, William Prince; *constable*, Bill McKinney; *Feyderspiel*, Michael Cavanaugh.

CREDITS

Produced by Robert Daley. *Directed by* Clint Eastwood. *Screenplay by* Michael Butler and Dennis Shryack. *Director of Photography*, Rexford Metz. *Editors*, Ferris Webster and Joel Cox. *Music*, Jerry Fielding. A Malpaso Production. Color by DeLuxe and Panavision. *Running time: 111 minutes.* Released by Warner Bros.

Eastwood's 1977 release for Warner Bros.' Christmas season was *The Gauntlet*, a contemporary police story in which he co-starred for the second time with Sondra Locke. Once again, Eastwood directed and starred in an action adventure, this one with a five-million-dollar budget, the most expensive film Malpaso had produced up to that time.

Despite its few good scenes, *The Gauntlet* is a poor film. The problem lies not in Eastwood's fine direction or in the performances, but mostly in the story (written by Michael Butler and Dennis Shryack). The script is laughable in its unbelievability, and there are holes in it big enough for Eastwood to drive a Greyhound bus (which he hijacks in the film) through. Audiences were expected to believe that the Eastwood charac-

Eastwood survives a beating in a boxcar.

Eastwood holds a group of motorcycle thugs at bay.

200

ter would voluntarily send his enemies his exact route into town so the entire police force could wait to annihilate him. The film takes on almost a comic atmosphere each time it attempts to become more serious. Virtually every time a new character is introduced, the audience knows the person is not to be trusted. Also, for a detective, Eastwood is mighty slow to realize that all the assassination attempts against him are more than coincidental.

With the film as a whole a shambles, it is not easy to find good elements of it to segregate for discussion, but they are there. For one, Eastwood's character is one of his most fascinating and promising—a down-and-out nobody who can be just as easily beaten as the man on the street. It's one of Eastwood's best performances, and he gives a range of acting not always possible for him to convey in other films. The visuals in *The Gauntlet* are magnificent. An aerial view of a chase between Eastwood on a motorcycle and a menacing helicopter is magnificently photographed and very exciting.

The U.S. grosses of *The Gauntlet* did not quite reach those of *The Enforcer,* but the film still performed remarkably well, and Eastwood could chalk up another box-office success.

SYNOPSIS

Phoenix police detective Ben Shockley (Clint Eastwood), an admitted alcoholic, reports to new police commissioner Blakelock (William Prince), who gives him the routine assignment of extraditing a prisoner from Las Vegas to testify at a trial. His prisoner is Mally (Sondra Locke), a tough young hooker who is to be the star witness in the probe of a political sex scandal involving several high-ranking public officials.

Eastwood and Sondra Locke prepare to film their motorcycle chase.

201

As soon as he takes her into custody, Mally warns Shockley that his life is in danger. She states that her testimony will incriminate many police officials who will attempt to prevent her from testifying by having her and Shockley assassinated. Shockley does not believe the story, even after a car mysteriously chases them in a gun battle. Several other attempts are made on their lives, the most spectacular of which is the wholesale destruction, by an army of police, of a house in which they hide. Shockley is now convinced that Mally is correct in her fears. He also comes to believe that Blakelock is behind the attempts on their lives. This proves to be the case, as he realizes after he learns that Blakelock will eventually be incriminated by Mally's court appearance.

Enraged, Shockley vows revenge through a daring plan. He hijacks a bus and sends Blakelock the exact route he is taking into town. The commissioner uses the information to order a police gauntlet to await the bus.

By this time, Shockley and Mally have fallen in love. Both are losers, and they feel they would rather die in the gauntlet in an attempt to expose Blakelock than live on the run for the rest of their lives.

Shockley runs the bus through the gauntlet of gun-firing police officers. The bus is torn to shreds, but Shockley manages to crash it on the steps of the building housing Blakelock's office.

As the pair emerge from the bus, they are surrounded by police officers, including Blakelock himself, now almost insane with disbelief that they survived the gauntlet. He orders the police to kill them, but his men refuse, apparently because of the hysterical actions of their boss and also because of Shockley's and Mally's bravery. In frustration, Blakelock wounds Shockley and kills his own aide before Mally manages to fire several shots into him, mortally wounding him. Mally and Shockley are then left to themselves to find new meaning in their lonely lives.

REVIEWS

Clint Eastwood . . . plays a character role. *The Gauntlet* has nothing to do with reality and everything to do with Clint Eastwood fiction, which is always about a force (Mr. Eastwood) that sets things straight in a crooked world. A movie without a single thought in its head, but the action scenes are so ferociously staged that it's impossible not to pay attention most of the time. Mr. Eastwood is talent in his style— unhurried and self-assured.

Vincent Canby, New York Times

The Gauntlet is the pits . . . a mindless compendium of stale plot and stereotyped characters varnished with foul language and garnished with violence.

Judith Crist, New York Post

Offbeat Eastwood film, but still violent enough for good respónse in the action market. At the very least, Eastwood tries something different and if the price of that is a run of formula programmers, let it be.

"Murf.," Variety

*Eastwood holds a
villainous henchman
hostage in the violent
climax.*

*On the set, Eastwood
practices up on some
shooting.*

Every Which Way but Loose (1978)

CAST

Philo Beddoe, Clint Eastwood; *Lynn Halsey-Taylor*, Sondra Locke; *Orville*, Geoffrey Lewis; *Echo*, Beverly D'Angelo; *Ma*, Ruth Gordon; *Tank Murdock*, Walter Barnes; *Clerk at DMV*, George Chandler; *Woody*, Roy Jensen; *Herb*, James McEachin; *Dallas*, Bill McKinney.

CREDITS

Producer, Robert Daley. *Director*, James Fargo. *Written by* Jeremy Joe Kronsberg. *Photography*, Rexford Metz. *Art director*, Elayne Ceder. *Editor*, Ferris Webster. *Music conducted by* Steve Dorff. *Sound-effects editor*, Joe Von Stroheim. In DeLuxe Color. A Malpaso Production. Released by Warner Bros. *Running time: 114 minutes.*

Songs:

"Every Which Way but Loose," written by S. Dorff, M. Brown; sung by Eddie Rabbitt

"I'll Wake You Up When I Get Home," written by S. Dorff, M. Brown; sung by Charlie Rich

"Behind Closed Doors," written by K. O'Dell; sung by Charlie Rich

"Coca-Cola Cowboy," written by S. Pinkard, I. Dain, S. Dorff, S. Atchley; sung by Mel Tillis

"Send Me Down to Tucson," written by C. Crofford, T. Garrett; sung by Mel Tillis

"Ain't Love Good Tonight!" written by G. Skerov, R. Cate, & G. Howe; sung by Wayne Parker

"Don't Say You Don't Love Me No More," written by P. Everly, J. Paige; sung by Sondra Locke, Phil Everly

"Honkytonk Fever" and "Monkey See, Monkey Do," written by C. Crofford, T. Garrett; sung by Cliff Crofford

"I Can't Say No to a Truck-Drivin' Man," written by C. Crofford; sung by Carol Chase

"I Seek the Night," sung by Sondra Locke

"Red Eye Special," written by S. Collins, S. Pinkard, T. Garrett; sung by Larry Collins

If Eastwood had allowed critical pans to worry him, then after the release of this film, he would undoubtedly have retired. Few major films have been attacked as venomously as *Every Which Way but Loose*. Critics shot barbs at what they considered one of the most ridiculous films of 1978.

204

Eastwood has said in the past, "With few exceptions, film critics don't know too much about movies. They're afraid to have a sense of humor." This attitude must have kept him sane during the early release period of the film. Almost all his confidants had advised him that the film wouldn't work and that he should drop plans to do it. Yet Eastwood saw something in the paper-thin storyline that he felt would appeal to people of all ages. With Warner Bros. financing it, *Loose* went into production in 1978.

This, too, was a large-budget film compared to most of Malpaso's products. Five million dollars was allocated to the budget, and there weren't any special effects, as there had been in *The Gauntlet*. There were some problems in the filming, most of which revolved around Eastwood's working with Clyde, the eleven-year-old orangutan who highlights the film. Clyde's trainers had warned Eastwood that they could control only so many of the lovable ape's movements through off-camera cues. Thirty percent of the time, the ape acted on his own. This caused a nearly deadly problem for Eastwood, when the ape grabbed him while he was driving a truck. Unable to break loose from Clyde, who was frightened because he could not see his trainers, Eastwood nearly lost control of the truck. The day was saved when the voices of Clyde's trainers calmed him over a CB radio.

Clyde makes a monkey of Eastwood.

For the boxing sequences, Eastwood received professional training from old friend Al Silvani, and the results worked quite well.

For the first time in a long while, Eastwood was nervous about a film's reception, because he had never appeared in an outright comedy before. There was also worry at Malpaso that the film would suffer from lack of publicity, since Warner Bros. was spending most of its money promoting *Superman,* the thirty-million-dollar spectacular that had been booked into most of the major theaters.

Malpaso and Warners agreed upon a staggered release pattern that allowed smaller theaters in more remote areas to get *Every Which Way But Loose* first. The strategy worked. The film opened in small towns, and word of mouth brought it phenomenal success. The movie never did find much of an audience in the larger cities, where audiences tend to be more selective, but for once that market was incidental. Eastwood claimed that he was appealing to the "bare-knuckled subculture," and that was the audience that stood in line to see his film. Not only was *Loose* Eastwood's most successful film to the time (it made back its production costs in three weeks), but it is also among the all-time top grossing films for Warners.

The film is juvenile; yet it never intends to be anything else. Eastwood, however, comes across well here, making his character likable enough to generate more interest than the script would seem to allow.

The film somehow works very well, with the ape stealing the show. Eastwood may have played second fiddle to an orangutan, but his share of the profits (estimated at an eventual fifteen million dollars) guarantees him more money than Marlon Brando made from *Superman,* thus making Eastwood the new title holder as the highest-paid actor in the world.

On the set with Beverly D'Angelo, Geoffrey Lewis, and Clyde.

Eastwood and his less-than-glamorous co-star Clyde.

Eastwood battles it out with a local bully.

SYNOPSIS

Philo Beddoe (Clint Eastwood) is a hard-fighting trucker who has an unusual sideline for making money: challenging the toughest men in each town to bare-knuckled fist fights. He is joined on his travels by his most faithful companions, Orville (Geoffrey Lewis), a dim-witted but good-hearted wrecker, and Clyde, a full-grown orangutan that Philo had previously won as a reward for winning a fight.

One night while cruising the local bar scene, the men encounter Lynn Halsey-Taylor (Sondra Locke), an attractive country-western singer. Philo immediately falls for the girl. Lynn leads Philo to believe that she is prepared to establish a meaningful relationship, but her fickle nature causes her to move away without notice. Philo is at first upset, but he is resolved to follow her, and Orville and Clyde join him.

Along the way, the two men encounter many adventures. Philo repeatedly wins local fist fights, but one such brawl leads to his making mortal enemies of two lawmen, who pick up his trail and attempt to do away with him. Philo foils the plot, but his problems are far from over. In the course of his travels he also evokes the anger of an aging Hell's Angels–type motorcycle group, which is also moving in on him for the kill. Philo encounters them several times and beats them in some humiliating fights, each time narrowly escaping serious harm.

As the two men's travels continue, they are joined by a former fruit seller named Echo (Beverly D'Angelo), an attractive young woman who aids them in their schemes and later proves to be a crack shot. Philo also accidentaly meets up with Lynn on an isolated road. She makes excuses for her past behavior, and the relationship takes up where it had left off.

It soon becomes clear, however, that Lynn is back to her old behavior. Philo gives her an ultimatum, and she admits that her feelings for Philo were always minimal and that she prefers the company of her more sensitive boyfriend. Philo is hurt and angered, but this time is steadfast in going home without her. As he leaves town, he gets badgered into a fist fight with the local champion, an aging, beer-drinking braggart.

He realizes that although this is just another fight to him, his opponent's entire reputation as a local hero is at stake. Philo has a surge of sympathy for the man, and he throws the fight, leaving the town hero with his reputation intact. He then turns for home, passing the battered remains of the motorcycle gang and the frustrated lawmen, who are returning home in disgrace.

REVIEWS

This film is way off the mark. If people line up for this one, and they probably will, they'll line up for any Clint Eastwood picture.

"Hege.," *Variety*

This is a redneck comedy with no stop pulled. If I could persuade my friends to see it, they would probably detest me. I loved it. Among the many virtues of *Every Which Way but Loose* is a bunch of superb acting jobs. . . . It's nice that in the context of making a career-saving movie Clint Eastwood has made such a happy, funny movie. Take a chance on it.

Stuart Byron, *Village Voice*

A Clint Eastwood comedy that could not possibly have been created by human hands. The proof is that the only decent part is played by an orangutan. One can forgive the orangutan's participation—he couldn't read the script—but what is Eastwood's excuse? That a star with his power in Hollywood would choose to litter the screen with this plotless junkheap . . . can be taken as an expression of contempt for his huge audience or an act of masochism.

David Ansen, *Newsweek*

The ape is amusing, and so is Ruth Gordon, but the picture itself is an unstructured shambles.

Gene Shalit, *Ladies' Home Journal*

The latest Clint Eastwood disgrace . . . an athropomorphic romance between Big Clint and an orangutan. . . . Anyone who sees it has suffered enough brain damage already.

Rex Reed, *New York Daily News*

Eastwood and Clyde sip a brew together.

Eastwood argues a point with Ma (Ruth Gordon).

Escape from Alcatraz (1979)

CAST

Frank Morris, Clint Eastwood; *Warden,* Patrick McGoohan; *Doc,* Roberts Blossom; *Clarence Anglin,* Jack Thibeau; *John Anglin,* Fred Ward; *English,* Paul Benjamin; *Charley Butts,* Larry Hankin; *Wolf,* Bruce M. Fischer; *Litmus,* Frank Ronzio; *Doctor,* Donald Siegel.

CREDITS

Produced and directed by Donald Siegel. *Screenplay by* Richard Tuggle. *Director of photography,* Bruce Surtees. *Editor,* Ferris Webster. *Music editor,* June Edgerton. Color by DeLuxe and Panavision. *Running time: 120 minutes.* Released by Paramount.

For *Escape from Alcatraz,* Eastwood reunited with Don Siegel for the first time since the two had filmed *Dirty Harry* in 1971. This film proved to be one of Clint's toughest assignments. Enormous legal problems were involved in getting permission to use the island of Alcatraz for filming (the former prison now attracts eight hundred thousand tourists a year). When permission was secured, the filmmakers were confronted with a large amount of work to get the decaying buildings to appear as they had in 1963. More than fifteen miles of cable were laid to provide electricity. The cold was numbing. The production designer noted, "We had to bring absolutely everything over from the mainland, handling every bucket of paint, every piece of plywood—every piece of material that we needed—seven times before it reached the cell-block area where we could use it." Many of the improvements made on the island were left intact as permanent displays—a tribute to the authenticity of the film.

A great deal of work went into *Alcatraz,* and Siegel made sure it was all visible on screen. The film was Eastwood's biggest critical success ever, possibly because it was a quality film that for once did not deal with controversial subject matter. Violence was kept to a minimum, although some critics were angered by a scene in which a prisoner is shown chopping off his fingers. Mostly, however, Siegel kept the emphasis of the story on the intricate escape plans, which are re-created in perfect detail (the screenplay is based on the true story of the only known escape from the prison).

Alcatraz is a refreshing vehicle for Clint Eastwood, and it comes as a reminder of the fine work he is capable of doing if given the right script and director. This movie was first rate in all aspects. Even the critics praised Eastwood's understated, totally believable performance, his best since *The Beguiled.* Eastwood's acting is more than matched by a brilliant performance by Patrick McGoohan, as the Captain Queeg–like warden

Eastwood is escorted to his cell upon arrival at Alcatraz.

Eastwood is frisked by guards in a routine check.

Eastwood rehearses for the courtyard fight.

Eastwood and director Don Siegel, who makes a cameo appearance as a prison doctor.

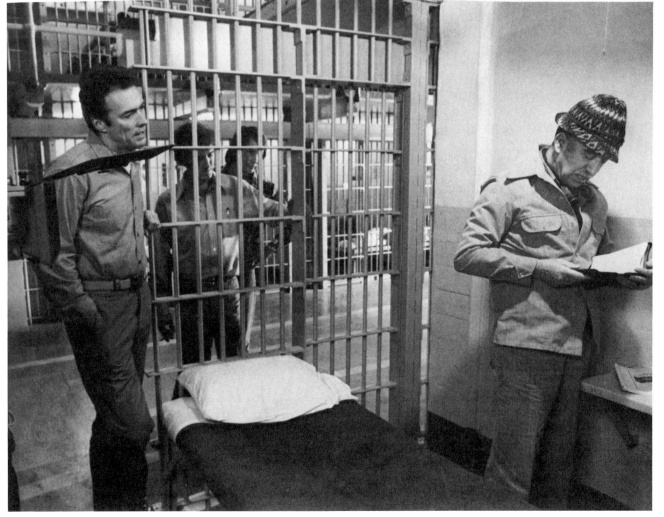

whose paranoid fears are reflected in his brutal treatment of the prisoners.

SYNOPSIS

In 1960, Frank Morris (Clint Eastwood) enters the maximum-security prison at Alcatraz. Having already escaped from several prisons, Morris is welcomed upon arrival with a warning from the warden (Patrick McGoohan): No one has ever escaped from Alcatraz.

Morris meets fellow inmates Litmus (Frank Ronzio), an old man who is inseparable from his pet mouse; English (Paul Benjamin), a black prisoner convicted in Alabama of murdering a pair of white rednecks; and Doc (Roberts Blossom), a peaceful older inmate who, after twenty years in Alcatraz, has only his painting to keep him going.

Morris also crosses paths with Wolf (Bruce M. Fischer), a hostile killer who attacks him with a shiv in the prison yard. When the guards break up the fight, both Morris and Wolf are sent to D block, the darkest, most solitary cell in the prison. Wolf promises revenge when he gets out.

Upon returning to the normal routine of the Rock, Morris meets Charley Butts (Larry Hankin), an inmate in the next cell. The prisoners are both stunned when Doc chops off his fingers after the warden takes away his painting privileges. When John (Fred Ward) and Clarence Anglin (Jack Thibeau), a pair of brothers Morris knew in an earlier prison, are transferred to Alcatraz, the group, along with Butts, begins to plan an escape.

Using makeshift tools, they manage to get through the ventilation grills that lead from their cells to a shaft running the length of the cell block, and from there to the roof. They make dummy heads for their bunks, complete with painted faces and hair from the prison barbershop.

As the day of the escape approaches, the warden prepares to separate Morris and Butts by moving one of them to another block.

At the final moment, Butts nervously remains behind while the others manage to carry out the escape. A massive search is conducted for Frank Morris and the Anglin brothers. Law-enforcement agencies are certain that their bodies will turn up. They never do.

Alcatraz was shut down less than a year after the incident on which this film was based.

REVIEWS

This is a first-rate action movie. Terrifically exciting. There is more evident knowledge of moviemaking in any one frame than there are in most other American films around at the moment. Mr. Eastwood fulfills the demands of the role and the film as probably no other actor could.

Vincent Canby, *New York Times*

Eastwood ponders his fate while in his cell.

Eastwood fights it out with bully Bruce M. Fisher in the prison courtyard.

Eastwood receives direction from Don Siegel.

Escape from Alcatraz is splendid!

Charles Michener, *Newsweek*

Escape from Alcatraz is a thoughtful, sobering, gratifying suspenseful "prison break" picture that bobs pretty close to the top of its genre.

Rex Reed, *New York Daily News*

Ingenious, precise and exciting. Audiences can rediscover the simple, classic pleasures of moviegoing. . . . Alcatraz's cool, cinematic grace meshes ideally with the strengths of its star. At a time when Hollywood entertainments are more overblown than ever, Eastwood proves that less can really be more.

Frank Rich, *Time*

Neat and suspenseful. Eastwood . . . shines with stony cynicism and indomitable self-confidence.

Ernest Leogrande, *New York Daily News*

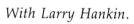

On location for Escape from Alcatraz.

The beginning of Eastwood's ingenious escape plan.

With Larry Hankin.

Upon arrival at Alcatraz, Eastwood is harassed by shouts from other inmates.

Eastwood behind bars.

Bronco Billy (1980)

CAST

Bronco Billy, Clint Eastwood; *Antoinette Lily*, Sondra Locke; *John Arlington*, Geoffrey Lewis; *Doc Lynch*, Scatman Crothers; *Lefty LeBow*, Bill McKinney; *Leonard James*, Sam Bottoms; *Chief Big Eagle*, Dan Vadis; *Lorraine Running Water*, Sierra Pecheur; *Sheriff Dix*, Walter Barnes; *Dr. Canterbury*, Woodrow Parfrey; *Irene Lily*, Beverlee McKinsey; *Lieutenant Wiecker*, Douglas McGrath; *station mechanic*, Hank Worden; *Edgar Lipton*, William Prince; *mother superior*, Pam Abbas; *Maid Eloise*, Edye Byrde; *reporter at bank*, Douglas Copsey; *sanatorium attendant*, John Wesley Elliott, Jr.; *cowboys at bar*, Chuck Hicks, Bobby Hoy; *boy at bank*, Jefferson Jewell; *bank teller*, Dawneen Lee; *chauffeur*, Don Mummert; *sanatorium policeman*, Lloyd Nelson; *cowboy in bar*, George Orrison; *King*, Michael Reinbold, *Mitzi Fritts*, Tessa Richarde; *Doris Duke*, Tanya Russell; *Sister Maria*, Valerie Shanks; *license clerk*, Sharon Sherlock; *bank manager*, James Simmerhan; *reporter at bank*, Robert Dale Simmons; *reporter at sanatorium*, Jenny Sternling; *bank robbers*, Chuck Waters, Jerry Wills.

Clint Eastwood as Bronco Billy, owner and star of a traveling wild-West show.

CREDITS

Executive producer, Robert Daley. *Produced by* Dennis Hackin and Neal Dobrofsky. *Director*, Clint Eastwood. *Written by* Dennis Hackin. *Photography*, David Worth. *Production design*, Gene Lourie. *Editor*, Ferris Webster. *Music conducted by* Steve Dorff. In DeLuxe Color. Released by Warner Bros. *Running time: 116 minutes.*

Clint Eastwood and Sondra Locke.

Songs:

"Misery and Gin," written by J. Durrill, S. Garrett; sung by Merle Haggard

"Cowboys and Clowns," written by S. Dorff, G. Harju, L. Herbstritt, S. Garrett; sung by Ronnie Milsap

"Bronco Billy," written by M. Brown, S. Dorff, S. Garrett; sung by Ronnie Milsap

"Barroom Buddies," written by M. Brown, C. Crofford, S. Dorff, S. Garrett; sung by Merle Haggard, Clint Eastwood

"Bayou Lullaby," written by C. Crofford, S. Garrett; sung by Penny DeHaven

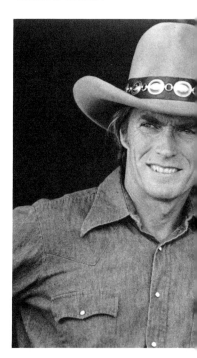

With *Bronco Billy*, Eastwood found himself behind the camera as director for the seventh time. Inspired by the success of his first attempt at a comedy (*Every Which Way but Loose*), Eastwood felt the script for *Bronco Billy* to be a sure-fire winner at the box office.

Eastwood quickly rehired many of the actors and technicians who

Clint Eastwood performs a riding and shooting stunt in his traveling wild-West show.

Scatman Crothers and Clint Eastwood take a break on the set of Bronco Billy.

usually compose what is growing to be the Clint Eastwood Stock Company. It marked his fourth screen appearance with Sondra Locke, and everyone agreed that their chemistry together in this film worked far better than in their previous efforts.

Eastwood shot *Bronco Billy* on location in Idaho, Oregon, and New York, while keeping the film on a modest budget. The film seems to have a genuine love for the Midwest and its people, while lightheartedly criticizing the Park Avenue establishment for its overemphasis on money. This point is further reinforced by the character of Antoinette, who is despicable when adhering to her big-city mores, yet lovable when she renounces then for the joys of working life.

Nevertheless, *Bronco Billy* is undoubtedly the gentlest film in which Eastwood has appeared. Its rollicking, good-natured theme makes it hard not to like; yet it has many flaws that seriously damage it. The script is often appealing; however, it is far too talky and predictable. We know immediately upon being introduced to the characters exactly what their problems are going to be and how they will be resolved. Yet Eastwood and Locke give some of their best performances, and some of their scenes together, such as when Eastwood coerces Locke into acting as a target for his vanishing knife-throwing skills, work extremely well, and Eastwood's direction captures a real feel for the life of the drifter.

SYNOPSIS

Bronco Billy (Clint Eastwood) is the owner and star attraction of a contemporary wild-West show that travels the Midwest. Time has not been kind to Billy and his performers, and as interest wanes in such sideshow attractions, so does Billy's profit margin. His disgruntled employees— Two Gun Lefty LeBow (Bill McKinney), Lasso James (Sam Bottoms), Chief Big Eagle (Dan Vadis), Doc Lynch (Scatman Crothers), and Lorraine Running Water (Sierra Pecheur)—have all been without pay for months. Still, the ragtag group is indebted enough to Billy's kind nature to continue the show and hope for better times.

Billy encounters Antoinette Lily (Sondra Locke), a spoiled society girl who has just married a man she despises in order to validate a claim to a fortune left to her by her father. Billy learns that when Antoinette's newly acquired husband, John Arlington (Geoffrey Lewis), discovered the reason for his wife's marriage vow, he left her stranded at an isolated motel. Billy agrees to help the desperate woman but only for a price; she must agree to act as a target for Billy's sharpshooting and knife-throwing act. Although infuriated by the virtual blackmail, Antoinette reluctantly agrees.

Meanwhile, John Arlington has been arrested and charged with the murder of his missing wife. A conniving lawyer, who schemes to get the inheritance money himself, convinces John to plead guilty to murder by reason of insanity, and John finds himself sent to a mental hospital.

Clint Eastwood performs his knife-throwing act on Sondra Locke.

Antoinette's and John's paths cross once more, after a disastrous fire that destroys Billy's tent. In the chaotic events that follow, John is cleared of murder and Antoinette returns to New York and her rich aunt's penthouse. In a short time, however, Antoinette discovers that it is not money she loves, but the quiet simplicity and honesty of Bronco Billy. She leaves the world of riches to return to Billy and his poverty-stricken wild-West show.

REVIEWS

Bronco Billy pokes along like an old plow horse with Eastwood doing comical slow burns and providing the movie with its best moments.
Kathleen Carroll, *New York Daily News*

Eastwood retains his customary calm when faced with almost anything. He's always in control. As director, Eastwood avoids arty excesses of any kind. His ability to avoid pretensions whether of mind, camera or sound stands him in good stead. He might be said to be champion of the commonplace, reducing all that plot to a movie-biz fable that uses two hours of your time with minimal demands upon your attention and sympathy.
Archer Winsten, *New York Post*

Oh, how good it is to have a comedy around for summer as genuinely funny as *Bronco Billy*, which is sophisticated enough and common enough to appeal to a broad audience, perhaps introducing Clint Eastwood to new fans as a comic actor and director, even if he doesn't need them. . . . This is the third picture together for Eastwood and Locke and the chemistry is still working.
Variety

Clint Eastwood taking a shot at some bank robbers.

Any Which Way You Can (1980)

CAST

Philo Beddoe, Clint Eastwood; *Lynn Halsey-Taylor*, Sondra Locke; *Orville*, Geoffrey Lewis; *Jack Wilson*, William Smith; *James Beekman*, Harry Guardino; *Ma*, Ruth Gordon; *Patrick Scarfe*, Michael Cavanaugh; *Fat Zack*, Barry Corbin; *Moody*, Roy Jenson; *Dallas*, Bill McKinney; *Frank*, Dan Vadis; *Glen Campbell*, Glen Campbell.

CREDITS

Executive producer, Robert Daley. *Produced by* Fritz Manes. *Directed by* Buddy Van Horn. *Written by* Stanford Sherman. *Cinematography by* David Worth. *Music*, Snuff Garrett. *Editors*, Ferris Webster, Ron Spang. Released by Warner Bros. *Running time*: 117 minutes.

Eastwood followed up the mild box-office success of *Bronco Billy* with *Any Which Way You Can*, a sequel to his top-grossing comedy *Every Which Way but Loose*. Warner Bros. wisely used the same marketing techniques for this film as it had for the predecessor. It opened at Christmastime with heavy advertising aimed at appealing to rural audiences. The film was also heavily promoted on country radio through Glen Campbell's hit title song.

A rare moment of tranquillity for Eastwood, with Sondra Locke.

Critics did not heap praise on this film to the extent many of them had *Bronco Billy*, perhaps because here, Eastwood was returning to safe ground rather than trying something new. However, reviews were far less scornful than had been the ones generated for *Loose*. Critics had apparently accepted that for the time being, Eastwood was returning to his niche as king of the action genre.

The film did get a few glowing reviews, with most critics praising Stanford Sherman's screenplay for allowing the characters to become more gentle and human, rather than just obnoxious fighting machines. Regardless of critical reaction, audiences responded to the film with the same enthusiasm they had showed for *Loose*. Within a week of its release, Warners was taking out ads in the trade papers boasting of the record-breaking grosses the film had achieved.

The film was relatively undistinguished for Eastwood and the rest of the cast, all of whom went through their roles with a minimum of effort and, apparently, a maximum of fun; however, it was notable in that it marked the feature-film directorial debut of Buddy Van Horn, previously a second-unit director on several Eastwood films over a period of fifteen years. Van Horn brought the film in relatively overnight. Production started in the summer of 1980, and the film was being shown in theaters that Christmas.

Although no one proclaimed the film a masterpiece, Van Horn can claim that his first effort became one of the highest-grossing films in recent years.

Preparing for another street fight.

SYNOPSIS

Tired of using his bare knuckles to make a living, street fighter Philo Beddoe (Clint Eastwood) swears off using his boxing abilities to make money. However, the mob offers him a deal that would make it extremely lucrative for him to participate in one more fight: a knock-down fight to the finish with an old nemisis named Jack Wilson (William Smith).

With so much money riding on the fight, the gangsters seek to ensure Philo's participation by kidnapping his girlfriend, country-western singer Lynn Halsey-Taylor (Sandra Locke). The reluctant Philo finds that he has no choice but to engage in the fight.

Philo's troubles do not end there. He is consistently plagued by the misadventures of "Ma" (Ruth Gordon), Philo's tempermental old landlady. In addition to these worries, he is forced to tangle with the Black Widows, a tough but inept motorcycle gang that has been humiliated by Philo in several previous fights. During one incident, Philo also discovers that his best friend and companion, Orville (Geoffrey Lewis), has been shot by mobsters. (Orville manages to recover, however, and falls in love with a nurse.) To cap off the problems, Philo must also keep watch over his pet orangutan, Clyde, who has a way of attracting trouble (and lady orangutans).

When Philo meets Wilson, the two men come to a mutual admiration for one another and band together to rescue Lynn. They succeed and

In action.

decide to cancel the fight. However, each man realizes that only one of them can actually be champion of the street fighters, and they therefore agree to go through with the fight once and for all. The brawl is a robust affair that eventually takes the men through the entire length of the town, ending when only one of them can truly claim the title of the greatest brawler of all time. Not surprisingly, that man is Philo Beddoe.

REVIEWS

What about a motel scene between two orangutans? If that breaks you up, head right over to *Any Which Way You Can.* . . . This sequel has more loony moments than its predecessor because there isn't as much time devoted to the tight-jawed romance between Clint Eastwood and Sondra Locke as there was in the first. When the movie gets into the bare-knuckle fighting . . . it loses its looniness and turns into a humorless exaltation of the world of macho men.

The biker gang . . . is given more rope in this movie to be ridiculous and their antics help bolster the slapstick quotient.

Ernest Leogrande, *New York Daily News*

A benign continuation of *Every Which Way but Loose* . . . Each subsequent film in Eastwood's two previous series, the Dollars westerns and the Dirty Harry actioners, grossed more than the one before, and only time will tell if the pattern repeats itself with these monkeyshines. . . . [The film] substantially moderates the reckless violent tone of *Loose*, bringing it closer to the genial nice-guy mood of star's last pic *Bronco Billy.* . . . First half is pretty funny as these things go, but film runs out of steam. . . . Clearly, this sort of thing exists on a plane either beyond or beneath criticism, and as it seems to be the main reason for the enduring popularity of *Loose*, there's no reason to believe that it won't prove equally satisfying for audiences who come back for more.

"Cart.," *Variety*

On the Any Which Way You Can *set with director Buddy Van Horn.*

Eastwood, who can be a compelling, charming screen actor, seems content here to watch the other performers pamper their eccentricities while he stands off to one side, as glum and immobile as a teamster's ashtray. . . . It says something about the American body aesthetic that Eastwood's previous picture, the innocently droll *Bronco Billy*, failed at the box office while Philo and Clyde, the Ape Man and the Ape, have moviegoers queuing and cheering.

Time

Eastwood on the set with his co-star Clyde.

Firefox (1982)

Disguised as a MIG pilot.

CAST

Mitchell Gant: Clint Eastwood; *Aubrey:* Freddie Jones; *Buckholz:* David Huffman; *Upenskoy:* Warren Clarke; *Semelovsky:* Ronald Lacey; *Kontarsky:* Kenneth Colley.

CREDITS

Executive Producer: Fritz Manes; *Produced and Directed by* Clint Eastwood. *Screenplay by* Alex Lasker and Wendell Wellman, *based on the novel by* Craig Thomas. *Camera,* Bruce Surtees. *Art Direction,* John Graysmark and Elayne Ceder. *Editor,* Ferris Webster and Ron Spang. *Music,* Maurice Jarre. *Special Effects,* Chuck Gaspar. Released by Warner Bros. *Running time: 136 minutes.*

Clint Eastwood in a big-budget, high-tech adventure with sci-fi overtones? As inconceivable as this may seem, Eastwood's film version of Craig Thomas's best-selling novel *Firefox* brought this unlikely event to reality. At an estimated cost of $21,000,000, "Firefox" represents one of Eastwood's few large-budget films in recent years, and, curiously, the only project which is not officially credited as a Malpaso production.

Shot on location in Austria, England, Greenland and the U.S., the film is truly an international affair, boasting a large cast of European actors in supporting roles. Eastwood recruited legendary special effects wizard John Dykstra, who provided the stunning visuals for *Star Wars*, *Star Trek* and *Moonraker* to design the actual Firefox plane, a sleek and deadly machine capable of extraordinary offensive and defensive mechanisms. The result is a film that looks first class, but is not without flaws.

At first glance, *Firefox* looks like an uneasy combination of *Star Wars* and James Bond, as the screenplay can't seem to decide whether it wants to be a science-fiction film or an espionage thriller. The result is somewhere in the middle. The most serious flaw is the pacing, and part of this must be blamed on Eastwood, who also directed. Every time the climactic chase sequence begins to become suspenful, Eastwood cuts back to endless scenes of Soviet officials arguing over minor plot details, as well as explaining virtually every technical aspect of the plane itself. This weighs down the plot substantially, and Bruce Surtees' cinematography does not aid things. Some sequences are so dimly lit that it is almost impossible to see what is taking place. Eastwood's performance is also uninspired here. He goes through the motions, and looks convincing, but he doesn't appear to be enjoying himself. And the scenes in which he speaks Russian rank as the most inappropriate linguistics to appear onscreen since John Wayne portrayed Genghis Khan in *The Conqueror.*

Yet, *Firefox* has enough good points to recommend it for viewing a second time. On subsequent screenings, one is less overpowered by the

Eastwood flies the Firefox towards the West.

The furious air battle between the MIG and the Firefox.

special effects and more intrigued by the other positive elements, such as the many superb performances of the supporting cast, many of whom were hired directly by Eastwood. The sequences in which the Soviet dissidents discuss their passion to aid Eastwood even in the face of certain death are truly inspiring, as is Eastwood's actual theft of the Firefox—a thrilling scene that highlights the film.

Firefox took nine weeks to shoot, over a period of one year, and although the effort is not entirely successful, it represented yet another daring departure for Eastwood, and a refreshing one at that. It is also interesting to note that ABC-TV which has generally butchered Eastwood's films for broadcast standards, actually added sixteen minutes of previously unseen footage for the TV premiere of *Firefox*. One wishes it had set a precedent, as there is undoubtedly a great deal of interest in what Eastwood must leave on the cutting room floor.

SYNOPSIS

When Western intelligence forces learn that the Soviets have developed the most sophisticated warplane of all time, they recruit retired ace pilot Mitchell Gant to steal it and return it to the NATO alliance. Code named the Firefox, the plane is capable not only of achieving unprecedented speeds, but also of allowing the pilot to fire its armaments through thought patterns.

Gant is reluctant to attempt the mission, as he often suffers from a mental disorder which sometimes leaves him disoriented and incapable of functioning. Upon arriving in Russia, he poses as an international drug smuggler, and fakes his own death to gain access to his contacts. He is met by several dissidents who sacrifice their lives so that Gant might steal the Firefox. He does so, but is pursued by a Soviet pilot in an identical plane. Gant must overcome his own psychological problems as well as the other Firefox in order to succeed. A fierce dogfight eventually ensues, with Gant narrowly avoiding death by using his thought patterns to activate armaments which destroy his adversary and allow him to fly the Firefox back to the NATO alliance.

Incognito as a Soviet soldier.

REVIEWS

(A) sagging, overlong disappointment, talky and slow to ignite. It is the first time that Eastwood the director has served Eastwood the actor-icon so badly, and it is unnerving.

Sheila Benson, *Los Angeles Times*

Firefox is a pulse-quickener from every point of view, subject, action, flight, patriotism and danger unlimited.

Archer Winsten, *New York Post*

Firefox is fun, little more and not appreciably less. It may offend people who believe in their heart-of-hearts that all Russians are harmless leprechauns magnified out of proportion by fearmongers like Truman and McCarthy in the 50's and Reagan and Weinberger in the 80's. But the Russians-are-leprechauns contingent cannot be considered as part of Clint Eastwood's potential audience under any circumstances.

Andrew Sarris, *The Village Voice*

Evading a search by Russian soldiers.

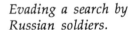

Firefox the movie, is, on balance, rather like Firefox the plane; it is at its best a clean, well-designed, fast-moving machine, at once practical, fanciful and capable of stunt flights that verge on the ecstatic.

Richard Schickel, *Time*

It's a good thing for the West that Clint Eastwood is available for the job. There's a bit of suspense as he slips past the entire Soviet security system, and a bit more as he skedaddles with the coveted craft. But most of the way, this is a very talky film, stretching a slim plot into more than two hours of familiar Hollywood maneuvers.

David Sterritt; *Christian Science Monitor.*

Red Stovall visits Whit's family. Whit was played by Kyle Eastwood, who is standing by his real-life father.

Honky Tonk Man (1982)

CAST

Red Stovall: Clint Eastwood; *Whit:* Kyle Eastwood; *Grandpa:* John McIntire; *Marlene:* Alexa Kenin; *Emmy:* Verna Bloom; *Virgil:* Matt Clark; *Arnspriger:* Barry Corbin; *Snuffy:* Jerry Hardin.

CREDITS

Executive Producer; Fritz Manes. *Producer;* Clint Eastwood. *Directed by* Clint Eastwood. *Screenplay,* Clancy Carlile, *based upon his novel, Camera,* Bruce Surtees. *Editors,* Ferris Webster, Michael Kelly *and* Joel Cox. *Music,* Steve Dorff. *Production Designer,* Edward Carfagno. Technicolor. A Malpaso Production. Released by Warner Bros. *Running time: 122 minutes.*

Singing is a talent that leaves performers the most naked. Unlike acting, there is no room to bluff a performance. A person can either carry a tune, or he or she will appear foolish trying. After Eastwood's less than auspicious singing debut in *Paint Your Wagon,* few would have thought he would ever tackle a similar role again. Yet, Clint Eastwood has never been afraid to take chances, and did not hesitate to translate the novel

Honky Tonk Man to the screen, assuming the lead role of a talented, yet dissipated country singer.

Shot on location in the Sacramento delta region of California, as well as Carson City, Nevada and Nashville, Tennessee, *Honky Tonk Man* evokes a richly textured feeling for the American southwest of the Depression era. This can best be attributed to Eastwood's insistence upon actual location photography to enhance a sense of period, as well as some wonderfully realistic sets by production designer Edward Carfagno, who had to learn to adapt to Eastwood's lightning-fast filming schedule.

It is doubtful Eastwood thought *Honky Tonk Man* would be a box-office smash, and indeed it was not. It remains his least-seen film in recent years, suffering from almost total audience rejection. This seems a pity, because *Honky Tonk Man* is in many ways a fine film, and remains one of Eastwood's most impressive directorial and acting accomplishments to date. Without a hint of violence onscreen, one might think Eastwood would appear to be like a fish out-of-water. Yet, his interpretation of the rowdy Red Stovall provides enough poignant moments to make the viewer unaware of just how little is occurring in the story.

The film was greeted with critical indifference, with some reviewers granting grudging praise that at least Eastwood tried to expand into new ground. The most savage appraisals were reserved for Eastwood's son Kyle, who in his acting debut, made many critics note that a dynasty of Eastwood thespians did not seem like an inevitability. These criticims seem unduly harsh, as the younger Eastwood gives a perfectly acceptable performance. The film is also enhanced by a series of vignettes enacted by a wonderful cast of character actors.

As for Eastwood's singing, suffice it to say that Sinatra probably did not lose any sleep. However, Eastwood delivers his songs in a low-key manner which does not strain credibility. The audience can accept him as a rising country star. It's a multi-faceted performance which deserved far more attention than it received.

Honky Tonk Man was highly praised in Europe, and among it's American defenders was no less than Norman Mailer who justly called it "the finest movie made about country plains life since *The Last Picture Show*....One of the saddest movies seen in a long time, yet, on reflection, terrific." Perhaps the film will ultimately be seen by its elusive audience through videocassette.

Two generations of Eastwoods, Clint and Kyle.

Behind the camera for Honky Tonk Man.

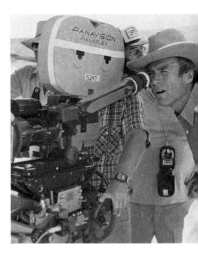

SYNOPSIS

Red Stovall (Clint Eastwood) is a modestly successful Depression-era country singer determined to make it to the Grand Ol' Opry. Among his obstacles, however, are a lack of money, a dependency on liquor, and a battle with tuberculosis, which he is rapidly losing. Accompanied by his nephew Whit (Kyle Eastwood), a 14-year-old farm boy whose mother tells him to care for and watch out for Red, the country singer begins his journey to Nashville, where the Opry has granted him an audition.

As Red Stovall, performing at a recording session.

Along the way, a strong affection develops between the young boy and his mentor, as they experience a variety of adventures.

Upon reaching Nashville, Red falls victim to an irrepressible cough during his audition, leading the Opry to reject him as a regular. However, a record company executive sees his potential and asks Red to record a series of songs. Against the advice of his doctor, Red endures the physically excruciating task of recording his favorite songs. The result is tragic, however, and he succumbs to the tuberculosis and dies the next day. As Whit prepares to move on to his family in California, a car radio plays Red's record, "Honky Tonk Man," indicating the fame which eluded him in life had found him in death.

REVIEWS

The pace is slow, very country, but it rises to touching moments. Eastwood never overdoes his acting—maybe he can't—always playing it very close to the vest. It works for the larger portion of the picture, falling somewhere between the Eastwood sincerity and changes of mood that put the picture in a special class, not all perfect by any means, but ultimately a story of occasional awkward truths.

Archer Winsten, *New York Post*

*With would-be lover
Alexa Kenin.*

Clint looks the classic country and western singer in dark suit, string tie, boots, 10 gallon hat. It would be great pleasure to report that his courage pays off. But the scenario's ultimate ambition is kitschy bathos, to make you weep in your popcorn...The mild humour of *Honky Tonk Man* devolves into the gross sentimentality of a Clint Eastwood *Camille*.

Joseph Glemis, *Newsday*

Eastwood has fashioned a marvelously unfashionable movie, as quietly insinuating as one of Red's honky tonk melodies. As both actor and director, Eastwood has never been more laconic than he is in this film. It reminds one...of *Bronco Billy,* although it disdains the farce and romance of that underappreciated movie.... If there are any people left who doubt Eastwood's accomplishment as a screen actor, they had better come around for this lesson in underplaying a long, strong scene.

Richard Schickel, *Time*

Sudden Impact (1983)

irty Harry Callahan.

CAST

Harry Callahan: Clint Eastwood; *Jennifer Spencer:* Sondra Locke; *Chief Jannings:* Pat Hingle; *Capt. Briggs:* Bradford Dillman; *Micky:* Paul Drake; *Ray Parkins:* Audrie J. Neenan; *Kruger:* Jack Thibeau; *Lt. Donnelly:* Michael Currie; *Horace:* Albert Popwell.

CREDITS

Executive Producer: Fritz Manes, *Producer and Director:* Clint Eastwood, *Screenplay,* Joseph C. Stinson. *Story by* Earl E. Smith and Charles B. Pierce, *based on characters created by* Harry Julian Fink and R. M. Fink. *Camera,* Bruce Surtees. *Editor,* Joel Cox. *Music,* Lalo Schifrin. *Production designer,* Edward Carfagno. A Malpaso Production. Released by Warner Bros. *Running Time: 117 minutes.*

Although he had stated earlier that he had exhausted all potential in the character of Dirty Harry, Eastwood decided to see if audiences disagreed with his assessment. After an absence of seven years, Eastwood picked up his legendary .44 Magnum, put on his "shades" and gamely stalked the streets of San Francisco acting as the world's only human magnet for trouble.

Sudden Impact is the quintessential Clint Eastwood film, as well it should be, since the actor directed as well as starred in it. It is violent, repugnant, completely without social value, and it presents social problems through the eyes of cartoon-like characters who find solutions through comic-book strategies. It is also a superb piece of entertainment, and in many ways, a better film than the original *Dirty Harry.* It's easy to see that for this effort Eastwood ignored all attempts to break new ground artistically, and decided to give his fans the most straightforward thriller he had made in years.

Sudden Impact proved to be appropriately titled, as it's impact on audiences was not only sudden, but tremendous in terms of box-office. Fans had been inundated with TV spots prior to the film's opening. They proved so effective that by the time *Sudden Impact* premiered across the country, audiences already knew Eastwood's now legendary phrase, "Go ahead, make my day!" Not since the days of "Get Smart's" "Sorry about that, Chief!' has a saying been repeated so often. At one point even President Reagan urged members of Congress to "make his day" when they threatened to challenge him on an issue.

That aside, *Sudden Impact* works perfectly in virtually every area. Eastwood is a consummate filmmaker who knows exactly what his audience expects, and in this fourth Dirty Harry adventure he blends the sadism with some intentionally hilarious dialogue and situations. He is supported by long-time leading lady Sondra Locke, who is very effective as a sort of Dirty Harriet—avenging both herself and her sister for a

brutal rape a decade earlier. It's also fun to watch Paul Drake and Audrie J. Neenan overact mercilessly—and appropriately—as the two most despicable villains in recent screen history.

"Go ahead, make my day."

It is ironic that this most violent episode of Eastwood's career enjoyed a surprising amount of critical success. At last reviewers seemed to get the idea that this was all harmless nonsense, and that no profound social messages were implied. Not that it mattered. *Sudden Impact* quickly became one of the great successes of Eastwood's career. There is not a false note in the film, and if it is not art it certainly is fun.

SYNOPSIS

San Francisco detective Harry Callahan (Clint Eastwood) finds himself in trouble with the police brass after his threats to an aging Mafia capo results in the man's death by heart attack. He is assigned to a small town to investigate a seemingly inconsequential murder of a local hood.

Upon investigation, however, it appears that he has arrived in the midst of a series of such murders, all perpetrated by Jennifer Spencer (Sondra Locke), an artist who has returned to town to avenge a brutal rape some years before which ruined the lives of herself and her younger sister.

Harry's attempts to find the killer are hampered by the local police

chief (Pat Hingle), who, it turns out, is hiding the fact that his now demented son was part of the group of rapists Spencer is seeking. Harry coincidentally meets and courts Spencer, only to discover later she is the killer. He cannot prevent her from shooting most of the remaining criminals, nor can he prevent the group's ringleader Micky (Paul Drake) from kidnapping her with the intent of murder.

After discovering Micky has killed the police chief, Harry himself is beaten mercilessly. He recovers in time to prevent Jennifer's death, and in a final spectacular shoot-out, destroys Micky and his gang. Feeling Jennifer's actions were justified vigilantism; he misleads the investigation and pin-points the prior killings as having been the work of Micky.

Sondra Locke as Jennifer Spencer.

REVIEWS

Directing the material himself, Clint Eastwood has attempted to retell the Dirty Harry myth in the style of a forties film noir. Much of *Sudden Impact*, including all the scenes of violence, was actually shot at night. In a stiff, sensational, pulp-filmmaking way, the mayhem is impressive: As the camera glides through the dark, sinister thugs emerge from the shadows, or Sondra Locke, blond hair curtaining her face in the style of Veronica Lake, moves into the frame, and violence flashes out, lightning in the air.

David Denby, New York Magazine

Sudden Impact has all the action anyone could want. . . . There's also heart-stopping sound accompaniment and Clint Eastwood looking leaner and tougher than ever. The man doesn't seem to age. His face is becoming pure granite—and his body sheds bullets like that same stone. This movie's a whirligig, an explosion, and absolutely senseless.

Archer Winsten, New York Post

The staging of the violent set-pieces is stylized, kinetic and visually inventive. . . . Whatever happened to the fear of boring audiences? Eastwood, occasional langueurs and all, has less to worry about in this respect than other filmmakers. When he stands poised for his civicly cleansing shoot-outs, no one in the theatre is likely to be dozing. I like Eastwood, always have. But then I even have a soft spot in my heart for law and order.

Andrew Sarris, The Village Voice

With Genevieve Bujold.

Tightrope (1984)

CAST

Wes Block: Clint Eastwood: *Beryl Thibodeaux:* Genevieve Bujold: *Det. Molinari:* Dan Hedaya: *Amanda Block:* Alison Eastwood: *Penny Block:* Jennifer Beck: *Leander Rolf:* Marco St. John.

CREDITS

Produced by: Clint Eastwood and Fritz Manes: *Directed by:* Richard Tuggle: *Screenplay:* Richard Tuggle: *Camera:* Bruce Surtees: *Editor:* Joel Cox; *Music:* Lennie Niehaus: *Set Decoration:* Ernie Bishop. *Technicolor.* A Warner Bros. Release of a Malpaso Production. *Running time: 117 minutes.*

Clint Eastwood is a man who knows his limitations. He has rejected many parts because he felt his audience would not accept him in certain roles. Over the years, he has turned down starring roles in both *Apocalypse Now* and *The Killing Fields,* leading detractors to claim he was afraid to venture too far outside of his established screen persona. Those criticisms were muted—at least temporarily—with the release of *Tightrope,* a suspense thriller which garnered Eastwood almost unanimous praise from reviewers around the world.

Seldom has a major film been shot in such a low-key atmosphere. With no advance publicity or even press announcements, *Tightrope* began shooting in New Orleans, and had virtually wrapped production before the industry became aware of its existence. A dark, brooding thriller, *Tightrope* was the brainchild of writer Richard Tuggle, who had previously done the screenplay for *Escape From Alcatraz.* He sent Eastwood the script, and asked if he could be allowed to make the film his directorial debut. In a phone conversation of less than 30 seconds, he had gotten his wish.

As Wes Block, a cop on the edg

Tightrope is an almost flawless suspense drama set against the back alleys and sordid nightlife of New Orleans. As Wes Block, the tormented cop whose own idiosyncrasies lean toward the kinky side of sexuality, Eastwood played his most multi-faceted character to date. This is no Dirty Harry—just a poor working stiff who comes to doubt his own sanity when his hunt for a psychotic killer makes him see he has far more in common with his quarry than he feels comfortable with. As events become more involved, even the audience begins to suspect that Eastwood might be a schizophrenic responsible for the murders himself.

The role represents a major departure for Eastwood. He plays a character who he is never sure of what to do next. He errs not only on the job, but also in his home life, leading his two young daughters to become the killer's next victims. It's a bold performance, and at times a brilliant one. There was genuine surprise when Eastwood failed to receive an Oscar nomination.

The film itself is not particularly original. Yet, Tuggle acquits himself admirably on all counts, turning what could have been a "run-of-the-mill" cop story into a nail-biting thriller that kept audiences on the edge of their seats. He also elicited fine supporting performances from Genevieve Bujold and Eastwood's own daughter Alison, who shows a strong and likable screen presence in her own right.

Tightrope was that long-awaited gem for Eastwood fans the world over—a film which critics responded to as well as Eastwood's legion of devotees. It also proved that the man they once said attended the Mt. Rushmore School of Acting was, indeed, a drastically under-rated talent.

SYNOPSIS

A homocidal killer of prostitutes is terrorizing New Orleans, and Detective Wes Block is assigned to head the task force devoted to locating the psychopath before he can strike again. Block, however, has his own problems. He is trying to cope with raising his two daughters from a previous marriage, as well as confront his penchant for kinky sex with submissive women.

As the body count increases, Block realizes a pattern is emerging: most of the victims are women with whom he has been sexually

236

Investigating a murder with Dan Hedaya.

involved. He attempts to stabilize his life through a relationship with Beryl (Genevive Bujold), the head of a women's rape crisis center. As the investigation continues, however, it becomes apparent that the killer is trying to frame Block for the murders, and that those closest to him might be the next victims.

Block's daughters narrowly escape death when the killer infiltrates the house. The investigation shows that the murderer is a former police officer named Rolf (Marco St. John), whom Block had arrested previously for sexual crimes. He arrives at Beryl's house in time to interrupt a furious struggle, during which Beryl manages to wound Rolf with a pair of scissors. A wild chase ensues, culminating in a hand-to-hand struggle between Block and Rolf. As the two men battle on railroad tracks, a speeding train kills Rolf, leaving shattered Block haunted by his nightmarish experiences.

REVIEWS

Eastwood is simply terrific, his lean and hungry face revealing all the right emotions... Alison Eastwood, the star's daughter, gives a remarkably convincing performance. *Tightrope*, thanks to the efforts of writer-director Richard Tuggle, is a raunchy but surprisingly intelligent movie, which at times scares the viewer as much as one of Hitchcock's tension-filled thrillers.

Kathleen Carroll, *New York Daily News*

237

Tightrope offers more intimacy, suspense and atmospheric color than most of Eastwood's other gumshoe safaris through the urban jungle. More importantly, it represents a provocative advance in the consciousness—self and social—of Eastwood's one-man genre.

Richard Schickel, *Time*

Opportunity to see the star in the relatively unfamiliar role of papa affords some very nice human moments which evoke both emotional warmth and tension....Becoming ever more daring, the killer goes so far as to set Eastwood up with a young man in a gay bar. Following every lead, Eastwood chats the blond fellow up, only to be overtly propositioned and asked how he knows he doesn't like boys if he hasn't tried them. "Maybe I have," Eastwood replies....Overall, action is well handled as Tuggle demonstrates ample story-telling talent and draws a multitude of nuances from his cast.

"Cart," *Variety*

With Jennifer Beck (left) and real-life daughter Alison.

238

City Heat (1984)

CAST

Lt. Speer: Clint Eastwood; *Mike Murphy:* Burt Reynolds; *Addy:* Jane Alexander; *Caroline:* Madeline Kahn; *Primo Pitt:* Rip Torn; *Ginny Lee:* Irene Cara; *Dehl Swift:* Richard Roundtree; *Leon Coll:* Tony LoBianco.

CREDITS

Producer: Fritz Manes. *Director:* Richard Benjamin. *Screenplay:* Sam O. Brown and Joseph Stinson. *Story by* Sam O. Brown. *Camera,* Nick McLean. *Editor,* Jacqueline Cambas. *Music:* Lennie Niehaus. *Production designer:* Edward Carfagno. *Set Decoration,* George Gaines. A Malpaso/ Deliverance Production. Released by Warner Bros. *Running time: 94 minutes.*

eynolds and Eastwood as lurphy and Speer.

From the mid-1970's thru the early 1980's, Eastwood shared his throne as king of the box-office with Burt Reynolds. But, around 1982, Reynolds star was beginning to descend. Unlike Eastwood, Reynolds did not have the foresight to see which genres audiences were tiring of. He continued to star in dated country-western comedies which featured little of his skills as an actor. Critics assailed him for taking his audience for granted, and fans began to stay away from his films in droves.

It was therefore with great expectations that the industry announced his co-starring role with Clint Eastwood in a 1930's action comedy titled *City Heat.* Surely, if this film couldn't revive Reynolds fans, the argument went, nothing could. Unfortunately, *City Heat* proved to be an ineffective vehicle for Reynold's much-anticipated comeback.

Plagued from the start with production problems, the movie kept changing titles throughout its filming, being called at various times, *Kansas City Jazz,* and *Kansas City Blues.* Then writer/director Blake Edwards either quit or was fired (depending on which version you choose to believe) due to "conceptual differences" with the studio. He was replaced as director by Richard Benjamin, but he remains credited with the story and screenplay under the oft-used pseudonym of Sam O. Brown. Marsha Mason was signed to a lead role, but bowed out and was replaced by Jane Alexander. Long before it hit the screens, *City Heat* was pegged as a dog.

Yet, despite it's faults—and there are many—*City Heat* remains a consistently amusing, sometimes very funny period comedy. It is one of Eastwood's least talked-about films, because, despite his first billing status, *City Heat* is really a Burt Reynolds movie. It is Reynolds who is given the most screen time, as well as some very witty one-liners. It's a deft and very underrated performance. Eastwood drifts through the film much like John Wayne in *The Man Who Shot Liberty Valance*—it's supposed to be his film, but his co-star has the meatier role.

With Jane Alexander.

Eastwood does score in two hilarious scenes, however. In one, he fearlessly walks into a blazing gunbattle in an amusing mockery of his own image, and brings the absurdley protracted action to a quick halt with a couple of blasts of a shotgun. The best gag in the film involves Eastwood and Reynolds trying to upstage each other by drawing upon some ridiculously elongated pistols in a not-so-subtle contest of phallic symbols.

The plot has more holes than a Swiss cheese, and the relationship and antagonism between both men is never really explained or developed, an obvious drawback of the film's many re-writes. Yet, *City Heat* is a fun way to spend 90 minutes with two engaging stars. The movie's grosses were respectable, but labeled "disappointing" by Warner Brothers. *City Heat's* relative failure did nothing to hamper Eastwood's popularity. However, as of 1988 Reynolds was still awaiting his "comeback" movie, which will doubtlessly materialize eventually. He took his long succession of flops with characteristic good humour, telling Johnny Carson, "I haven't had a hit since Joan Collins was a virgin!"

SYNOPSIS

In 1933 Kansas City, poverty-stricken private eye Mike Murphy (Burt Reynolds) learns that his partner Diehl Swift (Richard Roundtree) has devised a deadly plan to buy some confidential ledgers from the bookkeeper of gangster overlord Leon Coll (Tony LoBianco). He promises the ledgers to Coll's top rival, Primo Pitt (Rip Torn), for $25,000.

One of the many confrontations with Burt Reynolds.

However, when he attempts to sell them back to Coll for double that amount, he dies at the hands of Pitt's men.

Through a complicated series of events, Murphy gains access to the ledgers, only to find he has been marked for death by both gangsters. When Pitt kidnaps Murphy's girlfriend Caroline (Madeline Kahn) he must rely on the help of his former police force partner, Lt. Speer (Clint Eastwood). Now antagonists, the two men join together, and, in a wild gun battle, kill Pitt. When Coll kidnaps Murphy's secretary Addy (Jane Alexander), Murphy hands him a briefcase purporting to contain the ledgers. In fact, it contains dynamite, and as Coll drives away his car is blown to bits.

REVIEWS

Nothing that happens here...does anything to compensate for the structual awkwardness. Reynolds is smugly confirmed in his Cary Grant irresponsibility-with-charm persona, and Eastwood plays a teeth-gritting parody of himself that is crude by comparison with the parodies of *The Gauntlet* or *The Outlaw Josey Wales*. (Blake) Edwards, at least, might have made up for some of the writing weaknesses with a little more style in this department.

Richard Combs, *Monthly Film Bulletin*

I enjoyed *City Heat*, but I would be hard-pressed to say that the movie is about anything more than hats.... Burt Reynolds, doing his best work in several years is quite charming, but it's Clint Eastwood's movie. The director...allows Eastwood to be so straight, so single-minded that he achieves his own crazy kind of hipness.

David Denby, New York Magazine

Some of the repartee is relatively amusing, and the two stars with tongues firmly in cheek, easily set the prevailing tone of low-keyed facetiousness. Reynolds, working with great relish and rambunctiousness, seems subjectively to be on view considerably more than Eastwood, who nevertheless throws off so much star power and gets so much out of so little that he dominates whenever he's onscreen. Eastwood earned whatever he was paid just by the way he stalks down a street brandishing a shotgun and showing a nasty look in his eye.

"Cart," Variety

Actually, Eastwood is very funny in the second half, once he starts killing people and loosens up a bit, and once the screenwriters give him some good lines. They've concocted some surprisingly peppy banter between the two actors and while these superstar match-ups almost never produce a real movie, audiences bring a lot of goodwill to them....I dunno. Maybe I'm a yahoo, but I laughed. Burt's a crowd-pleaser, Clint's a crowd-slayer and the picture's going to pack them in. It's a Hope and Crosby movie for action freaks: *The Road to Mayhem*.

David Edelstein, The Village Voice

Resolving a crisis--the Eastwood way.

John Russell (center) and his deputies gun down a miner.

Pale Rider (1985)

CAST

Preacher: Clint Eastwood; *Hull Barrett*: Michael Moriarty; *Sarah Wheeler*: Carrie Snodgress; *Josh LaHood*: Christopher Penn; *Coy LaHood*: Richard Dysart: *Megan Wheeler*: Sydney Penny; *Club*: Richard Kiel; *Spider Conway*: Doug McGrath; *Stockburn*: John Russell.

CREDITS

Executive Producer, Fritz Manes. *Producer and Director*, Clint Eastwood. *Associate Producer*, David Valdes. *Screenplay*, Michael Butler and Dennis Shryack. *Photography* Bruce Surtees. *Production Designer*, Edward Carfagno. *Editor*, Joel Cox. *Music*, Lennie Niehaus. A Malpaso Production. Released by Warner Bros. Color by Technicolor. *Running time: 116 minutes.*

By 1985, the word had been out in Hollywood that the western had gone the way of Nehru jackets, polyester suits and the Bay City Rollers. The kiss of death was director Michael Cimino's 1980 mega-flop *Heaven's Gate*, a drastically underrated film that seemed to undermine the entire genre. To paraphrase an old saying, "The only difference between *Heaven's Gate* and the *Titanic*, is that the *Titanic* had a band." It was therefore a surprise to the industry when Clint Eastwood announced that his next film project would be a traditional western titled *Pale Rider.*

To say that *Pale Rider* is inspired by *Shane* would be the understatement of all time. It is, in fact, a virtual remake of the earlier film, with only

243

With Sydney Penny and Michael Moriarty.

marginal differences. (The most obvious being the substitution of a teenage girl in the Brandon DeWilde role.) The film also borrows liberally from influences from the Sergio Leone westerns, as well as Eastwood's own *High Plains Drifter.* Some critics charged Eastwood with borderline plagiarism, but it must be noted that Eastwood obviously wanted audiences to recognize the parallels between each of these films and *Pale Rider,* or he would not have them so apparant.

Shot on location in less than two months in Sun Valley, Idaho, Eastwood's film continued the trend of fast-paced, cost-efficient film-making which had become synonimous with the Malpaso name. If the film has a fault it is that it does itself an injustice by recalling the memory of other westerns. One is almost distracted from the storyline by trying to recall similar occurrences in the previously mentioned westerns. It makes *Pale Rider* a satisfying yet very predicatable affair upon first viewing.

Yet, this is an Eastwood film that is decidely better over a period of time. When seen again, one realizes just what an interesting and skillful production Eastwood has brought to the screen. In fact, one is almost startled to recognize that Eastwood's role is actually secondary to that of Michael Moriarty, who delivers a superb performance in what must be regarded as the Van Heflin role from *Shane.*

Of all Eastwood's films as director, *Pale Rider* is decidedly his most skillful in terms of getting memorable performances from his cast. There is not a false note in the ensemble. Carrie Snodgress and Sydney Penny are excellent as the women Eastwood must protect; and Richard Dysart creates an all-too-believable villain. Western veteran John Russell is well-cast as a dapper but moralless mercenary who enlists an army in a vain attempt to do battle with Eastwood.

As for Clint, the role of the mysterious drifter does not require him to build upon the acting skills demonstrated in *Tightrope*. It is, however, a humorous and highly polished performance.

Pale Rider did not ignite a flood of new westerns, but it did far better at the box-office than most had predicted, easily outgrossing the other big western of 1985, the enjoyable but overblown *Silverado*. With sweeping landscapes and magnificent cinematography, Eastwood got far more impressive results with a lot less money.

Critics were divided on the film, but most agreed it was great to see Eastwood back in the saddle. Overseas, reaction was even better, and the French showed *Pale Rider* in competition at the Cannes Film Festival. Truly, Clint Eastwood had arrived as a major force in the world cinema. It is also ironic to note that none of the critics who scorned Eastwood for borrowing so liberally from *Shane*, were as perceptive in 1987 when they failed to note that the hit film *Fatal Attraction* was an almost identical remake of Eastwood's *Play Misty For Me*.

SYNOPSIS

In 1850 California, a small group of independent gold miners and their families find themselves terrorized by Coy LaHood (Richard Dysart), who heads a powerful strip mining corporation, the future success of which depends upon securing the land held by the independents.

Desperate, LaHood begins using violence in an unsuccessful attempt to run the peaceful yet determined homesteaders from their land. Leading the homesteaders is Hull Barrett (Michael Moriarty), who dreams of a better life for himself, his girlfriend Sarah (Carrie

With Michael Moriarty.

Eastwood draws on LaHood's men.

Snodgress) and her daughter from a previous marriage, 14-year-old Meagan (Sydney Penny).

Into the lives of these strong-willed people rides a mysterious man known only as "The Preacher" (Clint Eastwood). He says little, divulges nothing of his past, but for a man of the cloth seems adept at handling weapons. He unites the miners and gives them the confidence to defy LaHood even in the face of mounting violence.

Although both Sarah and her daughter become enamoured of the preacher, he gently rejects their advances and makes them see that Hull is a less capable but far better man. After repeatedly defeating LaHood's men, The Preacher finds himself facing an evil marshall (John Russell) and an army of his deputies, all adversaries from his past. In a climactic battle, The Preacher slays each of his opponents, and Hull joins in the action, succeeding in killing LaHood. The Preacher then rides away as mysteriously as he arrived, with more than a suggestion that his presence may have had more to do with the supernatural than with fate.

REVIEWS

An entertaining, mystical new western.... Played absolutely straight, but it's also very funny in a dryly sophisticated way that—it's only now apparent—has been true of Mr. Eastwood's self-directed films and of the Eastwood films directed by Don Siegel. .... Like all Eastwood productions, "Pale Rider" is extremely well cast beginning with the star. Mr.

246

Eastwood has continued to refine the identity of his western hero by eliminating virtually every superfluous gesture. He's a master of minimalism. The camera does not reflect vanity. It discovers the mythical character within. *Pale Rider* is the first decent western in a very long time.

Vincent Canby, *New York Times*

On the whole, Eastwood's instincts as an artist are well-nigh inspiring in the context of the temptations he must face all the time to play it completely safe. Consequently, even his mistakes contribute to his mystique....Eastwood has managed to keep the genre alive...through the ghostly intervention of his heroic persona.

Andrew Sarris, *The Village Voice*

Easily one of the best films of the year, and one of the best westerns in a long, long time.

Jeffrey Lyons, *Sneak Previews*

Back in the saddle, Clint goes west in a six-gun classic.

Bruce Williamson, *Playboy*

Pale Rider is a slick attempt to revive the classic Hollywood Western in a traditional narrative style. This task is accomplished with a strong and fine cast, but there's no way of avoiding one central flaw: *Pale Rider* owes such a nostalgic debt to George Stevens' *Shane* that the similarities, scene by scene, become almost a parody.

Rex Reed, *New York Post*

Vanessa in the Garden (1985)

CAST

Byron Sullivan: Harvey Keitel; *Vanessa:* Sondra Locke; *Ted:* Beau Bridges.

CREDITS

Executive Producer, Steven Spielberg. *Producer*, David E. Vogel. *Associate producers*, Steve Starkey and Skip Lusk. *Director*, Clint Eastwood. *Written by* Steven Spielberg. *Photography*, Robert Stevens. *Production designer*, Rick Carter. *Editor*, Joe Ann Fogle. *Music*, Lennie Niehaus. *Theme*, John Williams. An Amblin Entertainment production.

Eastwood returned to television for the first time in many years to direct this episode of Steven Spielberg's much-anticipated fantasy series, "Amazing Stories," which was broadcast for two seasons on NBC. The Spielberg name was able to attract a wide range of talented actors and directors, most of whom limited their involvement with the series to one episode. Despite the high-priced talent and superior production values, however, "Amazing Stories" proved that even Spielberg's golden touch could be tarnished on occassion.

On the set of "Amazing Stories" with series creator Steven Spielberg.

The series was a sort of quasi-"Twilight Zone," with half-hour stories presented each week dealing with the supernatural. Spielberg, however, never seemed to make up his mind whether he wanted to frighten or enchant viewers, and most of the storylines became mired somewhere in between. Eastwood's episode was no exception. Burdened with the limitations of the show's time-slot, a predictable script, and strained performances from miscast Harvey Keitel and Beau Bridges, Eastwood could do little to make this occasion little more than a formula, bittersweet love story with supernatural overtones. It must be said, however, that the show is one of the most successful entries in a series which proved to be a major disappointment to sponsors, the network and viewing audiences. If nothing else, it did provide Eastwood the opportunity to direct Sondra Locke in something other than a violent thriller. Yet, even her talents are greatly hidden by a script which limits her dialogue to some brief, inconsequential romantic mumblings.

SYNOPSIS

Byron Sullivan (Harvey Keitel) is a rising 19th century artist who finds his wife Vanessa (Sondra Locke) to be the most fitting inspiration for virtually all of his romantic paintings. When she is killed in a riding accident on the eve of his first major exhibition, Byron destroys all of his paintings, as their depictions of Vanessa proves to be a torturous reminder of the woman he loved.

Byron becomes a reclusive drunkard, until he becomes haunted by fleeting apparitions of Vanessa. He soon learns that he can recapture his life with her by painting scenarios featuring them both. For every situation Byron paints, he is allowed to live it in reality with Vanessa. Motivated to resume painting, he turns out a tremendous number of works. His renewed creativity earns him fame and fortune, but his real—and secret—reward is the resumption of his life with the woman he loves through the miraculous gift of his talent.

Heartbreak Ridge (1986)

CAST

Sgt. Tom Highway: Clint Eastwood; *Aggie:* Marsha Mason; *Major Powers:* Everett McGill; *Sgt. Webster:* Moses Gunn; *Little Mary:* Eileen Heckart; *Roy Jennings:* Bo Svenson; *Lt. Ring: Boyd Gaines; Stitch:* Mario Van Peebles; *Choozoo:* Arlen Dean Snyder; *Fragetti:* Vincent Irizarry; *Aponte:* Ramon Franco; *Profile:* Tom Villard; *Quinones:* Mike Gomez; *Collins:* Rodney Hill; *"Swede" Johnson:* Peter Koch; *Col. Meyers:* Richard Venture.

CREDITS

Executive Producer, Fritz Manes. *Producer and Director*, Clint Eastwood. *Screenplay*, James Carabatsos. *Photography*, Jack N. Green. *Production designer*, Edward Carfagno. *Editor*, Joel Cox. *Music*, Lenny Niehaus. A Malpaso Production. Released by Warner Bros. Color by Technicolor. *Running Time: 130 minutes.*

"I piss napalm!" exclaims Clint Eastwood in his twelfth directorial effort. As we first see Eastwood, it's not difficult to believe his is quite capable of this dubious feat. Our initial view shows him greying, with a weathered face, reflecting upon former sexual conquests from a small town jail cell. Within seconds he manages to beat a hulking opponent to a pulp, only to continue his tall tales virtually uninterrupted. Vintage Eastwood, audiences think.

Yet, *Heartbreak Ridge* shows us a very different side of the Eastwood persona. As aging Marine Stg. Tom Highway, Eastwood throughout the film conveys a sense of humanity often absent from his previous efforts. In fact, *Heartbreak Ridge* is not really an action film at all. It is basically a character study of a flawed but likable man. Estranged from his wife, with whom he attempts periodic reconciliations with varying degrees of success, Eastwood is also hampered by the growing knowledge that his years of service to the Marines are rapidly growing shorter. A Medal of Honor winner in the Korean War, he has failed to impress his superiors due to his maverick nature. His last meaningful assignment is to shape a motley platoon of misfits into a fighting unit. It is here, however, that the film's flaws become apparent.

The platoon is basically a standard group of clichéd characters direct from Central Casting. Every sequence is virtually borrowed intact from World War II era films, specifically *Sands of Iwo Jima.* Like John Wayne's

th Mario Van Peebles.

Addressing the platoon during basic training.

The Green Berets, Heartbreak Ridge is basically a World War II movie set in modern times. Unlike *The Green Berets*, however, Eastwood manages to snare success from the jaws of defeat and produce a flawed but ultimately engrossing film.

The weaknesses he has to overcome to do so include a rambling screenplay which cannot decide whether the character of Highway should be basically "hard as nails" with a glimmer of sensitivity, or a basically sensitive man with a glimmer of being "hard as nails." The result is a compromise which waters down the character, leaving Eastwood to struggle on his own. This he does in a very competent performance, although the gravelly voice in which he speaks his lines proves to be an unnecessary distraction. As a director, he is even more impressive, getting plausible performances from the young actors (whom he personally hired) who portray the members of his platoon. Memorable, too, is Marsha Mason as Highway's wife. It's a vibrant and sometimes vivid performance.

Heartbreak Ridge ran into well publicized difficulties when the Marine Corps, which co-operated entirely throughout the filming, became dismayed at what they felt were inaccuracies in the practices of Marine personnel. This failed to hurt the film, as it was already completed, but several charitable functions which would have benefited from Marine co-operation at the premiere suffered.

Critics were split, as usual with this latest effort from Eastwood. Some dismissed it as a hopelessly corny journey through territory best covered forty years ago. Others, however, were quite enthusiastic in their praise of Eastwood as both performer and star. Predicatably, the film did impressive business with audiences, and some people were once again startled when the film was ignored in all but one category (Sound) at Oscar time.

Overlong, often meandering, *Heartbreak Ridge* still represents a remarkable achievement in that it was shot in only eight weeks, and still maintains a "big budget" look. It also proved that Eastwood certainly has no ego problems. He has seldom looked so tired and worn in a role. As a reminder this is intentional, however, one almost gasps when he is viewed in full dress blues. Whether he likes it or not, in this sequence Eastwood appears not to have aged in the last twenty years.

SYNOPSIS

Sgt. Tom Highway (Clint Eastwood) is a Korean War veteran who gained prominence by winning the Medal of Honor for heroic action at a battlesite known as Heartbreak Ridge. He has failed to progress through the ranks, however, because of his maverick nature and disregard for orders with which he does not agree. He asks for, and receives, permission to return to his former base, where he is assigned the task of shaping a group of undisciplined recruits into a traditional Marine unit.

The job proves to be a challenging one, with each member of the squad challenging him at every step. He wins their respect, however, through a combination of strict discipline and human compassion.

Highway is less successful trying to win back the affections of his estranged wife, Aggie (Marsha Mason), who left him years before due to his surly nature. Eventually, she relents and their relationship resumes on better terms.

Highway constantly battles his much younger superior officers regarding the methods employed for training his platoon. When the U.S. invasion of Granada finds the group in combat, however, it is Highway's methods which see the men through to victory, leading to his commendation by the Marine brass. Upon returning to the States, he announces his intention to retire from the Corps in order to spend time with Aggie.

...ring the assault on Granada.

With Marsha Mason.

Eastwood forces the platoon to shape up.

He feels a sense of accomplishment, but he also knows his methods are archaic in the modern world.

REVIEWS

Heartbreak Ridge offers another vintage Clint Eastwood performance—this time within a flat and predictable story. There are enough mumbled half-liners in this contemporary war pic to satisfy those die-hards eager to see just how he portrays the consummate Marine veteran which should translate into bountiful box-office.... Notwithstanding the unsatisfying storyline, Eastwood's direction stands out in sure pacing through the latter two-thirds of the pic.

"Tege," *Variety*

What's surprising is that Eastwood doesn't let Tom Highway stride through the picture beating up everybody in sight, and winning the war single-handed.... (The Film) contains as much energy and color as any action picture this year, and it contains truly amazing dialogue..... "Heartbreak Ridge" doesn't aim as high as most current high-tech action movies, but it hits its target.

Roger Ebert, *New York Post*

At 56, Mr. Eastwood doesn't look especially young, but neither does he look old. Nor does he look preserved, or perhaps surgically improved, like some of his contemporaries. He looks as if he's absorbed the years and turned them into guts and grit.... This is something he shares with Cary Grant. His public personality is bigger than life. It is difficult to imagine Clint Eastwood as a television star today. It would take a half-dozen 21-inch screens, one atop another, just to show him in full-figure.

Vincent Canby, *New York Times*

Pure entertainment. Eastwood's best performance since *Dirty Harry*—tough, funny, credible, even tender.

Mike Clark, *USA Today*

The Dead Pool (1988)

As Harry Callahan

CAST

Harry Callahan, Clint Eastwood; *Samantha Walker*, Patricia Clarkson; *Peter Swan*, Liam Neeson; *Al Quan*, Evan Kim; *Harlan Rook*, David Hunt; *Capt. Donnelly*, Michael Currie; *Lt. Ackerman*, Michael Goodwin.

CREDITS

Producer David Valdes. *Director*, Buddy Van Horn. *Screenplay*, Steve Sharon. *Story by* Steve Sharon, Durk Pearson, and Sandy Shaw. *Based on characters created by* Harry Julian Fink and R.M. Fink. *Editor*, Ron Spang. *Director of Photography*, Jack N. Green. *Production Designer*, Edward Carfagno. *Music*, Lalo Schifrin. A Malpaso Production. Released by Warner Bros. *Running Time: 91 minutes.*

Following the record-breaking performance of *Sudden Impact* in 1983, Eastwood insinuated the hard-boiled detective would be retired to the cinematic hall of fame. It was a surprise, therefore, when Clint announced Harry would be resurrected once again for his fifth screen showdown with the forces of evil in *The Dead Pool*, a film that is somewhat low-key and leisurely paced in comparison to its "Dirty Harry" predecessors.

Critics were quick to complain that Eastwood was falling back on the Harry Callahan character at an age when actual policemen were probably seeking desk duty in anticipation of retirement. John Wayne suffered from the same types of cynical remarks when he made the contemporary actioners *McQ* (1974) and *Brannigan* (1975), despite the fact that both were good thrillers. Could Eastwood really bring a fresh perspective to the series, or simply milk the formula one more time? Refreshingly, Dirty Harry #5 turned out to be a witty and entertaining part of the Callahan canon, albeit the film has many faults.

The basic problem is that the screenplay is not overly involving. It works best as a series of engaging and disjointed segments that fail to satisfactorily mesh as a cohesive storyline. There are also few surprises. The primary suspect in the series of gruesome murders is despicable film director Peter Swan, played with lively villainy by Liam Neeson. However, Neeson is *so* detestable that, despite the script's attempts to camouflage the identity of the killer, we never suspect for a moment that it might actually be Neeson. The idea of keeping the villain's identity a secret only makes sense if his unmasking proves to be a revelation and there have been a multitude of suspects the audience can identify with. In *The Dead Pool*, when the killer is unmasked, it's a cheat since the audience has not seen him or heard about him previously. Harry's antagonist turns out to be from the Central Casting School of Bad Guys—just another sniveling psycho with a penchant for torture and murder, weakening the impact of the climax.

Yet, *The Dead Pool* is a worthy entry in the series. Eastwood's still youthful appearance negated critical speculation that Harry might have

In action with a typical Harry-sized weapon.

to chase the perps in a wheelchair. Some reviewers unfairly complained that Clint was sleepwalking through the part. The character of Harry is simply rather non-descript, save for the action sequences. Fortunately, *The Dead Pool* allows for a maximum of such scenes. Early in the film, there is an exciting car chase in which Eastwood uses his notorious 44 Magnum to dispose of some gangland assassins. Another highly amusing scene has Clint and his latest ill-fated partner, Evan Kim, annihilating a gang of ruthless thugs in a Chinese restaurant. It is here that Harry mutters, "You're shit out of luck" (this film's inevitable tag line), to the rather unfortunate recipient of his Magnum's force. (The line is amusing at first, but when it is repeated later it seems forced and self-indulgent.)

Stuntman Buddy Van Horn, in the director's chair for the first time since *Any Which Way You Can*, does a very credible job in staging action sequences, undoubtedly due to his years of handling the second unit and stunt work on many of Clint's films, and he fashions a neatly paced thriller with a good deal of humor. Witness the car chase through the San Francisco streets wherein Eastwood and Kim's vehicle is pursued at high speed by a bomb-laden remote control toy Ferrari. In less capable hands, the scene would look ridiculous, but Van Horn somehow makes it work (even if several camera shots look as though they were directly lifted from *Bullitt*). The sequence also dares to do the unthinkable: end in an (almost) tragedy with the heroes failing to find a convenient escape route. Other action highlights include a shootout in a glass elevator and an effective finale in which Harry amusingly utilizes the ultimate phallic symbol—a harpoon gun—to "make the villain's day."

The female lead this time around is Patricia Clarkson, previously seen as Kevin Costner's wife in *The Untouchables*. Clarkson does well in a not terribly demanding role that basically consists of getting into danger and having Harry rescue her (à la Lois Lane and Superman). Evan Kim

254

proves to more than just window dressing as Harry's reluctant partner, and he manages to upstage Clint on a couple of occasions, such as the scene wherein he utilizes his martial arts prowess. Lalo Schifrin's jazzy score fits the proceedings perfectly, and Jack Green's cinematography deserves recognition, particularly for the extraordinary car chase between Harry and Ferrari. (Green mounted a camera on the bottom of a motorcycle to get some impressive viewpoints.)

The Dead Pool opened against stiff competition in the summer of 1988. Following big, initial box office, it lost ground rather quickly, bringing in a less than blockbuster overall gross. Critics did not help, with most giving the movie unfavorable notices and saying that the series had run out of steam. Two notable exceptions were longtime Eastwood aficionados Roger Ebert and Gene Siskel who seemed to get the jokes and raved about the film's merits. We rate The Dead Pool below Dirty Harry and Sudden Impact, but ahead of Magnum Force and The Enforcer. However, coming a full seventeen years after first introducing the character, Clint proved that Dirty Harry still had plenty of life left in him. Eastwood now swears Harry is in "retirement" for good, but about the only thing we can expect from Clint is the unexpected.

SYNOPSIS

A series of gruesome murders leads Det. Harry Callahan (Clint Eastwood) to the film set of director Peter Swan (Liam Neeson), an ill-tempered man with a legion of enemies. It appears that the murder victims parallel the names on "The Dead Pool," a tasteless game of speculation devised by Swan for his own amusement. Swan and other

Harry reads the villains' fortune cookie and informs them: "You're shit out of luck!"

255

With Evan Kim, investigating the latest victim of The Dead Pool.

Harry is grilled by reporter Patricia Clarkson.

participants write up lists of prominent individuals who may die within the coming months, presumably from accidental or natural causes. The person with the most correct guesses wins the "pool." Swan, a director of low-budget sex and horror exploitation films, is the press's number one suspect, but Harry dismisses that notion despite his dislike for the man. His efforts to solve the crimes are slowed by his superior's insistence that he pander to the press through "escorting" television reporter Samantha Walker (Patricia Clarkson) about town to generate

As Rowdy Yates in Rawhide.

Rawhide *was a merchandising bonanza, as evidenced by this children's book from England.*

Original lobby card for A Fistful of Dollars *released in the U.S. in 1967.*

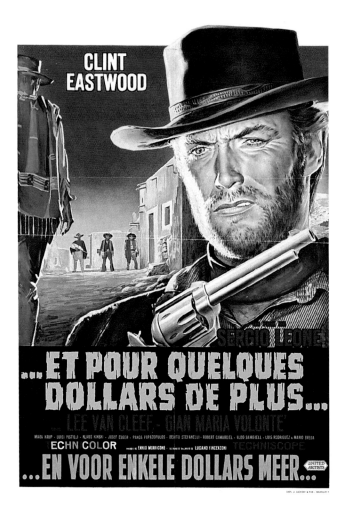

Belgian poster from For a Few Dollars More.

The Good, the Bad, and the Ugly *(1966) for Sergio Leone proved to be a classic.*

Clint and Maggie, late 1960s.

In action for Where Eagles Dare *(1969).*

Eastwood and an all-star cast marched Kelly's Heroes *to the top of the box office in 1970.*

Clint's debut as Dirty Harry for Don Siegel was a triumph (1971).

71/349

 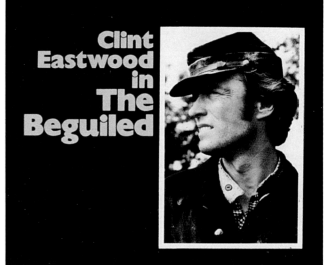

Eastwood's films have always been TV rating hits.

Lobby card for Joe Kidd *(1972).*

The return of Dirty Harry in Magnum Force *(1973).*

Scaling the Eiger (1975).

Clint's Malpaso office displays some favorite mementos, like the poster for The Outlaw Josey Wales

French poster for Tightrope *(1984).*   *In uniform for* Heartbreak Ridge *(1986).*

The star's popularity was recognized by the Eastwood Appreciation Society in Great Britain.

Relaxing at a beach in Carmel.

Directing Forest Whitaker and Diane Venora in Bird *(1988).*

Receiving the Cecil B. DeMille Lifetime Achievement Award from Richard Attenborough in 1987.

The director as director: White Hunter, Black Heart *(1990).*

As Will Munny in the acclaimed Unforgiven *(1992).*

favorable coverage for the department in the media. Harry and Samantha initially despise each other, but eventually a sexual relationship, if not a romance, develops.

Harry is ordered to take on Det. Al Quan (Evan Kim) as a partner. Quan proves to Harry that he can be an asset, although his well-placed fear of the fate that met Harry's previous partners becomes understandable when the killer uses a bomb-laden toy Ferrari in an assassination attempt that puts Quan in the hospital. The series of murders continues, and Harry suffers through more attempts on his life, in the process learning that his own name has been placed on the "dead pool" list. The villain is revealed to be Harlan Rook (David Hunt), a schizophrenic who once idolized Swan, but who is now trying to frame him in revenge for the director's refusal to film a screenplay Rook has submitted. Rook kidnaps Samantha and brings her to a deserted warehouse where he uses her as bait to lure Harry to his death. In a tense confrontation, Harry is disarmed, but manages to utilize a harpoon gun from a nearby film set to "terminate" Rook. The case solved, Harry walks away into the night with Samantha.

REVIEWS

Good news! This is quite a lively thriller in the Dirty Harry series, which had previously seemed to be fading into mediocrity. Crisply edited down to a tight hour and a half of hard hitting set pieces...Buddy Van Horn's best work as a director to date.

David Quinlan, *Film Monthly* (U.K.)

Dirty Harry Callahan isn't the best and brightest of cops but you can't kill him with cannon, mace and chain. *The Dead Pool* isn't the best and brightest of the Dirty Harry films, either, but it's just an invincible. Such things are hard to tell, but it's possible that Clint Eastwood and crew are just enjoying a bit of self mockery with this one. If not, and any one of them took this thing seriously for a moment, then the failure is monumental.

"Har," *Variety*

Eastwood, Smith and Wesson back in action.

Bird (1988)

CAST

Charlie "Bird" Parker, Forest Whitaker; *Chan Parker*, Diane Venora; *Red Rodney*, Michael Zelnicker; *Dizzy Gillespie*, Samuel E. Wright; *Buster Franklin*, Keith David; *Brewster*, Michael McGuire; *Esteves*, James Handy; *Young Bird*, Damon Whitaker; *Kim*, Morgan Nagler; *Dr. Heath*, Arlen Dean Snyder.

CREDITS

Producer and director, Clint Eastwood. *Executive producer and production manager*, David Valdes. *Screenplay*, Joel Oliansky. *Director of photography*, Jack N. Green. *Music*: Lennie Niehaus; *Editor*, Joel Cox. *Production designer*: Edward C. Carfagno. A Malpaso Production. Released by Warner Bros. *Running time: 161 minutes.*

Clint Eastwood's obsession with jazz has never been a secret, but there had been few opportunities for him to indulge in this passion onscreen. He did manage to sneak an extended sequence at the Monterey Jazz Festival into *Plan Misty for Me*, but even this played against the backdrop of the mad-slasher plot. In early 1988, Eastwood found financial backing for, and served as executive producer on, *Thelonius Monk: Straight, No Chaser*, a $400,000 documentary which utilized rarely seen footage of the jazz legend. The filmmakers were very gratified that the star and jazz aficionado had come to the rescue of this very non-commercial property, and were even more pleased that he did not interfere creatively other than suggesting the title and approving the final cut. In his book *Clint Eastwood/Malpaso*, Fuensanta Plaza writes of Clint, "Few filmmakers have such elegance or integrity."

The reason for the studio's reluctance to steer clear of the jazz genre was simple: virtually every movie to prominently feature this artform died at the box office. Eastwood has observed quite correctly that Europeans have shown more enthusiasm about many film ventures pertaining to U.S. heritage than domestic moviegoers. Thus the subject of jazz music had rarely been explored in-depth on screen, and even the once great American screen western has only recently shown signs of a resurrection.

Eastwood's film *Bird*, which examines the rise and fall of jazz genius Charlie Parker, is indeed an American tragedy. Eastwood had been fascinated by Parker's music and life, having become "hooked" on *Bird* at an early age, telling critic Roger Ebert: "I became a Charlie Parker fan when I was a kid, back in 1947. I saw him in *Jazz at the Philharmonic*. They'd have these big tenor saxes—Coleman Hawkins, Flip Phillips—and then this alto sax player stepped out and he was really amazing." He later reflected to *Esquire*, "It's unexplainable, there was nobody like him.... There was something about his music that was unbelievably well played. And he looked like somebody special, different from the other guys. They were great, they were giants, but here was somebody different."

Years later, after emerging as an influential force in Hollywood, Eastwood became interested in a script that had been written about Parker's life, recalling: "I always wanted to make a film about jazz, because I never thought a really good one had been made. Then one day...the script to *Bird* came to my attention. It was originally a project for Richard Pryor over at Columbia, but for one reason or another he'd become disassociated with it and the whole project was in limbo." The option on the script belonged to producer Ray Stark, who ultimately "traded" it to Clint for another property. Eastwood chuckled at Stark's reaction to the news the *Bird* project would be purchased by Clint: "He asked, 'Now how is Clint Eastwood going to play Charlie Parker??'" Fortunately, Dirty Harry doing an Al Jolson blackface approach to *Bird* was not in Eastwood's plans. He very definitely wanted to use relative unknowns in the film, and cast Forest Whitaker, a supporting actor from *Good Morning, Vietnam*, in the role of Charlie Parker. The choice proved to be inspired, as Whitaker gives a performance that is nothing less than brilliant.

With Bird *stars Forest Whitaker and Diane Venora.*

The supporting cast is also quite astonishing, with Diane Venora mesmerizing as Parker's long-suffering wife, Chan. Equally impressive is Michael Zelnicker as Red Rodney, Parker's caucasian protégé with whom "Bird" pleads to avoid taking the self-destructive path he himself has chosen. The film is populated by any number of letter-perfect characterizations, and to risk a corny pun, it's safe to say none of them hit a false note. Characteristically, Eastwood insured there was no waste in the budget, and somehow managed to bring the film in under schedule—quite remarkable—for less than $9 million, despite the expensive look of the movie.

Moreso than most Eastwood films, however, the talents of the behind-the-camera artists feature prominently. Cinematographer Jack N. Green's work is remarkable. The *film noir* atmosphere is perfectly captured in a mesmerizing panorama of camera angles, complemented by Green's highly imaginative lighting. Equally impressive is Edward Carfagno's outstanding production design, which almost physically transforms the viewer to the forties and fifties. Perhaps the most dazzling technical achievement is composer Lennie Niehaus's method of blending Parker's original recordings with new background music performed by contemporary musicians. This "cleaned up" the technically inferior master tracks thus allowing Parker's actual sound to be appreciated by audiences.

Clint's direction of Bird *would win him his first Golden Globe Award.*

There can be no overstating Clint Eastwood's directorial accomplishment with this very personal project. He makes no compromises in the name of commerciality. When someone questioned whether the film was too full of references familiar only to jazz buffs, he simply replied that this was the movie he envisioned making and "Either the audience gets it, or they don't." Joel Oliansky's screenplay, undeniably confusing at times, jumps back and forth in time, revealing Parker's all too few moments of bliss, coupled with his almost ceaseless battle against self-destruction. Eastwood crafts an amazing work, filled with many memorable images and sequences. He allows the film to run a leisurely 161 minutes and insures that each of Parker's jazz numbers is heard in its entirety. *Bird* remains tasteful, despite the many opportunities to provide lurid images. The early sexual spark between "Bird" and Chan is acknowledged without any graphic sequences. Likewise, Parker's drug abuse is talked about constantly, but Eastwood refrains from showing us clinical close-ups. Eastwood seems to relish the dialogue-heavy script, and indeed, there hasn't been this much nonstop, engrossing conversation on celluloid since *Who's Afraid of Virginia Woolf?* Ultimately, *Bird* emerges as a dark, depressing, but thought-provoking film, that is somehow joyless without being humorless.

With cinematographer Jack Green.

While it's doubtful either Clint or Warner Brothers expected this very specialized movie to be a box-office hit, *Bird* appeared to have the

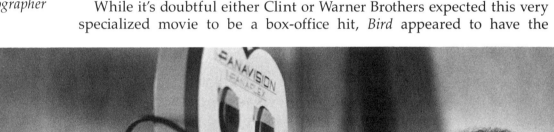

potential of becoming a commercial success. Shown in competition at the Cannes Film Festival, Eastwood's film was hailed as a major cinematic achievement and won prizes for star Forest Whitaker and for the technical aspects of the sound recording. Diane Venora won the New York Film Critics Award for Best Supporting Actress, and Eastwood won the Golden Globe for Best Director. Critical reaction was outstanding with even the cynical Rex Reed proclaiming—some years after he accused Eastwood of being "out of style"—that Clint had now catapulted to the forefront of American film directors. The international box-office results were unfortunately dismal. The film also flopped in its U.S. engagements, which probably cost the movie the anticipated Oscar nominations the studio had geared up for. (It did win the award for sound-recording—the only category in which it was nominated.) The Motion Picture Academy's snubbing of *Bird*'s other obvious merits is but another example of the Hollywood establishment abandoning a movie that could not be salvaged at the box office.

Nevertheless, Eastwood had the satisfaction of seeing his longtime dream project brought to reality amidst the almost unanimous praise of those who generally dismissed him decades before as a "flash in the pan," one-note actor. *Bird* is a work of art, and under Eastwood's direction, it truly soars.

SYNOPSIS

The life of Charlie "Bird" Parker (Forest Whitaker) is traced from his origins in the impoverished South to his emergence in the 1940s as a major talent in the world of jazz. During the early days of his career, Bird courts and marries Chan (Diane Venora), a free-spirited independent woman whose views on morality prove to be far ahead of their time. Parker's climb to the top is slow and painful, but his problems only worsen when he finally finds the critical praise and audience appreciation he has sought for so long. His drinking and drug abuse become uncontrollable, costing him lucrative contracts and lessening the demand for his work.

Bird periodically reemerges as a considerate family man and talented musician, but always resumes his self-destructive excesses. His womanizing and drug problems lead to a reputation of being unreliable. He ignores the advice from his mentor Dizzy Gillespie (Samuel E. Wright) and finds that the adoring fans who once worshipped him now consider his music outdated—replaced by the "new" phenomenon known as rock 'n roll. Bird continues to find lesser gigs with his new band, which includes his protégé, Red Rodney (Michael Zelnicker), a talented young trumpet player who seems to emulate all of Parker's bad habits. (Rodney died in 1992.) On a West Coast tour, Bird learns the devastating news from Chan that their young daughter has died of an illness.

Shattered by guilt due to his absence from home and an affair he has been carrying on, Bird returns to attend the funeral. A suicide attempt fails, and Chan refuses doctors' suggestions to initiate shock treatments on Parker, as it would all but end his musical creativity. Shortly thereafter, however, Bird succumbs to a heart attack while enjoying a comedy routine on television. Although his life ends prematurely (March 1955 at age thirty-four), his legend will endure and grow over the decades to come.

REVIEWS

Clint Eastwood has had to chart bold new territory for himself as a director, and he has pulled it off in most impressive fashion. Sensitively acted, beautifully planned visually, and dynamite musically, this dramatic telling of the troubled life of a revolutionary artist will surprise those stragglers who believe Eastwood's talents lie strictly with mayhem and monkeys.... Outstanding scene piles upon outstanding scene.... Whitaker [gives] an excellent performance, with an especially riveting death scene.... Diane Venora is riveting.... Eastwood has tested himself with an ambitious labor of love and emerged standing taller as a filmmaker than he ever has before.

"Cart," *Variety*

To draw maximum pleasure from the producer-director Clint Eastwood's *Bird*, it's best to be a dedicated jazz buff. Forest Whitaker [gives] a compelling portrayal of Charlie "Bird" Parker, the late, great jazz sax player who died in 1955 at the age of 34, so wasted by drugs, depression, and economic woes that he looked old enough to be his own father. Diane Venora as his patient wife, Chan, limns a graceful and moving portrait of a woman whose loyalty to her mate demands superhuman strength. Clint's directorial labor of love is a dark, almost impressionistic weaving of musical highs and emotional lows in the short, unhappy life of the legendary Bird."

Bruce Williamson, *Playboy*

Pink Cadillac (1989)

CAST

Tommy Nowak, Clint Eastwood; *Lou Ann McGuinn*, Bernadette Peters; *Roy McGuinn*, Timothy Carhart; *McGuinn Baby*, Tiffany Gail Robinson/Angela Louise Robinson; *Waycross*, John Dennis Johnston; *Alex*, Michael Des Barres; *Billy Dunston*, Jimmie F. Skaggs; *Darrell*, Bill Moseley; *Ken Lee*, Michael Champion; *Mr. Barton*, William Hickey; *Ricky Z*, Geoffrey Lewis; *Bartender*, Bill McKinney.

CREDITS

Producer, David Valdes. *Executive producer*, Michael Gruskoff. *Director*, Buddy Van Horn. *Screenplay*, Michael Eskow. *Director of photography*, Jack N. Green. *Production designer*, Edward Carfagno. *Editor*, Joel Cox. *Music*, Steve Dorff. A Malpaso Production. Released by Warner Brothers. *Running time: 121 minutes.*

Eastwood and Bernadette Peters go for broke in Reno.

Never one to be called predictable, Clint Eastwood followed the critical success of *Bird* with what he hoped to be a surefire commercial success: *Pink Cadillac*. Obviously meant to be reminiscent of *Every Which Way But Loose/Any Which Way You Can* genre, this is a quirky comedy with a slightly harder edge than those two hits. While those films were populated by larger-than-life characters, *Pink Cadillac* presents its principal players as (mostly) realistic, everyday people whose idiosyncrasies only occasionally lapse into the theater of the absurd. The film was shot in northern California and Reno and its production displayed all the elements of Malpaso's abilities for making movies on tight schedules and economical budgets. With winter approaching, director Buddy Van Horn had a very limited number of daylight hours in which to shoot, but managed to bring *Pink Cadillac* in on time.

  Pink Cadillac turned out to be Eastwood's biggest box-office flop since *The Beguiled* in 1971. Unlike that film, however, it is doubtful that critics will one day "discover" this as an important work in the Eastwood canon. It was released in the summer of 1989 among heavy-hitting competition such as *Batman*, *Indiana Jones and the Last Crusade*, and *Lethal Weapon 2*. With a handful of powerhouse films controlling the box office, many other traditionally popular series and stars posted disappointing results, among them the latest *Star Trek*, *Karate Kid*, and James Bond films. The grosses of these, however, still looked gargantuan next to the rental dollars generated by Eastwood's film (under $7 million).

  One can only speculate as to why audiences stayed away from *Pink Cadillac* in droves. The almost unanimously negative reviews of course did not help, nor did screenwriter Michael Eskow's uncertainty as to whether to make an overt comedy or an action adventure. The film features a number of amusing characters and situations, but it is difficult to find humor in many of the darker aspects of the script: kidnapping a baby and threatening her life; forcing a husband to hunt down and murder his own wife; and the inclusion of white supremacists and neo-Nazis. On the surface, one would have more laughs touring a morgue.

Pink Cadillac, despite of these setbacks, works largely because Clint Eastwood and leading lady Bernadette Peters generate unexpected sparks together and appear as though they are having a good time. For Peters, the film offered a rare opportunity to shed the dizzy bimbo-like image she has projected at least on screen over the last couple of decades. For Eastwood, the script allows him the chance to play comedy while creating a number of imaginative characterizations. Longtime Malpaso cinematographer Jack Green once stated that on reading the script, he felt that Clint was courting with disaster by having to impersonate a wide range of improbable alter-egos in his role as a modern bounty hunter. While such a challenge might appeal to Robin Williams, the idea of Clint Eastwood imitating a casino huckster in a gold lamé jacket, would give one pause. To Clint's credit, however, his work in *Pink Cadillac* is extremely amusing. His personifications of crazy deejays, clowns, and—in particular—a redneck dimwit often border on the hilarious. It's a wonderful, groundbreaking Eastwood performance that ironically is contained in one of his least-seen films of recent years.

When scriptwriter Michael Eskow sticks to the comedy, the movie works quite well. There are some deft barbs aimed at everything from Elvis impersonators to those squalid roadside motels with their "theme rooms." ("Eerie, isn't it, how much this place looks like Hawaii?" deadpans Peters as she and Clint check into an atrocious "Luau Suite.") Where the movie misses the mark is when it gets into the action genre. There are numerous pointless car chases, and the antagonists—a right wing group known as the Birthright—seem to pose no particular threat to anyone other than themselves. Additionally, the villains are disposed of rather easily when their car simply veers off the road in minor mishap,

Reluctant lovers: Tommy (Eastwood) and Lou Ann (Bernadette Peters).

making it appear that this portion of the script was written minutes before the cameras rolled. The story is far too slight to justify the two-hour running time, but one does admit the individual scenes generally are amusing.

Among the film's major virtues are Buddy Van Horn's handling of some impressive action set pieces, such as Eastwood's pursuit of a villain through Reno's streets and casinos, the abundant use of some catchy country songs, and Jack N. Green's superb cinematography. Although this is a minor work in the Eastwood oeuvre, it still deserves another look, as it seems to improve with subsequent viewings. A pity about the unsatisfactory climax, however. It causes the script to run out of gas long before the pink Cadillac does.

SYNOPSIS

Tommy Nowak (Clint Eastwood) is a tough-as-nails skip-tracer who reluctantly agrees to track down Lou Ann McGuinn (Bernadette Peters), a brassy woman who has absconded with her baby, Jennifer, following her indictment of possession of counterfeit money. What Nowak doesn't realize, however, is that Lou Ann is the long-suffering, victimized wife of Roy McGuinn (Timothy Carhart), a two-bit loser who as recently aligned himself with a gang of white supremacists knows as the Birthright. Although having nothing to do with the phony money, Lou Ann becomes the scapegoat when Roy hides it in their mobile home.

Depressed and frustrated, Lou Ann steals her husband's prized 1959 pink Cadillac and escapes to Reno, after temporarily leaving Jennifer in the custody of her sister and brother-in-law. Lou Ann discovers the car contains $250,000 in what she believes to be counterfeit funds, and she uses the money for a fling in the casinos. Here Nowak arrests her but is moved when she informs him of her hardships. He agrees to help her

Eastwood and Bernadette Peters rescue the baby from the Birthright camp.

Clint goes undercover as a redneck fanatic to infiltrate the Birthright organization

John Dennis Johnston (left) and Timothy Carhart get the drop on Clint and Bernadette.

and discovers that the supposedly counterfeit funds Lou Ann possesses are genuine dollars belonging to the Birthright. Enraged at having his treasury stolen, Alex (Michael Des Barres), the group's ruthless leader, orders Roy and a maniac named Waycross (John Dennis Johnston) to recover the money and do away with Lou Ann. With Nowak's help, Lou Ann escapes and Waycross is killed, but Jennifer is captured. With some assistance from Roy, who has had a change of heart, Nowak and Lou Ann plan a risky infiltration of the Birthright camp. They are discovered, and in a wild car chase and shoot-out, elude the villains and recover Jennifer. Nowak and Lou Ann decide they are in love and plan to resolve their legal problems and open their own skip-tracing agency.

Tommy Nowak jokingly intimidates his bailbondsmen boss.

REVIEWS

Mediocre duo-in-pursuit material only marginally brightened when Clint Eastwood parodies other personalities....May be the weakest Eastwood release ever. Here, to odd results, Eastwood tries to be both that laconic, stalwart persona, and strangely, kind of a pushover for an energetic damsel in distress (Bernadette Peters) with whom he develops little visible rapport and zero sexual chemistry....Film's redeeming moments come from a number of funny Eastwood turns—striking silly poses as a disk jockey, clown, and casino huckster, and rather amusingly, a lisping former Folsom prison inmate, all in an effort to foil his bait.

"Brit.," Variety

What is surprising for a Clint Eastwood action movie is its general torpid pace; its almost total lack of any cinematic energy...a 122-minute dozer.

Richard Freedman, Newhouse News Services

Pink Cadillac is possibly the most underrated of Malpaso films...an everchanging kaleidoscope of moods, and [Buddy] Van Horn excels at this type of film. Fun, sadness, excitement and downright comedy flash by in such quick tempo that we are continually disconcerted in our involuntary prediction of what will happen next—a delightful feeling, though possibly bothersome for anyone overly endowed with self-important.

Fuensanta Plaza, *Clint Eastwood/Malpaso*, 1991

White Hunter, Black Heart (1990)

As John Wilson.

Wilson embarks on the safari.

CAST

John Wilson, Clint Eastwood; *Peter Verrill*, Jeff Fahey; *Paul Landers*, George Dzundza; *Kay Gibson*, Marisa Berenson; *Ralph Lockheart*, Alun Armstrong; *Phil Duncan*, Richard Vanstone; *Miss Wilding*, Charlotte Cornwell; *Irene Saunders*, Catherine Neilson; *Reissar*, Edward Tudor Pope; *Basil Fields*, Richard Warwick; *Kivu*, Boy Mathias Chuma.

CREDITS

Producer and director, Clint Eastwood. *Executive producer*, David Valdes. *Screenplay*, Peter Viertel, James Bridges, and Burt Kennedy. *Based on the novel by* Viertel. *Director of photography*, Jack N. Green. *Art director*, John Graysmark. *Editor*, Joel Cox. *Music*, Lennie Niehaus. A Malpaso/Rastar Production. Released by Warner Brothers. *Running time: 112 minutes.*

Clint Eastwood did not have time to lick his wounds from the box-office failure of *Pink Cadillac*. Instead, he plunged immediately into one of the more offbeat projects of his career, *White Hunter, Black Heart*—rivaled only by *Bird* and *Breezy* as an uncharacteristic Eastwood movie. *Hunter* is based on a novel by writer Peter Viertel, who had accompanied director John Huston on location in the Congo for *The African Queen*. Huston, one of screendom's legendary mavericks, refused all studio pressure to film on a "safe" sound stage, and insisted on an expensive location shoot. As a confidant of Huston's, Viertel became repulsed, yet fascinated with the director's behavior on the set. Huston, alternately charming and brutal, made it apparent to all that completing *The African Queen* was less a goal for him than his real obsession: "Bagging" an elephant while on safari.

If there would appear to be a property less suited for Clint Eastwood than *White Hunter, Black Heart*, it would be difficult to imagine. Eastwood, a low-key actor, would seem to be too subdued to emulate the larger-than-life persona of Huston. Additionally, the screenplay is virtually all dialogue, despite the omnipresent splendors of the African plains. (The film was shot in Zimbabwae.) The traditional Eastwood action element was almost nonexistent. Yet, Eastwood proves to be a triple-threat winner with *Hunter*. Not only is his role of producer and director successfully fulfilled, but his performance—so uncannily like Huston, even down to the vocal timbre—is also an amazing achievement. At first glance, Eastwood's evident mimicking of Huston's mannerisms prove to be a distraction—much like watching an impressionist. Before long, however, he completely dominates the character and we are no longer aware that we are watching Clint Eastwood—certainly the greatest compliment one can give Eastwood the actor.

Surprisingly, although Eastwood and Huston were major talents in Hollywood during overlapping time periods, the two men never met. Eastwood explained how he became involved with this property: "I was a big fan of the [Viertel] book. I was surprised it hadn't been filmed before because it is one of the better stories based on the preparations of filmmaking, even though that's just the setting. The topic is obsessive behavior." Indeed, that obsession becomes apparent from the moment Eastwood's John Wilson prepares to go to Africa. He clearly has little enthusiasm for the film itself, and it is only because of his talents that he is able to use and abuse the studio brass who beg him to shoot the movie on a soundstage in England. Wilson has one primary goal: to get his elephant. His movie just represents the most logical way to justify running about Africa on someone else's money. Curiously, this seems to be exactly what occurred with Huston. While some directors become obsessed with making a particular film—Coppola with *Apocalypse Now* and Cimino with *Heaven's Gate* are the most notorious examples that spring to mind—Huston seemed almost hell bent on *not* beginning production of *The African Queen*. For all his bluster about the benefits of location shooting, he never seemed very interested in having the cameras roll.

Ironically, Eastwood himself faced studio pressure to shoot a key sequence from *Hunter* on the back lot at London's Pinewood Studios. The scene depicted Wilson's irresponsible decision to test the durability of the rickety craft to be used in his movie—a thinly disguised *African Queen*. Partly to gain a thrill, and partly to frighten the studio watchdogs sent to ride herd on him, Wilson recklessly drives the craft into rapids, a move that almost leads to tragedy. Shooting the sequence was quite hazardous and the studio tried to convince Clint that excellent rear-

As director John Wilson, next to The African Trader.

270

Wilson watches in horror as his safari guide is mauled by the elephant.

screen projection techniques would suffice. Eastwood would have none of it. He piloted the boat himself, and the scene works wonderfully because of the realism.

Eastwood as director also refrains from letting the exotic landscape overshadow the very personal nature of the story. Jack N. Green, a protégé of longtime Eastwood cinematographer Bruce Surtees, had been part of Clint's Malpaso stock company in recent years. His work on *Hunter* is quite stunning, not only in the outdoor sequences but in the interiors as well, yet it never distracts one from the dialogue. The supporting cast is chosen more for capability than box-office appeal. Jeff Fahey is marvelous as the Viertel character, here known as Verrill. He complements Eastwood's Wilson when necessary, yet is able to register the proper disgust with his friend's increasingly alienating behavior. The only other role of substance is that of George Dzundza's long-suffering studio executive whom Wilson humiliates at every opportunity. Another director might not have been able to resist being "cutesy" with the opportunity of having the Bogart and Katharine Hepburn figures on the set of the film-within-a film. They play no significant role in the story Viertel has to relate, but they do provide for an authentic atmosphere. Marisa Berenson's Kay Gibson manages to evoke a few Hepburn mannerisms, and Richard Vanstone's Duncan bears a strong resemblance to Bogart without slipping into an embarrassing Rich Little act.

This is Eastwood's movie throughout. His John Wilson is not a likable man, yet he is not without nobility. He thinks nothing of berating and embarrassing the very people who pay his salary, often for no reason at all. He pretends to be intrigued by a bubbleheaded starlet's absurd potential screenplay about a Rin-Tin-Tin type canine hero, while the real motivation is to use her sexually. He also puts his own obsession with prolonging a safari above the financial and emotional welfare of his cast and crew. Yet, there remains something enviable about him. He sabotages a potential sexual liaison by insulting the lady when he discovers her anti-Semitism. He later indulges in a brutal beating after initiating a fight to protest a bully's treatment of the black servants at a posh hotel. Clearly, Wilson is a paradox, and this makes for one of the most fascinating characters Eastwood has portrayed.

White Hunter, Black Heart would seem not designed to appeal to mass audiences, and it's doubtful Warner Brothers would have financed the film had it not been indebted to Eastwood for his long string of hits for the studio. Yet, this was not a vanity project for Clint. He produced a finished work that, like *Bird*, proved to be a prestigious and critically acclaimed film. Most reviews were quite enthusiastic. The film was shown at Cannes to wide acclaim, and the Chicago Society of Film Critics nominated Clint for Best Director. Undoubtedly, this film—and *Bird*— artistic achievements by Eastwood which were shunned by audiences at the time of their release (*Hunter* earned only $1 million in domestic rentals)—will be reevaluated by more perceptive and appreciative future audiences. When they are, there is little doubt that these two will help affirm Clint Eastwood as one of the major filmmaking talents of his time.

SYNOPSIS

John Wilson (Clint Eastwood) is a highly acclaimed motion picture director who has become increasingly impatient with his craft and the politics necessitated in getting his films financed by studios. A cantankerous, restless artist, Wilson reluctantly agrees to direct an adventure film *The African Trader*, to star box-office legends Kay Gibson (Marisa Berenson) and Phil Duncan (Richard Vanstone). Wilson, however, immediately alienates studio brass by chronically arguing with them and the film's harried producer Paul Landers (George Dzundza). Although the studio pleads with Wilson to shoot the film on soundstages in England, the director uses his clout to gain permission to use locations in Africa.

Accompanying Wilson is his longtime friend Peter Verrill (Jeff Fahey), a screenwriter hired to fine-tune the script. Once in Africa, Verrill is alternately amused and put off by Wilson's arrogant, erratic behavior. While Wilson nobly protests the bigotry inherent in the European nationals who still regard Africans as "the White Man's Burden," he also shows the cruel side of his nature to anyone who does not agree with him. Wilson confides in Verrill that his real reason for coming to Africa is to shoot an elephant while on safari, admitting that killing these magnificent beasts is indeed "a sin," but this only appeals to the rebellious side of his nature. When his targets prove to be more elusive than he imagined, he hires a tribesman named Kivu (Boy Mathias Chuma) to lead him on a time-consuming safari which seriously delays production on the film.

Despite Verrill's chastisements and pressure from Landers, who has arrived in Africa for a firsthand look at the location problems, Wilson becomes more obstinate than ever. With his career on the line and the fate of the film in the balance, he embarks on one last attempt to find an elephant. With a party of trackers, Wilson locates his prey, but ignores

Wilson argues the merits of his script with Verrill (Jeff Fahey).

Eastwood and Fahey arrange for their ill-fated safari.

warnings that the situation is far too dangerous to fire a rifle. The resulting tragedy leads to Kivu being gored to death after saving Wilson's life.

Returning to the film set in a daze, Wilson resumes production. It has taken a devastating occurrence to make Wilson aware of the price others pay for his conceits. As Kivu's grieving relatives mourn the senseless loss of the tribesman's life, someone in the crowd looks at the arrogant figure of Wilson and describes him in an African phrase reserved for Caucasian despots who besieged Africa: "White Hunter, Black Heart."

REVIEWS

Brilliant, witty and exciting.... Big Clint gives the finest performance of his career.... Eastwood impersonates [Huston's] every flaw with a characterization eerie enough to transcend tricks of voice and manner, offering a larger than life figure of Huston as artist and bully. This film not only gets inside the heart of the man, but explores the expatriate nastiness, anti-Semitism and white fascism among the posh safari clubs and jungles of Zimbabwae in the early '50s.... Clint Eastwood finally hangs up Dirty Harry's brass knuckles and, like a born Olivier, grafts the skin of a new talent onto himself. One of the best films of 1990.

Rex Reed, *Coming Attractions*

A gutsy, fascinating departure for Clint Eastwood.

Janet Maslin, *New York Times*

***** A masterful work. Superb entertainment.

Jack Garner, Gannett News Services

An intelligent, affectionate study...another film in which Eastwood is clearly trying to break away from the action roles that made him famous and establish himself as a serious actor. As a director, he has shown ever since *Play Misty for Me* that he is more than just a fine craftsman, and his willingness to tackle difficult subjects is commendable.

"Strat," *Variety*

The Rookie (1990)

CAST

Nick Pulovski, Clint Eastwood; *David Ackerman*, Charlie Sheen; *Strom*, Raul Julia; *Liesl*, Sonia Braga; *Eugene Ackerman*, Tom Skerritt; *Sarah*, Lara Flynn Boyle; *Garcia*, Pepe Serna; *Loco*, Marco Rodriguez.

CREDITS

Directed by Clint Eastwood. *Produced by* Howard Kazanjian, Steven Siebert, and David Valdes. *Screenplay*, Boaz Yakin and Scott Speigel. *Director of photography*, Jack N. Green. *Production designer*, Judy Cammer. *Editor*, Joel Cox. *Music*, Lennie Niehaus. A Malpaso Production. Released by Warner Brothers. Color by Technicolor. *Running time: 121 minutes*.

The failure of *Pink Cadillac* created industry speculation that that Clint Eastwood had lost his box-office appeal. Warner Brothers was therefore heartened when Clint decided to return to more traditional turf with *The Rookie*, an action adventure film of the "Dirty Harry" genre. Costarring Charlie Sheen, it would mark the first time since *City Heat* that Clint would be paired with another established leading man. Unfortunately, *The Rookie* would only add to industry concern that Clint's midas touch appeared to be in retrograde.

The Rookie has its moments, but it is never able to overcome one glaring flaw: that, despite the ample blood and guts, it is far more a comedy than a thriller. Eastwood and Charlie Sheen are no more suited for laughs than Clint and Lee Marvin were for warbling those tunes in *Paint Your Wagon*. The humor and lightheartedness look forced and pretentious, and the screenplay is vault of clichés that would have seemed stale twenty years ago. As with many action films of late, the writers seem far more preoccupied with creating a memorable tag line (à la "Make my day!") than in telling an engrossing story.

The film is crowded with talent, but virtually all of it is wasted or wildly miscast. For some mysterious reason Raul Julia portrays a *German* archvillain, and come off looking like an imitation of B movie bad guy George Zucco. One is so distracted by Julia's phony accent that the film should be retitled "Gomez Addams Joins the Third Reich." Equally absurd is the casting of Sonia Braga as Julia's lover and fellow terrorist. The vivacious Brazilian actress is given virtually no dialogue, and is seen merely sauntering around in sexy attire or blasting away with an Uzi. (One amusing sequence, however, finds her first terrorizing, then practically raping Big Clint. It's the most effective near-castration scene since Sean Connery was menaced by that laser beam in *Goldfinger*.)

The less-than-enthralling screenplay for *The Rookie* rips off so many scenes from far better films that it plays like two hours of trailers from

Eastwood is less than pleased to be assigned a rookie (Charlie Sheen) as his partner.

golden oldies. There's an absurd sequence in which Eastwood and Sheen are terrorized by a speeding jet which pursues them through a wheatfield, obviously meant to resemble the classic *North by Northwest* crop-dusting sequence. It doesn't work because jets can't turn on a dime and we wonder why Clint simply doesn't just step out of the way. The climatic shootout in the airport is such a carbon of the finale to *Bullitt*, we half expected to see the ghost of Steve McQueen pop up and put an end to this nonsense. The central plot—about a deadly car jacking ring—was done more effectively in *Black Moon Rising* wherein Robert Vaughn's villain hit all the notes Raul Julia fails to. Charlie Sheen has a scene in which he gets to shatter a mirror in frustration, but daddy Martin had beaten him to the punch ages ago with a similar stunt for *Apocalypse Now*. A well directed bar fight showcases Sheen's tough-guy abilities but seems like a rip-off of Clint's own *Coogan's Bluff*.

Eastwood and Sheen don't generate much chemistry, due to the clichéd relationship of their characters. The stunt work is spectacular, however, and despite the film's many flaws, it's not too difficult to stay awake. The Eastwood back-of-camera stock company is present, with occasional director Buddy Van Horn handling the second-unit work this time around. Even Clint's son, Kyle, is credited with cowriting an original song. Eastwood's direction is effective in the action scenes (particularly the impressive opening car chase), but is otherwise uninspired. His preoccupation with a *film noir* mood—appropriate in the likes of *Bird*—becomes tedious here. Critics were generally ruthless in their appraisal, and box-office results were very disappointing. A decade ago, a nondiscriminating actioner such as this with Eastwood's name above the title would likely would have been an inevitable hit. However, with Clint's newfound respect as an actor and filmmaker, audiences and critics now expected considerably more of him.

SYNOPSIS

Det. Nick Pulovski (Clint Eastwood) is a man obsessed with bringing a ruthless stolen car ring to justice in retaliation for the murder of his partner. An old-time cop with a penchant for throwing away the rule book and taking any risk to capture his prey, he is reluctantly assigned a rookie cop, David Ackerman (Charlie Sheen) as a new partner, and the two men initially have a tense relationship. Pulovski is a "blue collar" type while Ackerman is trying to shed his image as the blue-blooded pampered son of a millionaire industrialist (Tom Skerritt).

The veteran and the rookie learn that the masterminds of the car ring are Strom (Raul Julia), a ruthless German criminal, and his lover Liesl (Sonia Braga), whose sensuousness is only exceeded by her zeal for murder. Despite some important setbacks, Pulovski and Ackerman succeed in crippling the villain's operations. In desperation, Strom kidnaps Pulovski and demands a $2 million ransom with which to flee the country. Ackerman, haunted by his inability to save his younger brother from dying when they were children, is determined not to let the

A kinky moment with Sonia Braga.

276

same fate await his partner. He borrows the ransom money from his father and, in defiance of police brass, arranges to meet with the villains.

Meanwhile, however, Pulovski has freed himself but not before Strom and Liesl have fled to an airport where a private jet awaits. The detectives arrive in the nick of time and engage in a bloody shoot-out which leads into the main airline terminal. Ultimately, both Strom and Liesl are gunned down. Pulovski, long critical of police brass, is ironically rewarded with a promotion to captain. His first decision is to assign Ackerman—whom he now has learned to respect—to be paired with a rookie cop.

REVIEWS

Overlong, sadistic and stale even by the conventions of the buddy pic genre, Clint Eastwood's *The Rookie* may fill the cupboard with some early box-office coin, but won't survive long in the big leagues. Toe-tag this as one of the season's major holiday turkeys. Eastwood has always repaid Warner Brothers for underwriting his artistic aspirations with bread-winning action fare, but never with anything as relentlessly dim-witted as this.... A flabby two hour roller coaster ride. Eastwood

As Nick Pulovski.

the actor seems rightfully bored with the material.... Surprisingly in light of Eastwood's normally superb craftsmanship is the shoddy technical quality....

"Bril," *Variety*

A knockout! The best action film since *Lethal Weapon 2*.... The best bone-cruncher in years.

Gary Giddens, *Village Voice*

The Rookie is an astonishingly empty movie to come from Mr. Eastwood. As a director he sometimes overreaches himself (*Bird*) but his ambitious ones are unusually noble (*White Hunter, Black Heart*). When not thinking grandly, he has made some effective, entertaining Westerns and action movies, including *Pale Rider* and *Heartbreak Ridge*...but, as social nuisances (and movie subjects) go, this one ranks alongside pigeon feeding.

Vincent Canby, *New York Times*

Directing The Rookie.

Unforgiven (1992)

As Will Munny.

CAST

William Munny, Clint Eastwood; *Little Billy Daggett*, Gene Hackman; *Ned Logan*, Morgan Freeman; *English Bob*, Richard Harris; *The Schofield Kid*, Jaimz Woolvett; *W. W. Beauchamp*, Saul Rubinek; *Strawberry Alice*, Frances Fisher; *Delilah*, Anna Thomson.

CREDITS

Director and Producer, Clint Eastwood; *Executive producer*, David Valdes. *Screenplay*, David Webb Peoples. *Director of photography*, Jack N. Green. *Production designer*, Henry Bumstead. *Editor*, Joel Cox. *Music*, Lennie Niehaus. A Malpaso Production. Released by Warner Brothers. Color by Technicolor. *Running time: 130 minutes.*

By 1992, many in Hollywood establishment had decided that Clint Eastwood's days as a potent box-office draw had ridden off into the sunset along with the western genre with which he rose to fame. (Excluding, of course, politically correct Westerns like *Dances With Wolves*.) Eastwood, always a maverick, sought to prove them wrong by dusting off a script from the mid-1970s that harkened back to the glory days of the traditional western: David Webb Peoples' *Unforgiven* (originally titled *The William Munny Killings*, and unrelated to John Huston's *The Unforgiven*). The property was an unlikely vehicle for Eastwood to reclaim his box-office standing, but the actor/filmmaker has always said that his foremost goal is succeeding artistically, even at the expense of commerciality.

Eastwood, who failed to connect with younger viewers with the pretentiously "hip" *The Rookie*, went full circle with *Unforgiven* by handpicking a cast that hardly seemed appealing to MTV aficionados. But, what a glorious cast it is: Gene Hackman, Morgan Freeman, and Richard Harris. Along with Eastwood, these men have forgotten more about acting ability than most younger thespians will ever learn. Hackman at first refused to do the film because of its violent content. Eastwood argued: "There is maybe an antiviolence statement in there that could be profound if we executed it properly." Hackman read the script, agreed, and signed up. Richard Harris signed immediately. (Prophetically, he was watching *High Plains Drifter* on TV when the call from Clint came through.)

In a style typical of most Malpaso films, *Unforgiven* was shot and completed expeditiously, but efficiently. Clint, who was also producing and directing, chose Calgary, Alberta, Canada, as the site of the fictional town of Big Whiskey, Wyoming, where most of the action would take place. Oscar-winning production designer Henry Bumstead completed construction of the entire town in thirty-two days. Eastwood insisted that all the scenes be filmed on location, and—to maximize the feeling of the period—refused to allow modern vehicles on the set. (The cast took horsedrawn wagons to the filming sites each day.) As is customary on an Eastwood set, Clint worked his cast and crew hard, but always insured that a sense of camaraderie and humor prevailed. A scant fifty-two days after production began, principal filming wrapped.

Eastwood explained why he delayed making *Unforgiven*: "Current events. That's why I chose to make this movie after it had been around for fifteen years. It's more timely now with the world's desensitization to violence, and the misinterpretation of justice." Eastwood also forestalled the project until he was of an age to lend credibility to his world-weary character of Will Munny. It proved to be a wise decision, as Eastwood's performance is arguably the best of his career. His Munny is possibly the most complex character he has yet to embody. There is little sentiment to this man, and he is haunted by omnipresent demons of his violent and shameful past.

As with the Dirty Harry, Munny only gets the audience's sympathy because his adversaries are even more heartless. Yet, he is not entirely without a conscience. He resumes his violent past reluctantly and only with the noble goal of feeding his children. However, the script does not beatify the character. Once back in the world of violence and gunplay, he unhesitatingly undertakes the killings both methodically and ritualistically. He is not so much motivated by bringing to justice the men who mutilated a prostitute as he is in collecting the reward money. It's a bold and courageous performance, and it is not an overstatement to say that only Eastwood, the last major star weaned on the western, could portray the character so convincingly. Eastwood's work as an actor here is only exceeded by his directorial skills.

Munny and Logan (Morgan Freeman) set out on the bounty hunt.

Little Billy (Gene Hackman) confiscates Munny's weapon.

Munny and the Schofield Kid (Jaimz Woolvett) ambush their prey.

The supporting cast is peerless. Gene Hackman gives a brilliant, scene-stealing performance as Little Billy, the charming but vicious sheriff whose totalitarian control over Big Whiskey sets in motion the climactic showdown. Only an actor of great skill could embellish a character with such savagery and still make him somewhat likable. Morgan Freeman is equally excellent as Ned, Eastwood's onetime partner in crime who embarks on the bounty hunt more out of sentiment than for gain. It's a joy to see Richard Harris in a meaningful role, as he does wonders with his brief appearance as the bogus "legendary" gunslinger English Bob, who is shamed and disgraced by Little Billy. Harris appears far too briefly, and one wishes his character was made more integral to the story. Eastwood the director also evokes wonderful work from Frances Fisher as the prostitute who vows to avenge her mutilated friend, and Jaimz Woolvett as the glory-seeking paper tiger known as the Schofield Kid.

With *Unforgiven* Eastwood—ironically criticized for glorifying gunplay in previous films—succeeds in making the ultimate statement against violence. Will Munny's world has no glory and little peace. There are no gunfights at high noon in the center of town. Instead, people are mercilessly shot down when they are most vulnerable. Some suffer horribly, and the perpetrators of these actions—Eastwood and his accomplices included—must live with their deeds. As Munny tells the Schofield Kid after the latter's less than glorious introduction to a gunfight, "It's a hell of a thing, killing a man. You take away all he's got and all he's ever gonna have."

On a technical level, *Unforgiven* boasts some of the finest achievements of the Malpaso regulars. Cinematographer Jack N. Green does his usual yeoman work and western landscapes have rarely looked so breathtaking. Praise should also go to editor Joel Cox, a longtime Eastwood collaborator, who allows the film to run a leisurely 130 minutes without a single dull moment. Lennie Niehaus contributes a haunting score, done in part as a collaboration with Eastwood.

Unforgiven opened with little fanfare or publicity in the summer of 1992, when the industry was primarily preoccupied with *Batman Returns* and *Lethal Weapon 3*. It immediately was hailed as the high-water mark of Eastwood's career as both actor and director. Critical consensus was almost unanimously enthusiastic, and the film proved to be one of the top grossing films of Eastwood's career. By year end, it had been named one of the best films of 1992 by over two hundred critics, and Eastwood and Hackman had won numerous awards for their work.* The film won the Oscar as Best Picture of the Year and Clint won as Best Director. (He was nominated as Best Actor, too, but lost to Al Pacino.) Clint also was chosen Best Director by the Directors Guild of America. Hackman and Joel Cox also received Oscar recognition.

Eastwood has returned the western to its glory, and presented us with the best film of this genre since Don Siegel's *The Shootist*, which, as John Wayne's final film, was the last word on truly great westerns until now. (Appropriately, Eastwood dedicates the film to the memory of mentors Siegel and Sergio Leone.) This may not be the last Eastwood western, but it may be the last *great* Eastwood western, as it's doubtful he can top *Unforgiven*—a true classic of the modern cinema. Doubtless, he probably plans to try.

Severely wounded, Munny is comforted by the prostitute (Anna Thomson) he has come to defend.

*It received five awards from the Los Angeles Film Critics Association: Best Picture, Best Actor, Best Supporting Actor, Best Director and Best Screenplay. The National Society of Film Critics named it Best Picture of 1992 and Eastwood Best Director.

SYNOPSIS

As impoverished Will Munny as a retired gun-fighter.

Munny avenges Ned's death in the climactic battle in the saloon.

After Delilah (Anna Thomson), a prostitute in Big Whiskey, Wyoming, is mutilated, the perpetrators of the crime are released with virtually no punishment by the town sheriff, Little Billy Daggett (Gene Hackman). Delilah's fellow prostitutes, headed by Strawberry Alice (Frances Fisher), post a reward for the murder of the criminals. The bounty money draws an odd assortment of gunmen to town, much to the consternation of Little Billy. He prides himself on keeping a safe town through totalitarian methods. Among the would-be collectors of the reward are English Bob (Richard Harris), a pompous gunslinger who is accompanied by his biographer W. W. Beauchamp (Saul Rubinek). Daggett brutally exposes Bob's accomplishments as creations of the press, but retains Beauchamp's services to aggrandize his own achievements.

Reluctantly drawn into the hunt for the killers is William Munny (Clint Eastwood), a once murderous outlaw haunted by the crimes of his past. Munny has attempted to make a legitimate living as a pig farmer, but the death of his sainted wife has left him unable to support his two children. Although having foresworn violence years ago, he straps on his guns one last time in hopes of earning the bounty. Munny enlists the aid of Ned Logan (Morgan Freeman), his former partner in crime, of late a semi-retired farmer himself. They are joined by the Schofield Kid (Jaimz Woolvett), a young braggart who yearns to emulate the violent ways of Munny's past.

RACING ★ ★ ★ FINAL

WIN $500,000
PLAY **LTTL$$T** PAGE 37

DAILY ◉ NEWS

40¢ NEW YORK'S HOMETOWN NEWSPAPER Tuesday, March 30, 1993

CLINT

Wins Best Director & Best Picture for 'Unforgiven'
SEE PAGES 2 & 3 PLUS EXTRA SECTION

284

The quest proves to be a tragic one for all concerned. Munny finds that his return to gunplay reopens old psychological wounds that threaten to destroy him. When finally confronted with actually using his guns, the Schofield Kid is reduced to a shattered wreck of a man. While succeeding in tracking down their prey, the three bounty-hunting gunmen run afoul of Daggett who makes an example of Ned by whipping him to death. Vowing revenge, Munny boldly "invades" the town's saloon where he single-handedly wins a gunfight with Daggett's cronies. He then manages to render Daggett helpless, and coldly shoots him dead. Munny returns to his family, perhaps no better of a man than when he left, but certainly somewhat wiser. A postscript notes that he moves his family to a distant location in the hopes of starting a new life far removed from the violent world which has threatened to destroy him.

REVIEWS

Eastwood's finest hour as a moviemaker. It's likely to become an American classic, and it towers over every other film in current release.

Bob Campbell, Newhouse News Services

A classic western for the ages. Clint Eastwood has crafted a tense, hard-edged superbly dramatic yarn that is also an exceedingly intelligent meditation on the West, its myths and its heroes.... Playing a stubbly, worn-out has-been outlaw who can barely mount his horse at first, Eastwood, unafraid to show his age, is outstanding in his best clipped, understated manner.

Todd McCarthy, *Variety*

A great western. One of the year's best films. Eastwood deserves an Oscar nomination for directing.

Joel Siegel, ABC-TV

At first sight, *Unforgiven* seems a very fitting arrivederci to Eastwood-the-director's two great mentors...[but] owes much more to Eastwood's non westerns as a director since the early '70s....[It's] his best western—the most distinguished film he has appeared in and directed—since *The Outlaw Josey Wales*.

Christopher Frayling, *Sight and Sound*

One of the best films of the year. A profound work of art.

Rex Reed, *New York Observer*

A gripping and haunting work of art that should finally establish Eastwood as one of America's finest directors.

Kathleen Carroll, New York *Daily News*

In the Line of Fire (1993)

CAST

Frank Horrigan, Clint Eastwood; *Mitch Leary*, John Malkovich; *Lily Raines*, René Russo; *Al D'Andrea*, Dylan McDermott; *Bill Watts*, Gary Cole; *Harry Sargent*, Fred Dalton Thompson; *Sam Campagna*, John Mahoney.

CREDITS

Director, Wolfgang Petersen; *Executive producers*, Gail Katz and David Valdes; *Producers*, Jeff Apple and Bob Rosenthal; *Screenplay*, Jeff Maguire; *Director of photography*, John Bailey; *Editor*, Anne V. Coates; *Production designer*, Lilly Kilvert; *Music*, Ennio Morricone. A Castle Rock Entertainment production in association with Apple/Rose Films. Released by Columbia Pictures.

After the obviously grueling pace set by Clint while producing, directing, and starring in *Unforgiven*, Eastwood opted to concentrate on his acting skills alone in the thriller *In the Line of Fire*. The film, cofinanced by Columbia and Castle Rock, is a departure for Eastwood in that it represents his first movie away from Warner Brothers and Malpaso since *Escape From Alcatraz* in 1979.

Eastwood portrays Frank Horrigan, a retired Secret Service agent who was part of John F. Kennedy's tragic motorcade through Dallas. Although officially out of service in "the field," Horrigan is recalled to active duty to help thwart an assassination attempt against the current president. The film is directed by noted German filmmaker Wolfgang (*Das Boot*) Petersen.

SYNOPSIS

Frank Horrigan (Clint Eastwood) is a sixty-ish Secret Service agent who has been haunted for thirty years by his inability to save President Kennedy, whom he was assigned to protect in Dallas. Uncovering a potential presidential assassin named Mitch Leary (John Malkovich), Horrigan sees an opportunity to redeem himself. Leary, a former CIA hit man, plays an ingenious cat-and-mouse game with Horrigan, capitalizing on the agent's sense of guilt over the JFK murder, and filling him with doubt about whether he truly has the courage to sacrifice his life for the current president. When his partner, Al D'Andrea (Dylan McDermott), is murdered by Leary, Horrigan becomes obsessed with bringing the killer to justice. He finds sympathy from fellow agent Lily Raines (René Russo), with whom he becomes romantically involved. However, his zeal makes him overreact on occasion, and he is reassigned to other duties on the very day Leary has threatened to kill the president during a fund-raising appearance at a Los Angeles hotel. At the last minute, Horrigan's detective work allows him to identify Leary, who is posing as

286

a campaign supporter, and with seconds to spare, saves the president's life. Leary takes Horrigan hostage, and in a furious battle atop a glass elevator, the agent throws the would-be assassin to his death. Now a national hero, Horrigan can erase the demons of his past and begin a new life with Lilly.

Horrigan in a scene that is literally cliff-hanging.

Horrigan engages in a rooftop chase to foil an assassin.

Clint with René Russo, playing a Secret Service colleague.

Clint, as Frank Horrigan, escorts the presidential limo through the streets of Washington, D.C.

Clint Eastwood at the Box Office

Clint Eastwood has been a box-office icon for four decades. The following chart illustrates the dollars generated from his films as ranked in *Variety*'s All Time Rental Champs listing. The figures here should not be confused with box-office *grosses*, which are inevitably much higher. Rather, the rental dollars indicate the all important amounts that are actually earned by the studio. In reviewing the chart, one should remember that Eastwood's earlier films show rental figures that are modest by today's standards. However, at the time of release they were generally considered to be extremely profitable.

TITLE	*Rental Dollars*
EVERY WHICH WAY BUT LOOSE	$51,900,000
ANY WHICH WAY YOU CAN	40,500,000
UNFORGIVEN	36,000,000
SUDDEN IMPACT	34,800,000
FIREFOX	25,000,000
THE ENFORCER	24,000,000
TIGHTROPE	22,500,000
HEARTBREAK RIDGE	21,600,000
ESCAPE FROM ALCATRAZ	21,500,000
CITY HEAT	21,000,000
PALE RIDER	20,800,000
MAGNUM FORCE	20,100,000
THE DEAD POOL	19,000,000
DIRTY HARRY	18,000,000
THE GAUNTLET	17,700,000
BRONCO BILLY	15,000,000
PAINT YOUR WAGON	14,500,000
THE OUTLAW JOSEY WALES	13,500,000
THE ROOKIE	10,000,000
THUNDERBOLT AND LIGHTFOOT	9,202,000
HIGH PLAINS DRIFTER	7,451,433
WHERE EAGLES DARE	7,131,431
PINK CADILLAC	6,800,000
HANG 'EM HIGH	6,777,922
THE EIGER SANCTION	6,736,616
THE GOOD, THE BAD AND THE UGLY	6,111,962
JOE KIDD	5,827,402
KELLY'S HEROES	5,239,644
PLAY MISTY FOR ME	5,048,643
TWO MULES FOR SISTER SARA	4,638,733
FOR A FEW DOLLARS MORE	4,346,201